# Intensive Scare

# Intensive Scare

## Skullenia Book 6

**Tony Lewis**

*For Mike and Darren, my two amazing brothers, without whom I wouldn't be the person I am today. Twisted, vaguely malevolent, in possession of an imagination worthy of psychiatric review, strangely wary of darts and forks, and more grateful that I was able to grow up with you both than you'll ever know.*

*And to James. Thanks for the title.*

Nurse Parsnip signed the bottom of the medical chart, hung it back onto the hook at the end of the bed, tucked her pen away into the left breast pocket of her uniform, and let out a long, but satisfied sigh.

Currently, she was about three quarters of the way through her last round of the shift, after which she would wend her weary way home for a well-earned rest, a refreshing brew, and a spot of dinner, and by that I mean a glass of freshly squeezed A Rhesus Negative, a length of intestine lightly seared in a tangy bile sauce, and a modest portion of chips, and by chips I mean fingers, and not the chocolatey kind either.

Now, for those of you out there in reader land who consider yourselves to be human (although, if you regard Love Island as quality TV, labour under the illusion that the letters 'th' are pronounced 'f', and think a sophisticated night out involves meeting Bazza, Dazza, Shazza, Tezza, Fatboy Oinks, and Ming Mong Mandy at The Dog and Doughnut for a bag of pork scratchings and a jug of Woo Woo, you've kind of ruled yourselves out by default), and therefore tend to think along more traditional lines when it comes to the ingestion of food based items, you might be wondering, and quite rightly so, why the good nurse wasn't going to indulge in a big, fat bacon sandwich loaded with enough butter and brown sauce to clog a giraffes arteries, a bowl full of strawberry Angel Delight, and a large mug of tea.

Well, in actual fact, she *could* have that if she wanted, but as nice as that delightful culinary spread might sound it would definitely have a minor disagreement with her ghoulish internal organs the results of which would be a bloated belly, extended visits to an increasingly distressed toilet, and the chunk by chunk appearance of a partially digested and rather fragrant mess capable of rising to the surface of the water quicker than an asthmatic free diver. And by that I mean a free diver who has asthma, not a diver who's perfectly healthy, can hold his breath for three and a half weeks, and who is, to all intents and purposes, asthma free (and as I've mentioned a diver I could have said to all intents and porpoises, but I won't because that'd be rather cheap and inordinately silly).

Anyway, I know it's only a small lexicological detail, but it's one that does need pointing out I feel. I mean, there wouldn't be any point in making a comparison to something that has no correlation to what you want to compare it to now is there? That would be like saying, 'Oh look, that red car over there is exactly the same colour as my green one'.

That's unless you're colour blind of course in which case they'll both look identical whatever hue they're adorned with. Not that you should be driving anyway for goodness sake. The traffic light sequence isn't greeny/red, greeny/red and amber, greeny/red, amber, greeny/red. Unless you're in France that is, where even a visually challenged moose can get a driving license, and obeying traffic signals and road directions of any description is entirely optional.

The pastries are nice though. Just don't cross the road to get one.

Nurse Parsnip glanced up at the clock on the wall (she did have one of those upside downy chest ones, but she always felt a bit odd looking at her boobs whenever she wanted to know the time). Ten past three in the morning. That was good. At least she wasn't behind, a fortuitous circumstance that meant there was every possibility that she'd actually get off on time which, if you know anything about hospitals, is usually as likely as getting into one in the first place.

The potential for a late finish, a potential that was realised every now and again, was because, as part of her duties on this particular shift, Nurse Parsnip had to see to everyone in the Accident and Emergency Department and send them on their way once they'd been treated. Luckily, that hadn't taken very long tonight as it hadn't been very busy down there. Then again it never was really. If every creature that got injured on a nightly basis in Skullenia visited the hospital when it got a scratch, a cut, or had a couple of its limbs removed, the place would be full to bursting on the very same nightly basis.

(Ironically, full to bursting was a complaint that she'd dealt with the previous evening. It was a strange ailment that usually afflicted young, inexperienced vampires out on a binge who hadn't yet worked out what their capacity for blood intake was. Consequently, not only did this lead to the waiting room being full of pasty faced whingers moaning about their upset tummies, it also gave rise to some very interesting and colourful modern art renditions on the marble floor that took several hours and a gallon of industrial strength bleach to clean up. And regarding the A&E Department, the only time it got really busy was when Count Jocular got all bloodlusty and decimated the odd village or three. Or had new carpets put in, the effect was just the same. There were always life changing injuries, copious amounts of body fluids, wailing and screaming, missing appendages, and at least a couple of swatch booklets that needed removing after they'd been roughly inserted into places where the patterns would be quite hard to discern and all the same shade of muddy brown).

Anyway, as we've already established, it hadn't been too busy, and the only creature that the good nurse had seen in there tonight had been Fordwyche the troll, who'd presented himself at the medical establishment with a nasty cut to the hand. It wasn't his hand. It was one he'd found in the bin at the back of Mrs. Strudel's cafe (no doubt a remnant from one of her ghastly recipes. In fact, such was the diverse and eclectic nature of her rubbish, if Dr Frankenstein ever decided to come out of retirement, he wouldn't have too far to go to find everything he needed to get back into the reanimation business. There wasn't a night that went past that her bin wasn't overflowing with neatly lopped off extremities of one sort or another. Essentially, Doris Strudel's waste was like a Lego set for the ever so slightly deranged so if you ever find yourself at a loose end and needing to construct something fleshy, you can always pop round the back and have a go at cobbling something together. And let's face it, whatever you come up with is bound to be better than anything created using the foot destroying, multi-coloured plastic alternative, be it

Tower Bridge, the Taj Mahal, or a vague, pointy tube that's supposed to be a plane. Not that I'm decrying the use of Lego of course. I'm sure it has its place, but then so do straightjackets, padded cells, rubber helmets, soft crayons, and extremely heavy doses of prescribed medication. So, what can we conclude from all this? On balance, I think it's that you have to be a particular type of person to partake of the little Swedish building blocks and everything that miniature world has to offer. There is a technical term for it. What is it now? Oh yes. Dull).

Fordwyche wanted the hand sewn up because he was going to hang it above his front door (cave entrance) for good luck (it brought flies). He also liked how it smelled (although how he was able to detect any odours was a mystery to one and all seeing as how he stank like, well, like one of Mrs. Strudel's bins). As it turned out it wasn't a technically difficult procedure to fix the damage, so she'd happily obliged with a couple of stitches and sent him on his way.

Stifling a yawn, Nurse Parsnip gazed at the sleeping figure in the bed before her. Soft snores emanated from it that rippled the sheets and ruffled his moustache, which made him rub his nose because it tickled.

Great Flat-Top the mountain ogre, for 'twas he that lay recumbent under the covers, was a rather special case. He was one of a very select number of patients that had been admitted to the hospital over the centuries, one suffering from a malaise so rare that the staff had had to look it up in the medical texts and have a meeting to decide on the best course of action. So, what was the exact nature of the debilitating condition that'd stumped Skullenia's esteemed medical community? I hear you ask. Well, I'll tell you shall I (which would make sense seeing as how I'm the author and everything).

Much to the amazement of Dr Zoltan (he's the esteemed medical community I mentioned), Great Flat-Top the mountain ogre actually had something wrong with him, a state of affairs that was virtually unheard of in the wards and side-rooms of Aesculapian establishments all over the world.

(And if you don't believe me, ask a nurse, who will readily confirm that most hospital beds are occupied by either whinging malingerers with ingrowing toenails, barely functioning adults who've got a bit of a cold, or overweight lollygaggers who've got suspected food poisoning in their massive bellies because they've had their seventeenth take out of the week and it's only Tuesday).

So, our ogre. In his spare time, Great Flat-Top, a community minded sort of a chap, did a bit of showing visitors around the local area whilst they took in the chequered history, questionable architecture, and eerie landscape of the surrounding villages and countryside (I could have said he was a tour guide, but I do have a word count to reach you know), and it was doing this that had landed him in the hospital.

So, how did showing tourists round, answering a few questions, and generally being a stout and knowledgeable fellow make him so ill? Well, he would gather foreign looking people together, offer to show them about for a very reasonable price, pretend that he knew what he was talking about, and then escort them all to a cabin in the woods where they could have a nice sit down and something to eat. Or, to put it another way, he would eat every last one of them in a gluttonous, blood drenched frenzy, and then have a nice sit down.

Now, whilst you may think that his methods of guiding aren't strictly traditional, (but let's be honest here, they've got to be better than sitting on a coach with a bunch of sun burnt holiday makers and being shouted at a by an orange woman called Tracey who thinks local history is restricted to how many men she's slept with and how long The Tequila Mockingbird has been open), he did manage to secure (well, kidnap really, but that's just splitting bones) a fair bit of trade and was busy most days of the week. And it was all going rather nicely thank you very much. Up until a week ago that is. After finishing with a group of Glandian boy scouts, Great Flat-Top had felt a bit of discomfort that had refused to go away. Eventually, unable to find relief and with the pain steadily increasing, he'd been admitted to hospital and diagnosed with the worst case of constipation that Nurse Parsnip and Dr Zoltan had seen since Flug had pounded down one hundred and sixty seven Sticky Nutty Nut Bums.

(The introduction of so much refined sugar had caused the poor reanimates bowels to go into a cataclysmic spasm, and they'd remained in that immobile state for nigh on a week and a half causing Flug to suffer some nasty bloating, a few burst sutures, and a certain amount of fragrant leakage more suited to the bottom of an industrial pig bin. Anyway, thanks to copious amounts of water and not a few tummy rubs, his innards had finally begun to relent which was when Ollie and Ronnie had quickly ushered him outdoors where, to this day, there's an area in the forest that's strictly off limits, except to those with the stoutest of souls, the strongest of stomachs, and the sturdiest of shoes).

So, to ease his congestion, Great Flat-Top was on thrice daily doses of Skullenian Prune juice, a liquid so adept at shifting all things stubborn that it had once been used to clear up a lava spill. As good as it is though, the exact time that it's curative properties begin to take effect can be somewhat difficult to predict which is why, in expectation of the inevitable result, next to the ogre's bed was a mop, a bucket, a bag of sturdy pegs, and a quarter of a ton of sand. When he eventually went it was going to be a veritable jamboree with cloth caps, camping badges, and partially digested woggles all over the place.

Of the other patients currently languishing in their beds there was Enid Bottletop, an elderly witch who was becoming rather forgetful, and who was in hospital more for the benefit of the townsfolk than anything else. She'd been brought in by Constable Gullett after he found her perched on a windowsill, purring, and asking for a saucer of milk. The seriousness of her condition was clearly evident. The poor thing was at the wrong house. She usually got her lactose at Mr. and Mrs. Doom's.

Then there was Ascension White, a newly turned golem who'd contracted a nasty dose of stone fungus, although seeing as how he was still on probation it wasn't strictly speaking his fault. The warlock who'd placed the enchantment in his mouth was to blame for that. He hadn't taken the necessary precautions re handwashing and the like, and so had passed the infection onto poor Ascension. He should've known better really. There're leaflets everywhere about safe hex.

And lastly there was Obidiah Dickens, a poor unfortunate soul of a poltergeist who'd gotten caught up in a drinking game at The Bolt and Jugular, and then gotten caught up in the ceiling fan of the same establishment when he sneezed and catapulted himself upwards at quite an impressive speed. He was currently resting in half a dozen plastic bags that were tied to the bed with string, whilst Dr Zoltan tried to figure out how to stitch mist together.

So, all in all, on balance, when all's said and done, and whatever the hell else people say when things aren't going too bad, it wasn't going too bad. They had their busy times of course, but that was usually around the holidays, or when Mrs. Ladle decided to try out a new cake recipe.

Nurse Parsnip was just about to tuck in an errant corner of freshly laundered bed sheet when a noise from the pharmacy at the end of the ward attracted her attention. It sounded like bottles clinking together, but it couldn't be that because she'd finished her medicine round over an hour ago and locked it up.

Forgetting the untidy bed cover for the moment, she walked quietly towards the dispensary, because it took her past the other resting patients.

The little room had windows, but they were frosted, but that didn't make a whole lot of difference because it was dark anyway. As she approached, she squinted in the way that all people do when trying to see something more clearly (which is just silly. I mean you wouldn't talk more quietly to make yourself heard, or slow down if you were in a hurry, would you?), but it didn't help.

Strangely, despite the continuing noise coming from within, she couldn't see any actual movement, but as already noted, the glass and the darkness would be a major hindrance to that.

She momentarily wondered if it was Dr Zoltan in there, engaged in some night-time experimentation or research. He sometimes liked to fiddle about with all the various potions and tinctures in an effort to come up with more effective treatments for the particular type of maladies that could befall the residents of Skullenia. Well, that's what he told Nurse Parsnip anyway. If the truth be known, the good doctor could barely remember how to make a pot of tea, so the chances of him inventing a cure for say, Ghoul Rash or Warty Troll Syndrome, were about as likely as UKIP employing a Polish MP with special responsibility for bringing in as many of his countrymen into Britain as was feasibly possible.

No, the reason that Dr Zoltan often pottered about the medicines was that he had a bit of a crush on the lovely Nurse Parsnip you see, and he would sometimes hide in the dispensary and peek through the keyhole at the female ghoul as she went about her nursely duties. And whilst I know that sounds a tad creepy, it was only because he was a little bit shy when it came to matters of the heart. In other words, when he tried to speak to a lady, he turned into a gibbering wreck who couldn't have got a coherent sentence out if his life depended on it. Not that anyone would've noticed. He was scatty at the best of times, a state of being that saw him once prescribe an aggressive course of hormone replacement therapy for Hector Lozenge to help him with his alcohol problem. It hadn't helped the old boy of course, but then how could it have done? What was he going to do with a pair of boobs and a worrying craving for chocolate? On the other hand, Mrs. Throb, the lady who'd received his addiction counteraction remedy got on brilliantly. She's a professional wrestler now and can roll up a frying pan with her bare hands.

Anyway, Zoltan had considered telling her about his feelings, but he was worried that she might find him a bit too old and set in his ways, and if she rejected him it may make their pleasant working relationship a bit tense.

Nurse Parsnip rejected the idea of the physician being in attendance though, because Zoltan had told her earlier in the day that he was going on a house call that evening. Derek Strudel had dropped one of his mum's smaller saucepans on his foot and broken twelve bones and the concrete floor that he'd been standing on. He needed some painkillers, a spot of physiotherapy, and a hefty dose of 'stop making such a fuss you great big girlie man'.

She reached into her pocket, took out her keys, and sorted through them for the right one. It took a couple of minutes because she had them all, from the smallest cupboard in the basement, to the vast atrium on the third floor where the patients went for a bit of R and R after treatment (reeling and rocking if it was Hector Lozenge, ranting and raving if it was a witch, and wandering about like a wally if it was Flug because he couldn't spell).

With the correct key in hand, Nurse Parsnip approached the door. As she put the key towards the lock the door banged noisily in its frame. She let out a yelp of surprise and jumped backwards a couple of feet.

"Alright," she said, her voice sounding far more confident that she actually felt. "That's enough messing about for one night. I'm coming in there right now and if you haven't got a decent excuse for being in attendance there's going to be trouble."

Without any further hesitation she slammed the key into the lock, threw open the door, and flicked the light on.

Nurse Parsnip screamed.

\* \* \*

Noggin was on the prowl. As a vampire cat he absolutely loved being out and about, but the fact that it was an integral facet of his nature wasn't the only reason for his unalloyed pleasure. What made it especially thrilling was that he could never tell what was going to happen. He literally had no idea where he'd end up, who he'd bump into, or what juicy titbits might be found lurking in the dark recesses of the night. And bearing in mind the size of his territory that could be anything from a wandering Blue Badger to a fully grown troll. And what with Noggin being, well, Noggin, he had no compunction whatsoever in taking down whatever poor, unfortunate creature it was that was unlucky enough to cross his path, and taking it home to his 'owner', Mandrake. Not that Mandrake could claim to be the 'owner' of the psychotic feline of course because like most cats, Noggin was very much his own person, so to speak, and would hang around somewhere as long as it was warm and cosy and he got a tickle under the chin every now and again.

By nature, Noggin was a happy go lucky sort of a cat, in that he was happy to rend into bloody ribbons anything covered in flesh and you were lucky if it wasn't you. He had a murderous streak to rival Eric 'The Eviscerator' Edwards, last year's winner of the Serial Killer World Championships, and a lust for blood that would make a Central African dictator go running for the sick bucket.

A consummate predator he had many, and various hunting methods at his disposal, ones that were always guaranteed to net him his prey. They included, but were not limited to, the marauding, 'all out frontal assault involving lots of noise, slashing claws, and razor sharp fangs,' the patient, 'stalk through the grass, watch for a bit, then pounce when you're not looking,' and, of course, the beautifully stealthy and infinitely more terrifying, 'hanging about on a bird table pretending to be a peanut'.

He came and went as he pleased, not that anyone or anything would argue with him. Why, just the other night he'd had a run in with a large Forest Hound who'd had the temerity to use Noggin's favourite scratching post as a makeshift toilet. On discovering this most foul of desecrations, Noggin had turned into a fifty-six-pound ball of fur and claws that had trounced the much bigger animal in three seconds flat. And then, to add insult to considerable injury, Noggin had used the battered canine as a combined scratch post and cat litter, providing proof that cats have a finely honed sense of irony.

Tonight, though, he had eschewed the dank perils of the forest and was hunting in and around the town square, because at this particular time of night there was a very good chance that he could snag some staggering drunk, rough him up a bit, and deposit him on Mandrake's front step.

Many was the morning that Mandrake would open his front door to get the milk only to find a semi-conscious and heavily lacerated creature staring up at him in bewilderment with Noggin sat proudly on their chest. On one occasion he'd found Ten Foot Teddy out there, face down in a pot plant with an ear and most of his trousers missing. Quite how Noggin had managed to overpower the enormous golem and get him to the house was a mystery, and it would remain as such because no one was daft enough to investigate the matter. Not without arranging their funeral and making sure that their affairs were in order anyway.

After having a sniff at the fountain (which occupied him for about twenty minutes what with blood having the same effect on a vampire cat that catnip has on an ordinary moggy), making sure that his territory was still adequately marked (he didn't have to travel too far to do this. He could put a fire out at three hundred yards), and depositing what, on first appearance, seemed to be a five foot length of rope on the pavement outside Mrs. Strudel's café (a mistake that her son, Derek would make later that day when he tried to pick it up), Noggin swaggered over to The Bolt and Jugular. It was almost time for the pub to close and the shouts from the landlord and the complaints from the patrons were signal enough to draw Noggin in.

As he neared Skullenia's only pub, his senses were overawed by the various aromas emanating from within. It was a subtle combination of bad food, pungent and highly corrosive alcohol, and body odours that wouldn't have been out of place in a morgue where the cooling system had broken down. (Or a teenage boy's bedroom for that matter because that's just as bad. That's if you can get in it of course. Obviously you'd have to negotiate a mountain of clothes, some items of which may actually be clean, some questionable and, quite frankly, revolting substances that could only be identified in a laboratory, and a well-thumbed collection of exotic periodicals containing ladies in minimal clothing, tradesmen of one sort or another, and some very informative articles that are about as likely to be read as Philo the Dwarf's guide to the Slam-dunk).

Noggin watched the exiting drinkers, studying each one carefully before he made his choice. To be honest he wasn't overly bothered which one he was going to attack. Noggin would take on anything you see, be it a cowering mouse or a rhinoceros with an attitude problem. But whatever it was, it needed to be capable of putting up a bit of a fight, just for show if nothing else.

A moment later he had his target in sight, that being a reasonably sized demon that looked quite handy. He was heavily built, carrying a large club, and gave the definite impression that he hadn't had quite enough booze to turn him into a gibbering imbecile i.e. he was still vertical and was walking in a straight line. Mostly.

Noggin crouched down into what renowned naturalist Sir David Attenborough would call, 'a preparatory attack position', or what the casual observer would see as, 'psychotic cat getting ready to shred some poor bugger to chunks'.

Noggin inched forward, keeping to the shadows and so low to the ground that he was barely noticeable. It was then that he heard a noise to his right that made his ear flick. Still intent on his target though, he ignored it. Then it happened again.

Annoyed that it might be a rival predator trespassing on his patch (although in reality this was quite unlikely. There weren't many creatures in Skullenia brave enough to tackle the animal that had once skewered a cow to a shed), Noggin turned his head. The noise was coming from a dark alley that ran between the pub and the house next door. Patiently, he stared into the gloom, but even with his enhanced night-time vision, Noggin couldn't make out what was causing it.

Now the feline faced a dilemma. Should he go after his intended quarry, or investigate the alleyway? It was only when the noise came once more that Noggin abandoned his intended victim and boldly turned into the alley.

Still staying low, he padded forward softly and quietly so as not to give his presence away.

After a few minutes the moon appeared from behind a dense bank of clouds and shed its sepia like glow on to the world below, allowing Noggin to see what it was that had been making the noise.

For the first time in any of his lives, Noggin the vampire cat turned tail and ran away.

\* \* \*

Constable Gullett's size fourteen leather boots beat a rhythmic tattoo on the weathered, grey pavement. Well, they did for half a dozen steps or so before he had to stop and get his breath back. Although he was more than capable of solving any crime that came his way, and managed to uphold law and order in Skullenia all by himself with a natural skill, an unerring grace, and the utmost respect for the judicial system in general, he had let his physical fitness slip ever so slightly over the years. In fact, so unfit was the good constable that, not only was the average corpse in better condition than him (a dead one that is, not some ravening zombie hungry for a brain-based breakfast), but so was the average villain. Consequently, and somewhat contrary to the previous statement that Gullett could solve any crime that came his way (and let's face it, he wasn't going to go towards one. That was just silly, unnecessary, and totally irresponsible), what that actually meant was that every case that he applied his detective skills to was concluded with a simple, two line entry in his pocket book that read, 'Suspect got away', 'No witnesses'. It wasn't laziness you understand, it was just that Constable Gullett was exceedingly pragmatic, didn't believe in gilding the lily, and chose to use the word 'solved' in the same way that the Man Booker Prize judging panel employ the phrase, 'A nice, easy relaxing read'.

(No doubt that observation's ruined my chances. I reckon I could have been in this year as well. Hilary Mantel indeed).

At present PC Gullett was at the far end of town, just past Grendle's shop, a little way from Mrs. Ladle's house, and not too far from the road that led to Count Jocular's castle. He could see the vast and imposing edifice in the distance, shrouded as it was by mist, clouds, rampaging thunderstorms, bolts of lightning, bats, howls of anguish, screams of terror, scary unknowable thingamabobs, and yet more mist. Not that he was at all put off by its presence, you understand. As strange as it was, having the ancient, granite monstrosity nestled there was really rather comforting when all was said and done, and in spite of all the murder, torture, horrible deaths, grisly violations, and dubious decorative disasters that occurred within its gruesome walls, it was, and forever would be, a reassuring constant that spoke of a certain permanence and steadfastness. It said, quite simply, home.

He liked to stop here because it represented the halfway point of his tour around the town, and being such, it was, quite naturally, the most logical place to rest and have a quick bite to eat, and seeing that it was twenty six minutes and thirty eight seconds since his last intake of calories, he knew he was just about at his physical limit and very close to hitting the proverbial wall.

(To fend off that most terrifying of eventualities, Gullett made it his business to know to the nanosecond how long his various travels took, how far he was from the nearest eatery, and who to call on should the unthinkable happen and he run out of provisions. Thankfully, that had only ever happened once and such was the trauma of the nightmarish event that he'd needed the afternoon off work and a lengthy session of counselling in the shape of a fully loaded baguette that wouldn't have looked out of place in an aircraft hangar).

After commencing his beat, his first stop was always at Mrs. Strudel's where he'd pop in for a sit down, a well-earned cup of tea, and a moderately sized piece of cake (it was moderately sized to him, anyway. If it was presented to anyone else, they'd wonder why you'd asked them to eat an Ottoman).

He called in at the cafe because it was seven minutes and eleven seconds from the police station, and there was no way that he'd be able to continue his beat without further sustenance, especially after such a protracted length of time pounding the streets. (It wasn't that far distance wise, but then most people are a lot fitter than Constable Gullett and could make the short trip with consummate ease. Come to think of it most vegetables are a lot fitter than Constable Gullett. In that case I suppose they'd make the trip with consommé ease.

Now clearly, that overt generalisation about larger persons may or may not include those of you that have chosen to read this tale, but I can't spend all of my time singling out everybody, so if I've offended anyone then I most sincerely and humbly apologise. You may very well have the cruising speed of an arthritic parsnip but hey, there's nothing wrong with that and I'm not judging you in any way at all. Just don't ever queue in front of me at the supermarket).

At the end of the path was a small gate at the side of which was a stile, and it was onto this robust piece of woodland furniture that Gullett lowered himself. This he did gingerly, and with more than a hint of care for he was quite a stout fellow, one who'd been known to ever so slightly damage the odd chair or two in his time. (Actually, if we're being completely honest, and in the interests of transparency etc. he was actually a bit of a fatty who had no idea what anything below his belt looked like, and whose waist was far below where it should actually be. His trouser size could only be guessed at, but one pair took a fortnight to make and kept a Fibulan tailor in business).

He took off his helmet, removed a crinkly, brown package from within and placed it on the ground.

He then picked up the crinkly, brown package and put his helmet on the ground. It was dark after all and seeing as his sandwich was roughly the size of said headgear it was an easy enough mistake to make.

As he unwrapped the neatly covered package the aroma of ham and pickle stole into his nose. The filling was his absolute favourite and had been lovingly made for him by Doris Strudel. (Yes indeed. As well as maggot soufflé, Scapularian brain and noodle soup, blood trifle, and various other revolting concoctions straight out of The Evil Dead All You Can Eat Morgue, Skullenia's resident purveyor of undead victuals did, on occasion, make normal food as well. That's if pickle can be classed as normal food of course, and not as something that should be sealed in a lead lined box and cast away to the deepest depths of the ocean for all eternity where it won't be found until the sun goes nova and spreads the charred remnants of our planet across what remains of our decimated solar system. Or put in the bin, whichever's easier really).

As he chewed, he relaxed against the gatepost and listened to the night-time noises. Then, gazing upwards he chanced to see a shooting star blazing a fiery trail across the pitch-black sky.

His second bite faltered halfway to his mouth when he heard a rustle from the bushes to his left. Not that that was unusual of course. There were all sorts of creatures hiding, or skulking, or prowling about at this time of night, and even though Gullett knew most of them either socially or professionally, this was Skullenia after all. It paid to be cautious. And armed.

"Alright," said Gullett, popping the half-eaten snack into his helmet. "Who's there?"

RUSTLE. RUSTLE.

"Come on now. Stop buggering about. Don't make me come in there."

RUSTLE. RUSTLE. RUSTLE.

"Is that you again, Henge?"

Henge was a rather large troll who had a penchant for late night excursions into the woods where he would partake of the pungent and hallucinatory emanations of the Warbling Dollybush, a tall, spiky, blue leafed plant whose unique chemical composition caused it to have an adverse and somewhat relaxing effect on the brain cells of any creature that chose to imbibe its wispy emissions. Or, to put it another way that probably makes a lot more sense, if you smoked it you ended up smacked off your face, higher than a British bankers end of year bonus, and sillier than a room full of drunk clowns.

Consequently, and somewhat unsurprisingly, Henge could quite often be found blundering about in the dead of night either running away from some imagined horror or claiming to be something a bit odd. In recent times he'd been a spaceman, a carrot, October 1746, and, for some unfathomable reason, the colour yellow.

Around these parts most people called him Stoned.

The rustle was replaced by a thump, as if something very large, and very out of it, had hit the ground.

"Great," said Gullett, making sure his sandwich was safe before putting his helmet back on. "That's all I need."

He'd had to get Stoned home on several previous occasions. It wasn't an easy task and one that required a strong back, a lot of patience, and at some point in the proceedings, a block and tackle.

As he walked towards the undergrowth, he got out his torch and flicked it on. It lit up the night for the briefest of moments before going straight back out.

'Strange,' thought Gullett. He'd only put fresh batteries in the damn thing that very afternoon, not long before he came on shift actually, and that was only a couple of hours ago at the most.

(He couldn't remember precisely what time that was, but that was mainly because he didn't have an official start time, and although not arbitrary by any means it did vary on a shift by shift basis. As you can imagine, crime and disorder don't have a strict timetable so Gullett's working hours had to reflect that fact, and depended on numerous and varied technical and analytical factors such as crime statistics, the time of year, hours of available darkness, transient visitors to the town, which ale was guesting at The Bolt and Jugular and, most importantly of all, what time he got up).

"Come on then, let's be 'avin' you," said Gullett, his stentorian voice booming through the still night air.

Silence descended. Even the rustling had stopped.

"Look, if you want somewhere cold and miserable to spend the night, I'm more than happy to oblige. And I'm not talking about Mrs. Ladle's kitchen either."

Without warning, something that he wouldn't have been able to describe in his pocket notebook due to the lack of appropriate vocabulary, burst forth from the confines of its leafy hideaway and headed straight for the policeman, who hollered in surprise before fainting dead away.

* * *

Deirdre Clownpuncher sat bolt upright in bed and stared wide and bleary eyed straight ahead into the dark and mysterious recesses of her bedroom. (Obviously her bedroom didn't actually have any mysterious recesses because it was her bedroom and she was intimately familiar with it, but by describing it as such lends the paragraph a certain spooky gravitas that I have now, on reflection, completely ruined. It was dark though).

Despite the warmth of the night she shivered as if it were much colder, but that didn't prevent a thin sheen of perspiration from appearing on her forehead.

She flicked her bedside lamp on and studied her room. It all seemed normal. Well, everything was where it should be anyway, right down to her cat, Beanbag, who was curled up at her feet as usual (not that he'd be anywhere else. He was a beanbag by nature as well as by name and wouldn't have moved a muscle if he was sitting on top of an active volcano whilst a mouse did his, 'the thing about cats' comedy routine right in front of him).

Deirdre swung her legs off the bed, rubbed her eyes, and eased her feet into her slippers. For the life of her she couldn't figure out why she'd woken up. There were no disturbances going on outside, no noise coming from the Chimney family next door, and she hadn't been having any particularly vivid or worrisome dreams. It certainly was bizarre, especially when she was usually such a sound sleeper. Ah well.

She stood up and put her dressing gown on, deciding that a nice, hot cup of tea was the ideal thing to have before settling down again. And maybe a biscuit or three as well. There was nothing quite like a few dunked goodies for soothing one's mood. (I'm thinking of Bill Oddie on a ducking stool now).

Once in the kitchen, Deirdre popped the kettle on then sat down at the table whilst she waited for it to boil.

Her eyes drifted to the window, through which she could hear the gentle lapping of the water in the harbour, the ripple of sails in the wind, and the distant tolling of a ships bell. She'd lived in Shark's

Bay her entire life and never tired of its peaceful tranquillity.

Suddenly roused from her musings by the insistent whistling of the kettle, she realised she'd been lost in her own thoughts and that the small kitchen was rapidly filling up with steam.

Taking the kettle off the hob, she filled the teapot, gave it a few minutes to brew, popped two spoonsful of sugar into her best china cup, then filled it to the brim. And that was that. She took her tea without milk you see, enjoying as she did the acrid taste of the tannin as it danced across her tongue.

This particular way of taking her beverage was a remnant of her childhood, an age when money was scarce, and sacrifices had to be made. She had happy memories of those long-ago times, though, and never felt like she'd missed out on anything.

After placing a tea cosy over the pot lest she fancy another cup, she returned to her seat.

After taking a dainty sip she placed her drink onto the table and turned back to the window. (The cup itself went onto a stainless-steel coaster lest it scorch the wood. As in keeping with mature ladies all over the world, Deirdre had a mouth that was coated in asbestos, a physical trait that allowed her to imbibe liquids so hot even Hephaestus himself would need a couple of ice cubes and a straw). She furrowed her brow when she noticed something.

What she saw there made her wonder if she were dreaming and was in fact, at that moment, safely tucked up in bed and trying to stop Beanbag from nipping at her toes. Either that or the devastating stroke that had taken her mother at an early age had decided to pay her a visit.

The steam from the boiling kettle had clouded the kitchen window, apart from one area on the bottom right hand pane. It wasn't abstract and she had no clue how it had gotten there or what it meant.

There, in the dripping condensation, was one word.

SKULLENIA.

* * *

Ollie was about to knock on the door to Crumble's lab when he stopped, his knuckles a few inches from the wooden surface.

The reason for his hesitance was that the professor was becoming rather more eccentric of late, a state of affairs that made visits to his subterranean domain of lunacy somewhat more hazardous than usual, although on its own that statement is rather hard to qualify and needs a certain amount of clarification.

To say that the mad old fool was getting madder was like saying that a cup is getting cuppier, the floor distinctly more floory, or a table is getting more table like than normal. It's not a thing of flux, but a permanent state of being, one bestowed with a durable rigidity not subject to change or deviation. And, as is the way with these things, they simply are, always have been, and always will be. It's a happy status quo that reminds you no matter what happens, things can't be all that bad. Not as bad as Crumble anyway.

For example, just the other week Ronnie had popped down to the laboratory to see the good professor with the intention of finding out if Crumble had managed to further his progress into discovering that most challenging and elusive of alchemy's forgotten secrets, turning anything that he could get his hands on into tobacco. Sadly though, despite numerous efforts and vain attempts, the professor hadn't yet succeeded, but he had managed to make a mess on a scale not seen since something called Katrina turned New Orleans into a snow globe. When asked, Crumble hadn't been able to explain exactly what had happened, but poor Ronnie had ended up needing a dozen stitches, a stiff drink, and a course of robust antibiotics, and although Ronnie himself couldn't be completely sure of what had happened either, he was positive that it had something to do with a bowl of soup, a child's spinning top, two coconuts, and enough electricity to jump start Mount Everest.

Ronnie had left vowing never to enter, 'that bloody idiots madhouse' ever again. Not unless he produced the fags anyway.

"Professor," Ollie called out, sounding a hell of a lot more confident than he actually felt. "Is it safe to come in?"

"Indeed, it is, dear boy," came the reply from within.

Suitably reassured, or as much as he could be at any rate, Ollie prepared to venture in, albeit with a healthy dose of wariness, a hint of trepidation, and a teensy weensy measure of being about to run away in a mad panic as if the hounds of hell themselves were snapping at his cape.

He opened the door and stepped inside.

"Just watch out for the…never mind."

Ollie gazed down at his right foot and grimaced in disgust. His shiny black, patent leather shoe, the footwear for all discerning vampires everywhere, was now covered in something rarely seen outside of a low budget, 1950's science fiction movie, a handkerchief suffused with the bi-products of a heavy cold, or a microwave ready meal for one. It was otherworldly in colour (it was green and glowing), it didn't look quite right in a seriously wrong way (it was green and glowing), and, most disturbingly of all, it was moving (it was moving).

"Prof. What on earth is this…thing?"

"I'm not quite sure, actually," said the scientist, cheerfully. "But I think it moved in about a week ago. I've tried communicating with it and so far discovered that it reacts to sound, so if you ask it nicely to get off, it'll probably oblige."

"Probably?" said Ollie, doing a creditable version of the Skullenian Hokey Cokey (it was similar to the traditional Hokey Cokey except that when you put your left leg in, it stayed in. It didn't normally last for very long. Not more than five rounds anyway, by which time it was more of a Pushy Wushy).

"Yes. As long as you stop shaking your foot," said the professor.

Ollie did as he was told and stopped shaking his foot. He gave Crumble a look of dark and malevolent intent, one designed to convey his displeasure at being placed in such a predicament (which is a bit of a lie if I'm being completely honest; I only put it in because I liked the sound of it so much. In actual fact, Ollie's look was more of the pleading, pathetic, reserved for a toddler who's just seen a monster under his bed variety. Or that of his friend Flug, who would wet himself if he found a toddler under *his* bed).

"What happens when you shake it then?" asked Ollie.

Crumble put the cleaver that he'd been hefting onto his work bench and grabbed a glass beaker.

"Bits of it fly off," he said, approaching Ollie.

"That doesn't sound too bad," said the half vampire, somewhat relieved.

"And explode," finished Crumble, who was now on his hands and knees at Ollie's feet.

Ollie didn't offer any comment on this interesting little titbit. On hearing the news that some of the softer parts of his anatomy situated below the belt might be liable to suffer the indignities of a concussive blast at any moment and end up decorating the walls of the lab, he had ceased any and all bodily movement, to the point that he was less likely to move than a twelve year old girl told to sit on the lap of a 1970's DJ.

Crumble placed the beaker onto the toe of Ollie's shoe so that the open end was towards the seething, globular mass.

"Now, keep very very still," said Crumble, concocting a statement so patently stupid that he'd shortly become the world record holder as, 'Person who uttered the most ridiculous thing ever said ever in the history of everything ever said since people started saying stuff,' beating the current holder, Sergeant William 'Willy' Williams of the United States Marine Corps. On being presented with the captured Osama Bin Laden, the soldier had said, "Do you think we should let him off. He said he was sorry?"

And there've been others.

Take Dolly Kindle for instance, who sang songs about hats and collected wonky buttons in her spare time. On hearing the news that she was with child she said to her GP, "Are you sure it's mine? I don't even like milk."

Then there was Rhapsody Limb, a shopkeeper from Intellinnsidesville who told a burglar, "Of course I've got a safe. You don't think I'd keep all my money in the bank, do you? I'm not that stupid."

And who can forget Oxford Mole, a deceased chair stacker from Mimple who, before being found dead in the bath, had been heard to announce, "There's no way electricity can be that dangerous."

Now, I could conclude this searingly satirical section with some choice phrases uttered by your friends and mine, the politicians, but seeing as everything that every one of them has said since the dawn of time is stupid to the point of being barely believable, we'll take it as a given that they're out in front in the nonsensical statement business, although that fact is slightly skewed in that they do have a head start on virtually everybody else. They're all morons.

"Come on then, little one," cooed the Professor, who then proceeded to make kissy wissy noises. "Into the jar there's a good boy."

Ollie looked on in disbelief as the gelatinous blob oozed its way towards Crumble, much like a cat does when called by its owner (albeit a cat that's fallen into a blender, been whizzed around for a couple of minutes after which the resulting feline soup is decanted and neatly sewn into a translucent skin bag. Oh, my goodness that's disgusting. I really shouldn't write stuff like that. I feel sick now).

After a few moments, a dread filled span of time that was filled with a vaguely thick sucking sound that reminded the increasingly nauseous Ollie of the noise that the toilet made after it had been violated by Flug and his prehistoric digestive system, the sticky mass slipped into the beaker where it sat pulsating like a fleshy, emerald heart. Crumble put a lid on the receptacle and placed it on a shelf.

"I think I can say without fear of contradiction that that is one of the most disturbing things that I have ever seen in my life," said Ollie, which, when you take into account that he lived in Skullenia, saw death and mayhem on a nightly basis, witnessed first-hand just what Count Jocular got up to in his torture chambers, and accidentally saw a Christmas episode of Eastenders one year, was quite a statement.

"Oh, I don't know," said Crumble, returning to his bench and his cleaver. "I've seen worse."

"Really?"

"Oh yes. Believe me, Ollie, ever since I lifted the veil and had a peak and a poke at some of the horrors lurking in the faltering shadows of the nethers, there's nothing in this world that I find disturbing anymore. Well, not much."

"Still haven't got over the Egon incident then?" said Ollie, absently rubbing his right shoe on his left trouser leg.

Crumble shuddered and shook his head. Or maybe he shook, and his head shuddered. Whatever it was though, it was clear that a recent memory perturbed him.

"That, dear Ollie, is going to take some time," he said. "And perhaps a couple of sessions of hypnotherapy."

About a month ago the Professor had been summoned to Jocular's castle because the vampire lord had been having a problem with rats. Not that that was unusual in an old building the size of his, of course. In fact, it's normally a prerequisite, a distinct selling point, and something that's mentioned in the legal pack.

The problem with the current infestation was this. Rather than doing all of the normal ratty things like pinching food, pooing all over the place, and going 'squeak' the moment you try and go to sleep, this particular lot seemed to have taken a vitriolic dislike to Jocular's interior designs.

At first, the vampire lord thought that a couple of his flunkys had gone rogue, so that being the case, he abused them for a bit in a bid to force them to confess. Sadly, they didn't, and despite the horrific violations he inflicted upon their fragile little bodies, and their pleading protestations of innocence, he took their reticence to plead guilty as guilt. And yes, I know that's unfair but don't blame me. He *is* a vampire lord for goodness sake. It's not like he was going to send them to bed early without any supper.

Anyway, moral and ethical issues aside, Jocular had made his mind up and so ended their existences in rather a grisly fashion, as was his wont. And besides, he'd gotten his tools out and it'd seemed a shame to have gone to all that effort for nothing. (As you're no doubt aware, Jocular is a torturing aficionado, one so adept at inflicting pain and suffering that, not only does he instil abject fear and bone jarring terror wherever he goes, he makes the Spanish Inquisition look like a bunch of over ripe bollards performing the Argentine tango on a very soggy slice of Macedonian Fruit Bat. Goodness, how unusual was that analogy? I bet you weren't expecting that were you? Don't worry about it though. Nobody was).

When the damage had continued, Jocular had tasked Egon to get to the bottom of it, but in spite of all his efforts he failed miserably. Mind you, seeing as those efforts had mostly involved wandering around the castle, leaving bits of cake lying around, and saying 'here ratty ratty,' every now and again, it was hardly surprising.

He'd even tried the old Pied Piper of Hamlyn trick, although not having a pipe, a pair of overly tight and colourfully garish hose, a feathered cap, some curly toed shoes, or any musical talent whatsoever, he'd wandered about the castle like a dusty and unkempt vagrant, forlornly blowing into a makeshift kazoo until he'd turned purple and got a headache. He did try using a pie as well, but that just made a chickeny/mushroomy mess on the carpet when he'd blown into it and attracted more rats.

Anyway, despite the odds against him, it had actually worked. Well, it had up to a point. Instead of the rats it was The Children Of The Night that had been lured away from their subterranean dwelling, and such was their dislike of the racket produced by the offending instrument they'd stalked Egon for fifteen minutes, given him a ferocious mauling of such eye watering severity that he only had three thumbs left by the time they spat him out, and attempted to insert said noise-maker somewhere where it would be considerably harder to hear and in need of disinfecting.

And so, after all of that silly nonsense, Jocular was at his wits end, and particularly upset due to the fact that a pair of his favourite curtains had been torn to shreds (they covered one of his beloved torture devices, a machine so insidious that just to look upon it was enough to drive most creatures insane. Whilst skewering the eyeballs, slicing off the lips, and inserting a rather large and very hot poker into ones fundament, an attached gramophone repeatedly played a concert by Tone Deaf Thompson, a musician so dreadfully atrocious that ears had been known to spontaneously bleed when he played. Well, they did once the knitting needles had gone in anyway, but as Jocular always said, 'It is all in ze presentation no').

And so, with no idea what to do for the best, the vampire lord had called in Professor Crumble to take care of the problem. The scientist was always suffering from some sort of infestation or another and had therefore become quite adept at clearing his lab before things got out of hand. Or indeed if the hands got out. They were quite nimble once their fingers got moving.

Thusly charged, the professor had made his way to the castle armed with a bag full of his 'Double XL Super Duper Rodent Detention Devices (2018)' patent pending. (Don't expect to see them in the shops anytime soon though. The patent will be pending for quite some time to come. Forever in fact. This is due to them being rather expensive to produce, awkward to transport, and more danger-ous than not pretending to cry when a North Ko-rean leader pops his canvas slippers. Consequently, Crumble's design would be consigned to the bottom drawer in the patent office along with all the other inventions deemed unsuitable for release for one reason or another, although to be honest, it's usu-ally because of the adverse financial implications. Here's a few examples.

There's the cure for the common cold, a formula which would cause the entire pharmaceutical indus-try to collapse overnight because its main ingredient is cabbage.

The world's first perpetual motion device is in there, but that's a bit of a non-starter because elec-tricity is quite the money maker don't you know.

There's even a recipe for a decent tasting kebab that a sober person could enjoy. Now, you might think that would make sense, but no. Firstly, no one would believe it, and secondly, all the drunks would stop getting, well, drunk, just so they could eat one. After all, the only reason that people get sloshed in the first place is so they can have a kebab at half past two in the morning because let's face it, who's going to eat one if they haven't had fourteen pints of super strength lager and enough shots to drown an elk.

So as you can see, so inextricably linked are the two activities that the introduction of the tasty doner would lead to the collapse of the breweries, the inevitable closure of every inn and tavern in the world, the decimation of the crisp and nut industry, and the rendering of thousands, nay millions of people out of work who then can't afford to buy anything at all and thus sustain the economy. Then, because all the reformed drinkers have got nothing to do, the realisation of what society is really like will dawn on them and remind them of why they started drinking in the first place. Obviously, this will lead to civil disobedience and rioting in the streets due to a lack of alcohol, and it won't be long before law and order has completely and utterly broken down, transportation and communications systems become redundant, the very fabric of society collapses due to the lack of any viable urban infrastructure, and civilisation is reduced to nothing more than a few warring factions vying for control of Papa Craps' Kebab and Botulism House and the local offy.

So, as you can see, it's not oil, shares, money, or gold bullion that makes the world go around. It's kebabs. Take those away and the shish really would hit the fan).

And so, with the traps suitably deployed Crumble had headed down to Egon's quarters to apprise him of his progress, although the interconnected series of rooms were so compact that they should have been called eighths. Not getting a reply he'd let himself in, popped the kettle on, and gone into the bathroom to answer the call of nature. (He could've used one of the other toilets that were dotted around the castle of course, but they were absolute horror stories and only of any real use if you were suffering from severe constipation and needed a bit of a hand evacuating your torpid bowel. Upon entering you never knew whether you were going to be confronted by a mangled corpse, trapped for all eternity in a pseudo medieval death-trap, or surprised by paint of such a vibrant hue that it could give your shoes an epileptic fit).

There he was met by the sight of Egon stepping out of the shower, a vision that had shocked Crumble so much that he'd fled the castle in terror, leaving his traps in place, a mad professor shaped hole in the wall, and a portion of what little remaining sanity that his turbulent mind had left, in his wake.

Egon had visited him a few days later (fully clothed thankfully) to return the traps and to inform the professor that they'd been very successful. They never spoke about the shower incident though, and never would. In fact, such was the trauma that he'd suffered, Crumble hadn't even been able to tell Ollie about the specifics of what he'd seen; only stating that he would have nightmares for quite some time, and would never, ever be able to eat muesli again.

"Anyway, dear boy," said Crumble. "What can I do for you?"

"I just need a fuse for a plug. What's with the cleaver by the way?" said Ollie, wondering if Crumble had decided on a dalliance with serial killing. "You look like Cedric the Splitter."

Crumble gazed at the large and very sharp implement in his hand. He'd forgotten that he was holding it. 'Good job I didn't need to scratch,' he thought absently.

"Oh, I was just using it to chop up some pork belly."

"And why on earth would you be doing that? You don't usually cook anything down here. Not intentionally anyway," said Ollie.

"I've come up with a digestible product that combines the protein-based benefits of meat and the vitamin content of a fruity drink." He pointed to a large beaker on the bench. It contained a lumpy, orangey, thickly swirling liquid that looked like it'd been squeezed out of a boil the size of a space hopper.

"Of course, you have," said Ollie, recognising the familiar, acidic taste of nausea as it arrived to take up residence in his gag reflex. "And what is this culinary delight?"

"Squashage."

Ollie's nausea alighted from its chosen mode of transport and was checking in.

"Have you tried it?" he asked.

"Oh, good lord no," said Crumble with a rare glimpse of insight into his own particular brand of lunacy. "It looks absolutely disgusting. I did give some to a mouse though."

"And."

"I haven't seen it since."

"Mmm," murmured Ollie thickly, his nausea now unpacked and settled into its accommodation where it was ordering room service and raiding the mini bar.

Crumble put the cleaver down and pointed to something else.

"I've got high hopes for this though," he said cheerfully, ever the insane optimist. "I'm convinced it could be a real winner."

He was pointing to an ordinary bowl, the type you'd put your cereal or a nice bit of soup into. This one, however, didn't contain anything as easily identifiable as Weetabix, Cornflakes, or a serving of Mulligatawny. Whatever this was, it was red, a bit wibbly wobbly, and, more alarmingly, giving off wisps of grey/black smoke.

"I can't even begin to hazard a guess at what that might be," said Ollie keeping well back, although the back that he was attempting to keep well was entirely insufficient when it came to looking at anything at all in Crumble's Laboratory of Lunacy, especially if it was emitting fumes. The 'well back' that he should ideally have been keeping would have put him in the next village, and whilst that would have been an inherently safer option, it was obviously impractical.

Ironically, and some would say, not surprisingly, seventy five percent of the items in Crumble's lab actually did have the ability to blow you into the next village, although what condition you'd be in when you landed was anybody's guess. You'd be floppier than usual that's for sure.

"It smells vaguely of strawberries," said Ollie, taking a cautionary sniff.

"Indeed, it does, dear boy. That's because it's a cunning fusion of said fruit, sugar, gelatine, and water."

"Oh. That doesn't sound too bad."

"And just a touch of TNT."

"Ah."

Ollie shook his head and prepared himself for the inevitable. He didn't want to ask about it but knew that he was going to ask about it anyway, because the asking about it was slightly less of a hassle than the not asking about it. This was on account of Crumble being absurdly proud of his lethal inventions and his willingness to extol their virtues at every given opportunity. Ollie had tried not asking about one once, but this only caused the professor to follow him around for the rest of the day asking why Ollie hadn't asked him about something when he'd asked about so many things before. In response, Ollie had then asked him why it was so important that he ask him about everything, to which Crumble had said that he was only asking why Ollie hadn't asked him about his invention, because it was only by entering into a discussion that was preceded by Ollie asking him what something was and what it did, could he gauge what was thought of the item that he'd manufactured. Ollie had asked

Crumble to leave at that point, lest the half vampire lost what was left of his frayed temper and slaughter the old chap in cold, albeit ever so slightly deranged blood. When the professor had asked why he'd been asked to leave, Ollie had screamed, held his head in his hands, and flopped down into his chair. Crumble hadn't asked why. He'd just left the office, which had upset Ollie a little bit, actually. The professor hadn't asked him what the matter was.

Anyway, after silently praying to whatever unseen power that ruled this bizarre domain to be transported to an alternate reality where things like sentient slime and mad old men who'd had a chemistry set for their third birthday didn't reside, Ollie bit the bullet and asked the question.

"So. What is it then?"

"Jellygnite," said Crumble.

Good grief.

"So, very much a food-based theme today then. And how do you see this being deployed? Parties for naughty children perhaps? Terrorist themed costume evenings at the Women's Institute?"

"Ooh, terrorism, there's a thought," said Crumble. "I can see the advert now." 'Professor Crumble's Jellygnite. Putting the fun into fundamentalism.'

Ollie groaned, realising that the word mental was very much an integral part of it as well.

Deciding that he'd like to leave with all of his limbs still attached, Ollie reminded Crumble why he'd come down in the first place, took his fuse, thanked him and left the lab, making a note to have Ethan put some more locks on the door. About a dozen would do it. Crumble and his wandering mind were a combination that needed locking up. Securely.

* * *

Ronnie, Stitches, and Flug were sitting at the kitchen table. At present they were engaged in a game of Dragons and Stairwells, a fun game to play for all the family (Manson's, West's, Fritzl's…you get the general idea).

It was the same as Snakes and Ladders apart from the end result where the winner was allowed to physically abuse the losing players with a variety of household appliances that had been set on fire, move their bed ninety degrees to the right and set it on fire, and set fire to the their feet, if they weren't already on fire of course. Seeing as this was a game with friends though, they'd disregarded the medieval small print and just got on with it, as indeed they did with a lot of the games that they played. This was because the Skullenian rules for the game, as were the guidelines for most things in the town, were rather harsh.

In Skullenian Scrabble for instance, if you put a word down that wasn't a word and it was challenged successfully, the challenger could build an extension on your house and move his granny in. If you were made bankrupt in Skullenian Monopoly, you had to find the nearest ogre, kick it in the spherical objects, and ask it over for dinner. These pale into insignificance, however, when compared to what happens if you participate in a game of Skullenian Hide and Seek. Once you're found, your clothes are removed, your head is shaved, and you have to walk to Fibula whilst proclaiming that Count Jocular is a villainous, land-grabbing ghoul who dresses like a colour-blind fop. The last time it'd been played was just over seventy years ago, and such was the extreme nature of the punishment for losing, one player still hadn't been found. And he wouldn't be either. He wasn't taking any chances and had moved to a remote island somewhere in The Pacific Ocean where he now lived in a barrel.

Anyway, with all the savage regulations sensibly eschewed, they were well into their game and having a lovely time of it. Well, not really. At the moment, Flug was staring at the board and looking like a drugged ox.

"Flug, mate," said Ronnie. "It's your turn."

"Oh, okay."

"Off you go then."

Flug stood up and went to leave the room.

"No," said Stitches, "come back and sit down, you big dummy. God Almighty, a round the world cruise would be quicker than this."

Flug thudded back to his chair and plonked himself down, disturbing the table and the board.

"Right," said Ronnie, a cigarette clamped between his lips. "What you need to do is throw the dice remember?"

"Oh yeah," said Flug. "Me 'member now."

"Good."

"Ronnie."

"Yes, Flug."

"Wot are dice?"

Stitches picked them up and put them into Flug's hand where they sat like a pair of plastic cubes with numbers on them.

"Those are dice," said the zombie. "You throw them. Please tell me you *'member* that."

What happened next was obvious. Very obvious. In fact, it was more obvious than something very obvious indeed. More obvious for instance, than being told that a politician fiddles his expenses, that a dog really does look stupid when you put clothes on it, they're animals for goodness sake, and that no matter where you put a pair of slippers, your cat will always throw up in them. That's if your cat owns a pair of slippers of course.

Flug closed his banana like fingers around the dice, drew his arm back, and launched them as if they'd been fired from a cannon.

Ronnie instantly dived for cover and landed in a heap, narrowly avoiding a couple of broken ribs in the process (they were on the floor next to a skull, a femur, and a few ragged pieces of cloth. You guessed it. Noggin). Stitches though was slightly slower and took a glancing blow to the scalp that left a neat furrow in his flesh. It looked like a tiny farmer had ploughed his head.

Then, at just under the speed of stupidity, both dice smashed through the kitchen window and landed somewhere in the back garden.

"Do me win?" said Flug, jumping up and down excitedly and knocking over various items in the process (a couple of glasses, two chairs, and a brass band twelve and a half miles away).

In response, the next minute or so was filled with a variety of colourful metaphors that, if repeated here, would corrupt the young, offend the old, and annoy parents everywhere. Plus, it would have a serious impact on my reader demographics and consequently sales, so use your imagination for f*&^+s sake.

The end result of all this silliness was that Flug was sent to his room to calm down. Or, to be more precise, Stitches took him to his room to calm down. He'd only have gotten lost otherwise. He then guided Flug across his bedroom to his bed, because, yes indeed, you've guessed it, he'd only have gotten lost. Come to think of it there weren't many places that Flug could get to unaided because he had the unerring capacity to get lost just about anywhere. That's if he could get to anywhere in the first place without getting lost on the way of course. Anyway, where was I? I got lost there for a moment.

After all the fuss, palaver, and general chaos, Ronnie ended up standing in the garden with a torch. He was sweeping it back and forth trying to work out where the dice had gone but seeing as how the garden was like a primeval jungle it was like looking for some dice in a primeval jungle.

(He was trying to find them because, as with homes all over the world, it doesn't matter how many boardgames you own, you can only ever find one pair of dice. You could have every edition of Trivial Pursuit ever released, eighteen sets of Ludo, and be a professional craps player and you'd still only ever be able to find two of the numbered little buggers. It's my theory that they're in the same place as your missing socks, all those Biro's you bought, the TV remote you lost in 1998, the key to the back gate, your phone charger, that letter from the hospital with your appointment time on it, and your will to live when you realise that all of your stuffs gone missing and you can't have a game of Monopoly because the top hat's gone walkabout).

Ronnie scratched his chin thoughtfully and got down to business. By estimating the velocity with which they'd been thrown, calculating the distance from Flug to the window, the thickness of the glass, which would have slowed them down a tad, factoring in how much the dice weighed, and extrapolating the trajectory they would've taken once they'd left Flug's hand, Ronnie finally came to the conclusion that he didn't have a sodding clue where the bloody things were.

He took a long drag on his cigarette and watched as the smoke dissipated into the night sky. Looking for the missing dice was only a distraction anyway. He quite often stood outside and allowed his thoughts to wander (Stitches reckoned Flug had tried it once, but his thoughts had never come back).

Obviously, it wasn't the most tranquil of locations for introspection, but then again, nowhere in Skullenia was, really. Still, it was pleasant enough, especially now that Dendrite Globe had agreed to come over and tend to the overgrown patch of madness masquerading as a garden (and I don't mean he was going to visit whilst dressed as a rhododendron. He was going to tidy up a bit. Do I have to explain everything?).

And boy did it need tending to. And not only from an aesthetic viewpoint either. Health and safety was a big factor as well. Whilst exceedingly pleasing to look at, Skullenian plants can be vicious, you see, and therefore require some rather extreme horticultural intervention to stop them getting all snappy and bitey. Some of them could only be tamed with a flamethrower or a scythe the size of The Clifton Suspension Bridge, whilst others, in particular The Slathering Blood Rose of Doom and Qwango's Lily, need regular feeding to prevent them getting moody. They made triffids look like daisies. Ordinary ones that is, and not Whoppett's Belligerent Bellis for instance, a daisy so anti-social that it makes the plants that make triffids look like daisies, look like daises.

As he watched the various entities swooping overhead, Ronnie, as he often did, thought about the events that had led him here, so in the time honoured fashion of film and TV, let's engage the wibbly wobbly special effects and travel back in time for a bit (or failing that just shake the book from side to side).

Ronald Smalls been born in an ordinary town, to ordinary parents, and gone to ordinary schools where he'd received an ordinary education, and it wasn't until his late teens that he'd developed an interest in, and shown a remarkable talent, for physics and chemistry.

After getting excellent A level results he'd secured a place at a prestigious university, and it wasn't long before his natural ability was noticed and he was offered the chance to participate in a research programme (and I'm talking about proper research that is, and not the usual sort of research that university students tend to get up to. Ronnie's was of the academic variety rather than the usual, 'let's see how much I can drink before my liver decides it's had enough and moves out but in the meantime I'll piss about doing anything as long as it's not going to lectures' type so common to those indulging in what is laughingly known as a further education), one where he'd be delving into certain esoteric fields of study that were not only extremely interesting, but also rather diverse.

Knowing the opportunity was far too good to pass up, he readily agreed to take part, and it was to his unwavering delight that he found the subject matter to be not only ground breaking, but provocative, and not a little controversial, and as such not really falling within the boundaries of what would be considered a standard curriculum. (In fact, the boundary was so far away that even the Hubble telescope would've given up looking for it, grabbed its crayons, and drawn a nice picture instead).

That being the case, he had to keep his work a bit hush hush, but he wasn't overly concerned if he was tackled about it, though. Any probing questions regarding what he was doing, why he was doing it, and to what ends were easily fielded. Like all good men of science he could justify what he was up to by claiming the goals he pursued were for the good of the planet, the furthering of scientific knowledge in a quest to peek into the unknown and discover its secrets, and for the benefit of mankind in general blah blah blahdy blah.

Now clearly that would have been a bit of a fib, but isn't that what they all do? Surely all scientists tell lies about what they're doing. They have to. I mean, who wants to have to explain why they're trying to determine how many plankton will fit on the end of a pencil, work out the fat content of a mountain, or find out how long it takes a squirrel to do a Rubik's Cube?

Actually, and more accurately, Ronnie wouldn't have told a bit of a fib about his work, he'd have come out with a great big whopper of a lie. By his very nature he was driven by the allure of making as much profit as possible you see, so that being the case, he steered his research to those areas that he knew had the potential to reap the highest financial rewards. Of course, that meant extremely danger-ous work on the fringes of science, but he wasn't overly bothered about the risks because the pay-off would ultimately be worth it. Any discoveries that he made could be sold to the highest bidder, particularly those with military applications. They were worth a bomb.

And so, retreating to the confines of his lab, he'd got to work.

He'd tinkered with weapons, messed around with transport, and even had a stab at producing more palatable field rations for the soldier in battle, but none of those ideas really ignited his enthusiasm.

Then, after reading an article online about the dangers of covert operations, he'd finally settled on trying to develop new camouflage technology, because from what he could gather, it was woefully behind the times and not remotely fit for purpose. Further reading confirmed his thoughts, and he'd been left stunned that in this day and age, troops still wore uniform that only had a passing resemblance to their surroundings, and rather than concealing them, which was the point after all, it only served to make them stand out like...well...like troops trying to hide whilst wearing uniform that only had a passing resemblance to their surroundings. For all the good it did they might as well have been wearing day glow pink fatigues and carrying luminous green rifles.

(Interestingly, the combined fighting forces from the kingdom of Stanstanistan had tried that when

they attempted to invade their neighbouring territory. With breath-taking ingenuity, the leaders of
the Stanstanistanian military determined that the
enemy would be so surprised to see an army so
gaudily dressed that it would leave them floundering in disarray, and ripe for a quick defeat. Sadly
though, the plan didn't work out quite as well
as expected. Despite the entire massed ranks of
the Stanstanistan war machine making good and
steady progress, they only got about ten yards from
their barracks before they showed up on every radar
system from darkest Africa to a passing UFO that
had taken a wrong turn at Jupiter. Consequently,
and somewhat inevitably, they got blown into several thousand bloody, ragged, and very badly concealed body parts).

And so, after wrestling with his conscience, he
put his avarice to one side and forged on. Not that
it was a hard decision. Once he'd thought about
it, he quickly realised that he wasn't very comfortable with striving to improve methods of wholesale
slaughter, no matter how rich it made him, so he decided that the protection of life was what he would
dedicate his work to. And besides, what Army, Navy,
or Air-force in the world wouldn't want its person-
nel safeguarded? Also, if the opposing protagonists

were all nicely hidden, they couldn't kill each other as easily could they. Okay, so it was a relatively simplistic view of warfare, but the idea was well intentioned.

As his research progressed, Ronnie, like many of the great scientists before him who'd made astounding discoveries, had a fortuitous accident. He'd been trying to develop a camouflage vest that utilised iridescent colouring, one that had the effect of allowing the wearer to completely blend in with whatever background they happened to be standing near. It achieved this by bending light around its surface and incorporating the refracted light waves into its weave, and it was while he was testing said item that he managed to bombard it with a hefty dose of charged photons. He didn't mean to. He'd wanted to turn the kettle on and make a cup of tea but switched on the particle accelerator by mistake. Ah well. Hey ho.

(This sort of serendipitous occurrence has precedence of course. Alexander Fleming discovered penicillin on some dirty dishes because he'd run out of Fairy Liquid, whilst Florence Nightingale is credited with modernising outdated nursing techniques just because she couldn't see where she was going, stuck a candle in a bottle, and told a soldier to wash his hands after having a wee. And just to clarify, it was the soldier who'd had the wee and not Miss Nightingale. It would be unseemly to suggest that a lady of such grace and poise should have it within her to perform such an act in the presence of a bunch of rough, tough military types. Besides, she'd just had a massive poo in the corner and was feeling rather relaxed.

Surely though, one of the most celebrated and astounding discoveries ever made, one that still resonates to this day, has to be attributed to a young chap from Droitwich. Upon his return from a fortnights holiday in The Wirral, he discovered that he'd left his fridge door ajar, and such was the stench emanating from its interior that he vomited profusely, ruined his holiday flip flops, and passed out for seven hours. When he awoke and saw the rotting meat and produce that had stunk up his house, he had an inspirational idea. Ladies and gentlemen, I give you Dingdong Merryman. The creator of the Pot Noodle).

To Ronnie's amazement, the portion of the vest struck by the errant particles had completely disappeared. The light wasn't bending, refracting, dissipating, or anything else clever ending in 'ing'. There, slap bang in the middle of the garment, was a hole.

At first, he wasn't quite sure what he was seeing (or not seeing as the case may be), but a careful prod with his index finger confirmed what had happened.

Realising that this was a breakthrough of slightly larger than average proportions, Ronnie locked himself into the lab and set about trying to recreate the conditions present during the accident.

So, after making sure the vest was in the right position on its metal frame, he positioned the particle accelerator in front of the garment and switched it on.

Unfortunately, whilst he'd been manoeuvring the machine, his sleeve had caught on a dial and turned it to maximum output.

When he switched it on, the beam hit the vest with such energy that it exploded into trillions of infinitesimally small, and highly volatile charged particles, a high percentage of which slammed into Ronnie, penetrating his body right down to the cellular level. Thrown violently across the room and into a wall he banged his head and slumped unconscious to the floor.

Sometime later he came to. He didn't know exactly how long he'd been unconscious for, but he reckoned it must have been a good while because it was pitch black and there was no light coming in through the windows. All he could make out was the vague glow from the lampposts in the centre of the campus.

After checking himself for injury, he gingerly made his way to the door, taking care not to step on any of the broken equipment. It was bad enough that he'd blown up the lab; he didn't fancy adding receiving a serious injury to the list of stupid things that he'd done that day, and he was already getting upset at the thought of his grant going towards paying for the damage.

He unlocked the door and stumbled out into the corridor, which was lit, thankfully. He turned around and looked back into the lab. It looked like a bomb had gone off. A very big bomb.

Shaking his head and wondering how in the hell he was going to explain what had happened, Ronnie gazed up and down the passage and tried to work out what to do next. There were several options available to him, but they all involved a degree of sneaky underhandedness and the requirement to blame someone else, and that was a road he wasn't going to venture down no matter how much trouble he saved himself. And so, despite not really wanting to let anyone know about his embarrassing faux pas, he decided the best course of action was to take ownership of the situation and tell someone about it. After all, it wasn't the sort of thing that was likely to go unnoticed if he kept quiet and went home.

'I could try and cover it up,' he thought, but then rejected that idea as it wasn't any better than saying nothing. In fact, it was probably worse, as that course of action was likely to precipitate an outcome that he'd already rejected wholeheartedly, that being someone else getting into trouble.

No, he had no choice. He'd have to come clean and face the consequences. And besides, a laboratory that looked like it'd been targeted during the Dresden raids wasn't something that could be swept under the carpet, especially as the carpet had been incinerated and couldn't be used to cover anything much larger than a flash stick.

Just then he heard a door at the far end of the corridor bang open, and through it came Dr Julian Grant.

"Ah, Julian. Thank goodness you're here," said Ronnie, walking towards his physics lecturer. "Um, I think you better come and take a look in the lab. I've had a little bit of an accident, and I don't think Thomas and his dustpan and brush are going to be able to sort it out."

What happened next struck Ronnie as a bit odd.

Dr Grant stopped in his tracks, furrowed his brow as if he were confused, and looked around like he was trying to locate something.

"Hello," he called out.

"Julian. It's me, Ronnie."

Once again Grant glanced around. He then spun in place as if he thought that someone was behind him.

"Okay, who's hiding and playing silly buggers?" he said. His voice, whilst angry, had a certain tremor to it, as if he were on the verge of actually being frightened. "Is that you, Morris?"

Ronnie was at a loss as to why the teacher was behaving so strangely. He approached Grant, waving his arms in front of him.

"For goodness sake, Julian are you blind? I'm right in front of you."

Dr Grant shook his head and sighed.

"Right that's it," he said. "Once I find out who this is there's going to be trouble."

With that he marched off purposefully down the corridor straight at Ronnie who had to move out of the lecturer's way lest he get knocked over. He watched in amazement as Grant carried on his way, muttering under his breath about the irresponsibility of certain members of the student body and getting rid of the student bar once and for all.

Still not quite sure what to make of the incident, Ronnie went into the gent's toilet. Initially, he'd thought about going after Dr Grant but decided against it in the end. Julian was clearly distracted by something or another, so figuring that he might not be at his receptive best at the moment, he left it for now. He could find out later what the problem was.

He clicked the light switch, walked over to one of the sinks, and steeled himself to look into the mirror above it. As much as he thought he was okay he needed to assess any wounds that he may have sustained. At the very least he was expecting a few cuts and grazes. 'I just hope my nose is still in the right place', he thought.

Despite the situation, the idea that his nose could be stuck to the ceiling of the lab made him chuckle, but when he gazed into the mirror it died on his lips. What he saw staring back at him made his heart leap into this throat, where it settled like a dead weight, gagging him with its pulsing fleshiness.

Gone were the boyishly handsome features that he was used to seeing every morning. So too the blue eyes and faint crescent scar on his left cheek, the result of some teenage escapade or another. All he could see was the warm air hand dryer on the wall behind him. The warm air hand dryer on the wall *directly* behind him.

The ridiculous thought that the mirror wasn't working properly flashed through his mind, but it wasn't until he raised his hand to his face that he realised something was spectacularly wrong.

Overtaken by panic and fear he fled the tiled, off white and sterile confines of the toilet, sprinted along the lonely, echoing corridor, exited the building and didn't stop running until his muscles cramped with over exertion and his lungs were screaming for oxygen.

Physically spent he leaned back against a wall but ended up doubled over as he fought to get air into his exhausted system whilst trying to keep the contents of his stomach down.

Then, as if that wasn't enough, the heavens opened, and he was instantly drenched by a veritable torrent. In a moment of madness Ronnie rubbed his hands together in a vain attempt to wash away the affliction that had overtaken him. But it was to no avail. By the sepia, water dappled glow of a single, forsaken streetlight he could see that he was still…he couldn't believe that he was even entertaining the thought…invisible.

It sounded so ridiculous. To utter it out loud would be madness, to think it, outlandish. It was so far-fetched that he had trouble rationalising the very idea of it, but there was no escaping the obvious, fantastical truth. His experiment had gone wrong and how he now found himself was as a direct result of his mistake.

He straightened up against the wall and wept as raw emotion claimed him, and he wondered what the future now had in store for him. What sort of a life was out there for someone who couldn't be seen, if indeed there was one? Was he forever to be condemned to wrapping up as if it were a nuclear winter, and subjected to wearing a mask to cover up his missing face? Was he doomed to spend his time hiding away from ordinary people and only venturing out when decent folk were in their homes lest they shy away from his shrouded figure in horror?

As he regained his faculties his sorrow retreated to be replaced by a burgeoning rage, and as he stood in the downpour a seething anger very soon overtook him. It wasn't outwardly demonstrable, but focussed inwards, directed at himself for being so reckless and irresponsible, for being arrogant enough to assume that he was capable of harnessing the tremendous forces he'd been trifling with.

Unabated and completely out of his control his ire increased, as did his respiration and consequently his metabolism.

As his temper continued to flare though, a balmy warmth began to engulf him both internally and externally. It was almost as if he were being totally immersed and consumed by warm, gently flowing water. And what was that? In the periphery of his vision he could make out golden bursts of light that shone like mini supernovae, and yes, he could hear a faint noise that buzzed away merrily in his head like a distant alarm.

He lifted a clenched fist and prepared to strike out at the frigid and unforgiving brick wall when he suddenly froze in position and gazed at where the sleeve of his coat would have been. Could it be true? Were his eyes playing a perverse joke on him? Had his mind snapped or…? Was it really…? Yes. Yes, it was. He could see his hand. It was translucent and vaguely ghost like, ethereal in aspect and somehow fading in and out as if he were subject to a poor signal, but it was definitely there, floating before him like some spectral apparition attempting to force its way from another world into ours.

In a flash of panicked but jubilant inspiration it seemed to Ronnie that perhaps the rush of anger fuelled adrenaline that had surged through his system may have had something to do with the reappearance of his hand.

His thoughts raced. He suspected he'd been stricken at a micro-cellular level, so much so that his very essence, that unique biological make up that made him what he was, had been unutterably tainted, but if he were able to harness and ultimately control the chemical imbalances in his decrepit DNA, he may yet be able to master this most outrageous of torments.

Over the course of the next several weeks Ronnie practised the art of controlling his invisibility. At first, he couldn't achieve any semblance of command over it at all, spending the majority of the first few days completely see through from the knees up. Eventually though, after dozens and dozens of attempts, fighting severe exhaustion, and hiding out in a rented room lest he be the cause of reports of phantom legs wandering the streets, he did it and learned to disappear and reappear more at less at will.

The only downside he discovered, apart from the whole silly episode happening in the first place of course, was that he had to monitor his condition extremely carefully. He found that if he remained invisible for too long he very quickly tired, came over a bit faint, actually fainted, and became visible once more, a consequence that was confirmed on one memorable occasion when he was observing the post-match shenanigans at the local ladies hockey club (as you can see, it didn't take Ronnie long to put his newly found talent to good use. Or good as far as he was concerned anyway). Over-confident, Ronnie had totally lost track of the time (some of the players were rather robust women who could arm wrestle a gorilla and crack walnuts with their thighs) and passed out in a sweaty heap just outside the changing room.

When he reappeared and was discovered, he was greeted by a chorus of deep voiced protests about a male being in the building, although how they could have possibly singled him out would have been beyond even Sherlock Holmes' powers of deduction.

(At this juncture I would just like to point out that I am most definitely NOT stereotyping lady hockey players in any way, shape or form. It just so happens that lady's hockey is one of those activities that seems to attract persons of a particular persuasion, i.e. girls that favour the intimate company of persons of the same gender. And it's not just being involved in sport that's a bit of a giveaway. There's watching Bruce Willis films just for the fight scenes, being able to name all of the actors in the original Magnificent Seven, being able to get to grips with any task that involves the use of a hammer, and joining the police.

And just to balance things out, and in an effort to show that we'll have no sexism around here and that we're all very accepting and tolerant of other people's lifestyles, thank you very much, the same criteria can be applied to a gay gentleman. He'll tend to be drawn to things like hairdressing, being an airline steward, owning every recording that Judy Garland ever released, owning a yappy little dog called Streisand, and being in a Village People tribute act, although that last one could quite easily go on both lists. That Red Indian, excuse me, Native American, was definitely suspect on many, many levels).

Ronnie had left the hockey club sharpish. Still, the experience hadn't been a complete and utter waste of time. If nothing else he now had some idea as to time frames and the limits of his physical tolerance to his newly found talent, information that was going to be vital if he wanted to completely master it.

On a side note it also gave him an appreciation of what the business end of a hockey stick can do to the softer, trouser covered areas of a gentleman's anatomy, especially when it's wielded by a marauding, heavily muscled, and testosterone fuelled centre forward called Daphne.

Anyway, after three months or so he'd returned to the university claiming that his absence had been due to illness and that he had no idea what had occurred in his lab on the evening in question.

Obviously none the wiser, Dr Grant had said that Ronnie did look a bit washed out, an observation that amused him no end, and that the lab had been fully restored and was ready and waiting for Ronnie to get back to his research.

Try as he might though, Ronnie couldn't settle back into his previous existence. Any work that he was assigned seemed mundane, insignificant, and somewhat pedestrian, especially when compared to what he'd achieved before, but he dare not share what he'd experienced for fear of spending the rest of his life as a clinical study.

And so, with a hint of regret but excited as to what the future may hold for him, he left the academic world behind. Then, unsure of what to do next, he decided to go travelling. He reckoned six months away from the austere world of research would help to clear his mind and hopefully focus his thoughts as to where his future lay. It was also an activity made all the easier, and considerably more entertaining, in that he didn't have to pay a penny to get anywhere. It was the easiest thing in the world to disappear and slip onto a boat or a plane undetected. And did he behave? Of course, he didn't. He'd amuse himself by flicking switches and turning dials in cockpits, terrifying the other passengers with prods and pokes, and watching in silent hysterics as the captain panicked when he whispered phantom messages into his headset.

Eventually, he found himself in Eastern Europe. He'd gone there for a rest after a four-month spell in Amsterdam where, without being seen by anyone, he'd seen just about everything.

One day, whilst out with a couple of acquaintances that he'd met during a mammoth drinking session in a grotty bar adorned with the latest in fourteenth century decor, plague victims and all, they'd arrived in Skullenia on the umpteenth leg of a record breaking pub crawl that would have ruined a blue whale's liver and caused Alcoholics Anonymous to admit defeat.

Before they entered The Bolt and Jugular, however, Ronnie's two friends, who unbeknownst to him were a ghoul and a werewolf, suggested that they take a walk around town, because unbeknownst to him, the ghoul that he was unbeknownst about had the nasty habit of delivering waifs and strays to the vampire, Gorge the Corpsegrinder who, as unbeknownst to Ronnie as everything else he seemed to be unbeknownst about, had the equally nasty habit of grinding corpses, which kind of makes sense when you think about it, unbeknownst or not.

(Actually, and just to put things into perspective for a moment, there's quite a lot of things that Ronnie's unbeknownst about after he's downed a couple of gallons of ale and a vat of gin. Things like rational thought, how to talk to ladies, clear decision making, how to talk to anyone, appropriate use of currency, and how his legs worked are just some of the everyday activities that go straight out the window. As does he when he gets all silly).

And so, the two of them had arrived at a large building near the centre of town. (The werewolf had already left. He'd seen a cat and was currently chasing it across the roof of the town hall, a foolhardy venture because it was Noggin).

The ghoul knocked on the front door which was opened by a massive and haphazardly sewn together monster of a being who, on account of having a mouth full of sweets, was dribbling in seven different colours and at least that many directions.

They were shown to an office where a dusty looking mannequin, the ugliest, and greenest, woman that he'd ever laid eyes on (or anything else for that matter), and a pale, rather toothy gentleman sitting behind a desk were waiting.

Of course, being drunker than a Russian peasant after a half-price sale at Vodkaland, Ronnie was completely oblivious to his clearly strange surroundings, and the clearly stranger creatures that occupied those clearly strange surroundings.

As he was guided towards them the pale one behind the desk stood up. And kept standing up. In fact, it seemed to Ronnie that it took the fellow a good five minutes to get himself up to his full height he was so big, although at this juncture Ronnie's senses were so dulled by the copious amounts of alcohol that he'd imbibed he was starting to think what a nice place this was, how friendly the folks were, and how attractive the green lady was. (Yes, dear reader, he was that drunk, and therefore totally unaware that nothing animal, vegetable, mineral, or indeed, supernatural found the chartreuse hued woman alluring in any way at all, and wouldn't have found her pleasant to look at if she were the last whatever on wherever. Not without the aid of an extremely powerful spell, forty-seven pints of Ustinov's Waffling Treacle, or a ten-pound sledgehammer anyway).

The large, pale man was a lump it had to be said. And vaguely menacing as it happened. In fact, the taller he got the more menacing he became, which had the effect of sobering Ronnie up rather quickly.

Then, in a flash, the giant with the fangs was standing right in front of him. Bizarrely though, Ronnie hadn't seen him move a muscle, and there seemed to be enough of those attached to his bones to be seen from miles away. But despite that, here he was, face to chest with the pituitary enhanced freak.

A creeping chill stole into his very core, and a growing sense of dread festered and grew in his gut like a virulent cancer. He was just about to say something, (what exactly it would be he didn't know, it would just be a case of winging it and see what happened), when two things happened. Firstly, the chap facing him looked down and smiled, revealing a set of very white, very big, and very sharp looking teeth that were no doubt more than capable of chewing through granite (or a drunk and very confused research scientist for that matter).

Secondly, he heard someone say, "Bugger, we haven't put any plastic sheeting down."

Very quickly coming to the conclusion that he wasn't going to be asked to paint the ceiling, or whip up an impromptu sculpture, Ronnie fired up his insides, and just as the grinning demon before him reached out a baleful, taloned hand to grab him, he winked out of existence. Then, as if the hounds of hell themselves were hunting him down, he fled for his life. To the fireplace. Obviously, he'd planned to make his escape a tad more inventive, incorporating a suitable hiding place, extensive plastic surgery, and a distance measured in light years, but he could only see one open door and that was currently being obscured from view by the behemoth that had let him in.

"Well, there's something you don't see every day," said the dusty looking one.

"Indeed, you don't," said the menacing colossus. "And what a confounded nuisance it is. Do you have any ideas, Mrs. Ladle?" He sniffed the air. "My tummy's rumbling now. I was looking forward to having someone over for dinner."

Ronnie surveyed the scene and quite rightly wondered what the hell was going on. Then, two and a half seconds later, he realised he didn't have the first clue. Then, one point seven seconds after that, he decided he was more than happy with that state of affairs, wasn't interested in hints and tips no matter where they were in the queue, and needing to perform a disappearing act that would've made a nineteen year old dad from Romford proud. It was either that or hope and pray that he'd wake up lying in a gutter, covered in vomit, (his own hopefully, but that depended on who he was out with), and not knowing where he was. *This* reality, such as it was, could not be, well, real.

Unfortunately, such was his concentration on the five figures in the room and what his next course of action should be, Ronnie had neglected to give any thought as to what certain parts of his body were doing. And so, without realising it, he moved his right foot ever so slightly and knocked into a poker that was leaning against the fire surround. It was only a subtle movement, and no doubt it would have gone unseen by a normal person, but it was noticed by the ghoul that'd led him here.

Now, said ghoul was a bit of a goody three shoes (yes, he was that sycophantic), and in a shameful attempt to curry favour with all those present, he kept what he'd seen to himself and charged at the disturbance in the hope of catching the newly disappeared traveller and be rewarded for some excellent work.

Noticing the sudden flurry of activity, the others looked on, wondering what on earth the silly creature was up to. In fact, Mrs. Ladle was just about to enquire as to that very thing when the poker, seemingly of its own accord, rose into the air, swung backwards in a wide arc, and slammed into the ghoul's head, caving it in as if it were as fragile as an over ripe melon. He crumpled to the carpet where he twitched a couple of times before being still.

That's done it, thought Ronnie to himself, coming to the sad but inevitable conclusion that his life was about to come to an abrupt and, no doubt, very messy end.

"It's okay," said the green lady. Mrs. Ladle wasn't it? She lit a cigarette, took a drag, and blew a vast plume of smoke towards the ceiling. She cast her gaze over to the fireplace. "You can show yourself now. You won't come to any harm I promise. Skullenia's a town that appreciates beings with, how shall I put it, talents that are out of the ordinary. Isn't that right, Gorge?"

"Yes indeed," said the big, pale one.

"So, he's welcome to stay, isn't he?" said the green one.

"Yes indeed," said the big, pale one.

"His abilities could be useful, couldn't they?" said the green one.

"Yes indeed," said the big, pale one.

"He'll fit right in, won't he?" said the green one.

"Yes indeed," said the big, pale one.

"And you won't go tearing his throat out will you?" said the green one.

"Yes indeed," said the big, pale one.

"Gorge, don't scare the poor chap anymore then he already is," said the green one.

"Sorry. I couldn't resist it," said Gorge. He turned to the fireplace but didn't approach. "Come on then, young man. It's time to reveal yourself. There's no need to worry. You're amongst friends now."

Ronnie shook his head and put his hands over his eyes as he tried to block out the whatever the hell it was he was looking at. It didn't make a damn bit of difference of course. He might as well have tried to shield his vision with fresh air.

And so, finally, and with a crushing inevitability that drained whatever fight he had left in his system, he realised he was undone, and despite everything that his scientific brain was telling him, the freak show that he'd stumbled upon was still there right in front of him in all its dusty, green, stitched together, fangy glory.

From what he could tell, and he felt like a complete head case for even considering the possibility, the 'friends' that he was amongst consisted of a witch, some kind of zombie, a mobile post mortem that looked as if it'd lost an argument with a bulldozer, and…get ready to disembark at your final destination, room 23a at the Home for the Terminally Batshit Crazy…a vampire.

He was trapped and he knew it. Even invisible there was no way that he was going to be able to escape all of them.

Ronnie allowed himself to calm down, well, as much as he could of course, seeing as how he was marooned within the walls of this utter madhouse, and slowly reappeared.

Once he'd finally coalesced, the witch approached and offered him a cigarette that he gratefully accepted, never more grateful to be a smoker. Mind you, for all he knew the tobacco could be laced with some sort of poison. Or something worse come to that. Still, he wasn't overly bothered. All things considered he reckoned he was deader than Stripey the zebra out on a blind date with Leo Zebrakiller, the zebra killing lion, and chief zebra killer of the zebra killing club.

She offered him a light and he drew the toxins into his lungs.

"So, who's going to kill me then?" he asked.

"No one," said the witch.

"As Mrs. Ladle has already pointed out," added the vampire, "a person with an ability such as yours will fit right in around here." He approached Ronnie with arms extended to indicate their surroundings. "This tormented region that we call home is full of interesting and diverse creatures, a fact that you've no doubt worked out for yourself already. And let's be realistic here. Where else could you go and be accepted?"

"In other words," said the powdery being who looked like a refugee from Georgian England, "you're an abnormality. And as strange as it may seem you're in the company of some other abnormalities. Abnormalities who just happen to live in a town full to the brim with lots of other abnormalities. Don't worry yourself though. You'll get used to it. It'd be abnormal if you didn't. Anyway, if you'll allow me to play the genial host, I think some introductions are in order if no one else minds."

No one else minded.

"My name is Stitches, this lovely lady is Mrs. Ladle, the pasty looking chap is Gorge, and that large, upright, butcher's table over there is Flug. Say hello to…"

"Ronnie," said Ronnie.

"Say hello to Ronnie, Flug."

Flug stomped across the room like a perambulating wall, picked up Ronnie with ridiculous ease and gave him a squeeze that could have got juice out of a mountain.

"Hi, Ronnie Flug," he said. "You smell nice. Have you got sweeties?"

"You'll have to excuse Flug," said Mrs. Ladle. "He's got a heart of gold, but he is a little bit lacking in the intelligence department. I think it's got something to do with degradation of the brain stem or some such biological waffle."

"Or, to be more accurate, he's got the mental capacity of a radish," said Stitches.

"Me like, Ronnie Flug," said Flug.

"Don't worry about the name thing," said Stitches. "He'll get it after a month or so."

"Stay with us," said Gorge.

And so, he had.

Right. I suppose we better get back to the present. Time to shake the book again.

Ronnie blew the last of the smoke out and dropped his spent fag onto the floor. He was about to step on it when he heard a noise from the bush directly in front of him. Not that that was entirely unusual of course. You couldn't normally walk three paces in Skullenia without tripping on, stepping in, or getting jumped on by something or another, and that was just in Crumble's lab.

He walked towards the sound figuring it was just a drunken spirit who'd gotten lost, or a phantom who'd forgotten how to fly. Then again it could be Noggin lying in wait to attack him and drag him off somewhere secluded where he'd be used as a claw sharpening tool.

"Here, Noggin. Nice kitty."

It was then that something burst forth from the bush. A something so horrifying that Ronnie fled indoors in terror.

Whatever it was, it wasn't Noggin.

* * *

Deirdre Clownpuncher put her third best hat onto her head, stepped outside, closed and locked her front door, popped her keys into her handbag, and headed off into town.

(Her third best hat was a fluffy blue affair that was for general everyday use, as opposed to her second-best hat which she wore for tea with friends, going to the bingo, and hobnobbing with minor local dignitaries. It was a silky green, spiral accoutrement that looked suspiciously like a slightly gone off meringue. Her best hat was a different matter entirely though, and hardly ever came out of its box at all. It was made of fine purple velvet and once adorned, it perched grandly upon her head like an overgrown blackberry. It even had a feather on the top that danced around jauntily as she walked. It was as expensive as it was elegant which was why she'd only ever worn it on two occasions, once when she'd lost her glasses and put it on instead of her second best hat, and at her husband's funeral because he'd been a crotchety old bugger who'd hated the sight of it).

Outside, Shark's Bay was shrouded in a blanket of darkness, and it would remain that way for a good few hours yet, but that didn't matter all that much because she was having trouble sleeping anyway. She couldn't get the word Skullenia out of her mind, and knowing that she wouldn't be able to rest until she'd found out what it meant, she'd decided to pay a visit to the local library to conduct some research into the matter. Obviously, she'd rather stay indoors with a cup of tea, some chocolate biscuits, a good book in her hands, and Blobby at her feet, but such was her need to know about the strange word that she really had no choice. In fact, despite not knowing why, who, where, or what she may find out, it was almost as if she felt compelled to go, and that was a feeling that she hadn't experienced before. Usually, she was rather good at picking up on things, no matter how obscure or apparently irrelevant they were, but to not have a clue about something was a brand-new experience that was as disconcerting as it was alien. Why, even on the odd occasion that she was bereft of an answer, someone would normally come to her assistance. Sometimes they were still alive.

Deirdre was a medium, you see, and as such, had been able to communicate with the dead for as long as she could remember.

Her first encounter had been as an eight-year-old girl when she'd engaged in conversations with her recently departed grandfather. He would visit her at night after her parents had gone to sleep and they would chat for hours, she propped up on a couple of pillows and he sat on the end of her bed.

Since then she hadn't been able to go for more than five minutes without someone saying hello. Not that she minded of course. All the dead usually wanted of her was for a message to be passed onto their relatives (the living ones, that is. After all it'd be a bit silly if they needed to employ the services of a go-between just to have a chat with the spirit sitting next to them wouldn't it. No, the massed legions of the wandering deceased are more than capable of communicating with each other in the strange, ethereal world they call home. We call it Birmingham).

But with regard to what had happened a short while ago she was stumped, and without a word from the other side, the message embossed on her kitchen window still meant nothing to her. (If one of the dead knew what it was, they'd have told her straight away. Just because they'd passed didn't mean they weren't competitive and didn't like to be first).

"*Deirdre,*" a female voice as clear as a bell said to her.

"Yes, dear," she replied.

"*It's Mavis Balustrade.*"

"Hello, Mavis. What is it today?"

"*Can you tell Fred to wash the nets? The smoke from that awful pipe of his does stain them terribly.*"

"Will do, dear."

"*Thank you.*"

Mavis, as was the case with most of her other-worldly contacts, was one of her regulars, just an ordinary person who'd passed over, but who still liked to keep in touch with those still residing in the land of the living. And boy there were lots of them. So many in fact that she kept a diary with her at all times and a comprehensive address book at home. It simply wouldn't do to forget anything that she was told, and with the passing of the years and the inevitable onset of a slowly fading memory, jotting things down had become a necessity. She saw her ability as a wondrous gift and delivered every single message given to her no matter how trivial it appeared to be.

She took her diary out of her bag, made a note of Mavis's message and put it back before continuing on her way.

Due to the earliness of the hour Deirdre made good time and arrived at the library some twenty minutes later, a fact that she was eternally grateful for, because although she didn't know precisely what she'd find out, she somehow knew that her mission was of the utmost importance, an errand that she couldn't afford to ignore or allow to be delayed. Hence the reason for her predawn sojourn. If she'd made the same trip during the day it would have taken considerably longer. Deirdre was rather well known in Shark's Bay you see, maybe even close to being considered a minor celebrity, and although she would have pooh poohed that notion as so much tish and piffle it was nevertheless a statement of fact, a fact that meant a daylight excursion would have seen her being stopped every few yards and asked all manner of things, because when it came down to it, the living were just as tenacious as the dead when it came to matters of supreme unimportance. You know the sort of thing.

"Will I have good luck?"

"Will the weather be nice for my holiday?"

"How are you feeling tomorrow?" etc.

Deirdre couldn't answer any of those questions of course because she wasn't a fortune teller and couldn't have told you what was going to happen tomorrow if her life depended on it. Obviously, she wouldn't know if her life depended on it, of course because she wasn't a fortune teller and couldn't have told you what was going to happen tomorrow if her life depended on it because she wasn't a fortune teller. Good grief. That got a bit involved didn't it. Actually, I'm surprised I didn't see it coming to be honest. Then again, I'm not a fortune teller so, how would I? I couldn't tell you what's coming next if my life depended on it. On second thoughts, forget all that. I don't think admitting to not knowing what's coming next is a sensible thing to declare when one's an author. Methinks I'll leave that to the experts. You know. Train companies, The Royal Mail, DHL, a blind man in a tunnel.

(You can't blame people for being uninformed though, but it is a state of affairs that leads to people getting the meanings of words and phrases wrong sometimes. Take the main thrust of this missive for instance. In this case, medium is being used as a noun and not an adjective, to wit, it perfectly describes what Deirdre does and not what she is, but unless you're in the know, so to speak, you won't be aware of the difference. It's an easy mistake to make, however, and one that my wife, the delectable Mrs. Author, makes on a regular basis. Especially when she's trying on clothes).

When she arrived at the library, she waved cheerily to Mrs. Gondola, the chief librarian, and wended her way through the shelves to the reference section.

Her first port of call was Botley's Big Book of Everything; a title that ultimately proved to be rather misleading because it didn't have everything in it at all.

Next she tried the phone book, but all she found in that was Skullington, Skullpan, Skullkingabout, and Skullfracture, four names that she decided were rather silly when all was said and done (which is an interesting observation from someone called Clownpuncher, but then one never notices what's right in front of one's face does one? This fact explains, for instance, why Quasimodo, despite having a face like an electrocuted sausage and a body that looked like a sack of coconuts, thought that he was a bit of a handsome devil, that some people are under the misguided impression that Britain actually does have talent, and that Bobby 'The Torsoman' Steamchops is in training for his first triathlon, which is quite the feat when you consider that he has a few minor disabilities, physical quirks that, depending on how politically correct you're feeling at any given moment, his nickname may or may not allude to.

'And what on earth could he do that's vaguely sporty?' I hear you ask, 'especially when he looks like a pork chop with eyes.' Well, one, don't be mean, it's not his fault that he looks as if he fell off a butchers counter, and two, his chosen event involves disciplines specifically catered for someone of his ilk making him just as sporty as the next person. Okay, so the next person would need to have flippers and look like a lump of warm plasticine roughly moulded into the shape of a crippled penguin, but you get the idea. Anyway, he starts with a twenty-fathom sink, performs a ten-storey fall, and concludes with a fifteen-mile, downhill roll. There, weren't expecting that were you, dear reader? And there was you thinking I was going to make some cruel and sarcastic comment about a person with no limbs competing in an able-bodied sport. For shame. Nothing could be further from the truth and it would be ridiculous, unfair, and dare I say, somewhat patronising to even suggest such a thing. And besides, The Torsoman couldn't possibly have gone up against the professional athletes, anyway. He'd pulled a muscle in his left ear and was in a sling. He hoped someone would let him out of it one day. Ah well, back to the story).

The only other sensible place that she could think of looking in was Places, although using the word sensible was a bit of a stretch considering that the library contained such epic tomes as 'Famous Papua New Guineans', 'The Collected Humorous Verse of Dr Josef Mengele', and 'Things to do in Cardiff for under a Pound'.

Eventually, Deirdre found a book that may prove useful, or at least one that might actually contain some relevant subject matter on pages free of the usual abstract scrawl so prevalent in library reference books the world over, i.e. one that hadn't been used as a repository for information that wasn't strictly within the boundaries of academic study, and had the tendency to be a bit on the naughty side.

You know the sort of stuff. Anatomically incorrect and rather optimistic sketches of male genitalia, dubious claims about certain people's sexuality, and witty slogans such as, 'Mrs Timpkins is a man. Check out the hands, they're massive', 'Colin looks at bums in the changing rooms', and 'Trevor smells of wee'. And just to prove that most of these 'facts' are unfounded nonsense, that last comment about Trevor is completely false because what he really smells of is homeless people, out of date mince, and the pigeons who are his best friends in the whole wide world. Ironically, he can't stand homeless pigeons, won't eat mince, and isn't homeless.

Mrs. Timpkins is definitely a man, though. She can get one of those aforementioned hands around a pint glass.

The book in question that Deirdre was pinning her hopes on was Tangle Cactus's, 'If You Can't Find It Anywhere Else It's Bound To Be In Here'. It was heralded as a modern classic that was crammed with often overlooked explanations on all sorts of topics including, 'How do your clothes not disappear when there's a ten-pound ball of fluff in your tumble dryer?' 'How come the queue you're in moves slower than yours even if you change?' and 'Belgium. Why?'

Deirdre flicked through the pages until she got to S and ran her index finger down the list of chapter contents, passing 'Sandwiches, does the bread always need to be on the outside?' 'Safari parks. Home of natural wonders or voyeurism for weirdos?' and 'Selery, it really should start with an S.'

"Ah here we go," Deirdre said to herself. "Skullenia. A village/town. Mmm, so it *is* a place. Interesting."

She flipped over a few more pages until she located the entry. It wasn't very long. In fact, it was just a few lines and was only slightly longer than the heading that she'd already read.

'A small village/town in South West Transylvania. No major industry or viable functioning economy. Population eclectic and changeable on an hourly basis. Said to be a little strange. Take care if visiting.'

And that was it. It was scant at best and not really much to go on, especially when she'd just then come to the realisation that she had plans firmly in place to go there, which was odd because up until this precise moment she hadn't known it was a place at all and had no idea that she would be going there, consciously anyway, or even that it *was* a there. 'Ah well', she thought. 'At least it's a start. Of sorts'.

"*Deirdre.*"

"Yes."

"*It's Mavis again.*"

"Hello, Mavis."

"*I went there once you know.*"

"Really?"

"*Yes indeed. Many, many years ago. I'm sure it's different now but I do have one overriding memory.*"

"Please tell me it's a good one, Mavis because I have rather a strong urge to travel there," said Deirdre, hopefully.

Deirdre was answered by a cold, stony silence.

"Mavis."

"*Sorry, Deirdre, I was thinking about my nets again.*"

"I'll deal with that as soon as I'm done here, Mavis, I promise. Now, what can you tell me about Skullenia?"

"*Well, Deirdre, it's either one of two things but I'm not sure which one it is exactly.*"

"Oh, don't worry yourself about that, Mavis. Why don't you just tell me both."

"*Ooh, there's a good idea. Okay, it's either be careful what you eat or…*" Mavis let the sentence tail off. It was either that or her energy was waning.

"Are you still there, Mavis?"

"*… Yes, dear I'm here. Lost you there for a moment. Now, where were we?*"

"You said there was something you remembered about Skullenia, but you weren't quite sure what it was. It was either one of two things, you said, so I suggested that you tell me both."

"*Oh, yes. And what was the first one again?*"

"You said I should be careful what I eat."

"*A… es…*"

"You're starting to dwindle, Mavis. Come on, love. One last push now."

As the gloominess of the night was slowly being chased away by the dawning of a new day, Deirdre left the library and started her journey home. She needed that cup of tea now more than ever. Mavis had got back to her with her second recollection. It had been slightly muffled and a bit feint, but Deirdre was sure she'd heard it right, and that being the case she sincerely hoped it was the first option, although what either of them meant was a mystery. Before fading out completely, Mavis had said, *"Be careful you don't get eaten."*

* * *

Not for the first time, and it certainly wouldn't be the last by any stretch of the imagination, a group of disturbed and rather confused individuals were assembled in Ollie's office. After Ronnie had come crashing into the building following his curious incident with the bush in the night-time, several other people had descended on Ollie, and each of them had a strange and stunningly vague tale to tell.

Ronnie had mentioned seeing something that had made him jump, but for the life of him he couldn't remember what it was.

Nurse Parsnip had arrived muttering something about an experience in the hospital but, despite clearly being shaken by the whole incident, had no recollection of any of it whatsoever.

And finally, Constable Gullett had turned up talking about a ham and pickle sandwich that had gone to waste (a travesty that someone would pay for as soon as he could conjure up a suitable violation yet to be laid down in the statute books), a funny noise, and an unscheduled nap. Ollie would have pointed out that sounded like a normal shift for the policeman, but he refrained from making the observation as the officer, who wasn't actually afraid of anything apart from Mrs. Ladle's Holy Flan, looked extremely perturbed.

And so, Ollie was currently trying to get to the bottom of what had happened to three people who had no information about the incidents that they couldn't remember.

"Well isn't that handy," said Stitches, who had also been party to the tales of woe from the depths of his leather chair (he wasn't actually hearing tales of woe from the depths of his leather chair you understand. He was sitting in his leather chair when he heard the tales of woe. My goodness, English can be a strange language sometimes can't it. Maybe I'll try writing in Russian. All you have to do is turn the R's round the wrong way. Anyway, the chair was officially his now, hence the use of 'his'. This was because he'd spent so long sitting in it, that it'd developed a very particular bum groove that no other creature could possibly get comfortable in. This was due to the zombie's very unique and distinctive anatomy that nothing else could match. This is, of course, a nice way of saying he had a backside bonier than The Undead Skeleton Orchestra performing a sterling rendition of Ribby McPelvis's Spinal Column Concerto in C4 Flat).

"Mmm," said Ollie, attempting to look as if he had the slightest clue what to say next, when in fact, he didn't have the slightest clue what to say next but wanted to look like he did. Which he didn't. Fortunately, he was saved by another visitor so could stop attempting to look as if he had the slightest clue what to say next when he didn't have the slightest clue what to say next but wanted to look like he did. Which he didn't. Which was just as well. I think!

"Hello, Mandrake," he said, for once genuinely pleased to see the suicidal silly sausage. Hopefully, he'd divert the topic of conversation away from the randomly speculative and steer it towards something slightly more definable. "Everything alright?"

"I'm not sure to be honest, Ollie. Something weird seems to be going on," he said, dashing Ollie's hopes of a return to normalcy in an instant.

As he approached the desk Ollie could see that Mandrake had put on rather a lot of weight. Bizarrely, it was on his chest of all places and nowhere else.

'That's a strange place to get fat', thought the half vampire, although he thought it best not to mention it. Even the slightest of criticisms was liable to send Mandrake spiralling down into a bottomless pit of depression. Or cause him to have a bit of a moody anyway.

To be fair to him though, Mandrake had been doing rather well of late and hadn't tried to commit suicide for a good few months now, so Ollie was fully justified in his decision not to point out any flaws, physical or otherwise, that may give the chap an excuse to fall off the wagon (yet another method of self-extermination that he'd tried in the past. Okay, so the wagon in question was part of a child's train-set and couldn't have knocked over an unstable domino if it was travelling at top speed, but he had received a minor graze when a plastic steam locomotive had brushed passed his knee, an injury that required the attention of Dr Zoltan, who'd looked at the less than significant wound and declared, "Bugger off, Mandrake. I was more badly injured the last time I combed my hair").

He did seem to have turned over a new leaf though, which was obviously a good thing, and a step in the right direction if nothing else (as long as that step wasn't towards the edge of the three hundred page book that he was precariously balanced on, or into the path of an oncoming pensioner). In fact, ever since Ollie had had a little 'chat' with him at Jocular's castle, Mandrake had only had one slip up when he tried to end it all by running a bath, getting in, and dropping a AAA battery into the water.

Feeling a little guilty, and not wanting to let Ollie down he'd confessed his transgression to the half vampire, who, much to his regret, seemed to have unwittingly become Mandrake's unofficial, anti-suicide sponsor. (If it'd been made official, Ollie would have told him to drop dead).

And so, Ollie, ever the one for coming to the assistance of those attempting to face their demons or triumph over adversity (once you'd tried to help Flug use the bathroom effectively there wasn't a task on the planet that could faze you), had listened attentively, nodded encouragingly, made a few appropriate noises, and even had Mrs. Ladle cook his meals for a couple of days.

"Yuck!" I hear you cry, but wait and listen in. That was quite a shrewd move on Ollie's behalf believe it or not, and whilst it may have appeared a bit spiteful, it wasn't intended to be a sadistic and malicious gesture by any means (although on the face it, that's a conclusion easily reached. Being served up one of the good witches culinary disasters is the type of hellish, Lovecraftian act of evil likely to cause one to run mad, and bring back vivid and disturbing recollections of the horrors of The Salem Witch Trials, the pseudo-religious mass genocide that was The Spanish Inquisition, or the visually repellent and soul destroying monstrosity that is Len Goodman's Partners in Rhyme).

Anyhoo, after being served up a couple of dinners of questionable nutritional value and presented with a dessert that wouldn't keep still and kept calling him rude names, Mandrake had quickly recovered and been fine ever since (ever since his colon had cleared anyway. He couldn't believe that he'd been able to go to the toilet in the dark and still see clearly. What she'd put in her stew he didn't know, and quite frankly didn't want to find out, but any ingredient that made bodily extrusions glow orange was something that he never wanted to experience again. His children were still under the impression that they'd been visited by an alien spaceship. Or at least some kind of Unidentified Floating Object anyway).

Suddenly Mandrake's fat chest wriggled, moved down a foot or so, and stepped onto Ollie's desk.

In an instant, everybody in the room jumped two feet into the air, scattered like a group of startled birds, and disappeared out of the nearest available exit, leaving Mandrake standing by the desk and Noggin sitting on the keyboard of Ollie's computer (maybe he was after the mouse, ha ha).

"It's okay, guys," Mandrake called out to the very suddenly empty room. "Noggin's a bit subdued at the moment so there's really nothing to worry about. He won't hurt any of you." He didn't sound very convincing.

"That's all very well for you to say," said Stitches, who was sitting/cowering at the bottom of the staircase, "but pointing out that that cat of yours is subdued is like saying that a force ten gale might blow a tile or two off your roof and rattle your windows a little bit. Sorry, Mandrake but I kind of like my head where it is thank you very much. If that mad moggy of yours gets hold of me it's liable to end up in a different time zone and considerably less head like."

Mandrake left Noggin where he was and went over to the office door. He started to open it but had barely moved an inch when he was assailed by a collective and extremely loud "NO!" that nearly burst his eardrums.

From the brief glance that he got, Mandrake noticed that Stitches was curled up at the bottom of the stairs like a bunch of discarded rags (which, apart from the odd few pieces of desiccated flesh that he had left, he pretty much was), Nurse Parsnip was standing as still as a very still statue at the end of the hall pretending to be a hat stand (although seeing as how she had her nurses hat on there was every possibility that she was masquerading as either a statue wearing a hat, a hat stand that actually had a hat on it or, and maybe more realistically, in an option that we really should have considered from the outset given the available information, a terrified nurse who didn't want to get mauled to undeath by a large and borderline insane vampire cat whether there was a hat involved or not. Not that Noggin ever wore a hat of course, but that's another matter entirely), Constable Gullett had his truncheon out and was ready to beat into submission anything black and furry that came his way (so, no change there then. Extreme violence and asking questions later was a proven policing method that he always relied on), and Ollie was hiding in the cupboard under the stairs (and for all you clever dicks out there thinking how could Mandrake possibly know that Ollie was hiding in the cupboard under the stairs, his cape had gotten caught in the door. That and Stitches saying, "Ollie's hiding in the cupboard under the stairs.")

"It's absolutely and completely fine, honestly," said Mandrake. "Look."

He stuck out his chin and showed them his hands to emphasise the point (not to Ollie of course because he was hiding in the cupboard under the stairs remember, and he wasn't going to risk venturing out until the coast was clearer than a recently valeted vacuum).

"There, not a scratch," continued Mandrake. "And as you can see, I've still got all my fingers and legs. If Noggin was in one of his moods do you honestly think that I'd be handling him like I did in there? I'm not that brave."

"Fair enough, Mandrake," said Gullett, putting his baton away. "But if he comes at me for anything other than a tickle under the chin, I'll be using you as a human shield understood."

Five minutes later saw them all back in the office, reasonably happy that they weren't going to be mauled to bloody strips, tossed about like a sack of mince in a threshing machine, and subsequently relieved of any vital organs that happened to be flopping about. Except for Stitches obviously, whose need for organs, flopping about or otherwise, wasn't so much vital in that they were required for life to function, but necessary in order to keep him more or less three dimensional.

"So, what *are* you doing here then, Mandrake?" said Ollie. He was back behind his desk and watching Noggin like a hawk whilst thoroughly convinced that Noggin was watching him like a cat that had a particular taste for birds of prey. Say, a hawk for instance.

"Something happened to Noggin last night," said Mandrake.

"How do you know that?" asked Gullett.

"When I got up this morning, Noggin was sat on the back step by himself."

"What, not even a horse?" said Stitches.

Mandrake stroked his cat who reciprocated by rubbing his face up Mandrake's arm, an act that made them all realise that the feline wasn't in the right frame of mind, because if anyone were to show him such affection under normal circumstances, it was usually the catalyst for an all-out frontal assault resulting in the giver needing an extensive stay in hospital, a course of antibiotics so powerful that they could have cured the Plague, and ongoing counselling to deal with the inevitable PTND (Post Traumatic Noggin Disorder).

Mandrake shook his head. "Nope. Nothing. Something scared the little chap that's for sure. He was just sat there looking up me and meowing quietly."

"Noggin doesn't meow," said Nurse Parsnip, who had previous experience of the vampire cat. Or the results of his nocturnal genocides anyway. "He roars certainly, howls like a demon yes, and hisses like a mad volcano," she continued, "but he never meows."

"Meow," said Noggin, looking around the room as if to highlight Mandrake's point.

Gullett, Ronnie, and Nurse Parsnip then filled Mandrake in on what had happened to them, but it was just as sketchy as before. None of them were able to provide much more than, 'I think I saw something and ran away.'

Ollie shook his head, leaned back in his chair, and came to the conclusion that this had been a complete and utter waste of time, and that he could've gotten more information out of Noggin's litter tray (a patch of ground roughly the size of a small village that contained a variety of gnawed bones, mummified chunks of flesh, the remains of a flock of sheep, some unidentifiable clumps of lumpy and rather fragrant brown stuff, a ragged and bloody postman's uniform devoid of precisely one ragged and bloody postman, an assortment of chewed body parts, some of which were still twitching, and a frightened troll who'd inadvertently wandered into the open air burial vault in 1986 and was now too terrified to move).

"So, what do we think?" said Ollie to everyone, "because I sure as hell haven't got a clue. And to be honest it sounds like a normal night in Skullenia if you ask me."

"He's right. And at the end of the day it all comes down to evidence doesn't it," said Gullett. "And whilst there's no doubt that each of us has had a strange encounter, without any facts to point us in the right direction there's no way to solve it. I say we don't overly concern ourselves about it and put it down to experience."

"Maybe we're being haunted," said Nurse Parsnip.

"And which particular ghost, phantom, poltergeist, phantasm, spirit, or spectre would you like to single out and blame for that then?" said Stitches. "Because you've got hundreds to choose from."

"He's got a point there, Nurse Parsnip," said Mandrake. "I think an unexpected haunting is something that we can rule out with almost one hundred percent certainty. Maximus is in my attic right now. He only started his shift an hour ago."

What Mandrake meant was that every house, or indeed every building in Skullenia, notwithstanding the fact that the majority of them were already occupied by the undead, was haunted at some point or another to a varying degree (except Ollie's place that is. Odric the spectre had tried it once, but he'd scared Flug so much that the big reanimate had punched him out of existence. No one bothered after that and the building was declared a no haunt zone). This was because not only were there lots and lots of ghosts desperately in need of something to do, it was actually a job requirement. And let's face it, they couldn't just float around in people's homes all night making a nuisance of themselves now could they. Not without contractual obligations anyway. Sadly though, as with just about everything else in life, or unlife, there were rules and regulations that had to be adhered to (unless said being was a politician, a professional footballer, or a nondescript celebrity of some sort in which case they can do whatever the hell they want without fear of any consequences whatsoever), so if a person wanted to secure, and remain in gainful employment as one of the wailing deceased, once engaged in regular nightly work they had to achieve a certain level of output, or what was more commonly known as the number of 'Possessions In a Set Shift' (PISS).

It was a figure that had been agreed upon during some protracted negotiations between the 'Allied Ranks of Skullenian Entities' (ARSE), and the 'Noble Order of Stable Ectoplasm' (NOSE).

The NOSE had spoken to the ARSE and suggested what it thought was a reasonable amount of PISS, but the ARSE had fervently disagreed with the NOSE's proposal and kicked up a right old stink. And so, that being the case, the ARSE had been forced to come up with what *they* thought was a goodly quantity of PISS. Of course that was after there was a massive split right through the middle of the ARSE itself, when they argued amongst themselves about what the figure should be, but they soon got their act together when the arbitrator, a representative from 'Terror Industry Trade Solutions' (TITS), invoked clause 44DD and put the wind up them.

When the new figure was finally introduced by the ARSE, it was sniffed at by the NOSE, who stated in a memorandum that there was no way that they, or their members, could maintain such a high level of PISS for a full eight hours. That being so, additional talks were scheduled.

After many days and nights of further wrangling, during which the NOSE got rather snotty about the amount of crap that the ARSE was coming out with, they finally reached an accord on what exactly the PISS should be and how much of it they were willing to take.

Then, just as things were settling down, the proceedings were interrupted by a splinter group from the 'Ethereal League of Biologically Odd Wanderers' (ELBOW), who had barged their way into the meeting demanding to be heard. As unconventional a tactic as it was, they were allowed room to manoeuvre though, despite the NOSE smelling something fishy. The ARSE kept its own council on the matter though, but it would have been more than willing to rear end any outlandish proposals that the ELBOW tried to nudge in on the sly.

As it turned out, and to everyone's surprise, the ELBOW disagreed with the idea of having a PISS altogether, and wanted to introduce a system of their own involving keeping track of the number of 'Suitable Hauntings In a Total Set' (SHITS).

This, however, was met with complete derision from the other two groups. The NOSE looked down at the ELBOW and had a proper flare up, whilst the ARSE, who did have some previous experience with the SHITS, remained firm in its position of not allowing any third-party proposals in via the back door.

And so, the NOSE, backed up by the ARSE, finally agreed to take the PISS, after which they led the ELBOW from the room and wiped away any trace of the SHITS from the minutes.

"How is old Max by the way?" said Gullett. "I haven't seen him for ages."

"Oh, he's alright," said Mandrake. "Up to the usual sort of thing, you know. Rattling chains, moaning a lot, ruining my wife's best sheets."

"He was like that when he was alive," said Nurse Parsnip. "One of the worst patients that I've ever had to tend to in fact. I've never known anyone to have so many non-existent complaints. And that includes vampires." She winked at Ollie affectionately.

(In the same way that Dr Zoltan held a torch for the good nurse, she in turn rather fancied Ollie, which, it has to be pointed out, is a state of affairs that's straying a little towards the odd.

Being from distinctly differing backgrounds species wise, her affections were rather unusual, and for the unlife of her she wasn't quite sure what it was about him that made her feel that way. And do you know what? She's not the only one. I haven't got a clue and I'm the idiot writing this drivel. Still, in much the same way as King Louis XVI was heard to utter as he knelt in front of Madame Guillotine, if I have to stick my neck out, I'd have to say it probably has something to do with his rakish yet pasty faced vulnerability, his otherworldly charm, the way he always gets things done, and the fact that he looked absolutely splendid in a cape and fancy trousers. There, that'll do won't it. Well, it'll have to so tough. It's either that or I'll have to come up with some sort of Twilight inspired drivel guaranteed to make you vomit by the time you've reached the second paragraph on page one.

You can make up your own mind, of course, but I know what I prefer).

Ollie didn't react to the eye related gesture. By his own admission he was a bit naïve when it came to dealing with members of the opposite gender, therefore he was blissfully unaware of Nurse Parsnip's ill placed affections. And a good job he was too because he would have been absolutely horrified at the idea. To another ghoul, and a slightly batty physician with a dead body fixation, she might very well have been considered a bit of a catch, but to a vampire, and especially one with a distinctly human half, she was about as attractive as an infected liver.

Anyhoo, after all the unclear deliberations about the aforementioned, so called happenings, the group came to the inevitable conclusion that maybe they weren't so out of the ordinary after all. Even Noggin seemed to have recovered somewhat and was presently heading towards Stitches with a nonchalant air, a casual gait, and a happily swishing tail, all with the express intention of rearranging him ever so slightly.

That being the case, they all bid each other farewell and left, and as Ronnie said to Constable Gullett as they exited the building, "I don't know what I was so worried about now."

He'd find out soon enough, though. As would they all.

Meanwhile, down in the hallowed dankness that was his lab, Professor Crumble was embroiled in a quandary. At this precise moment in time he was slap bang in the middle of two different experiments and was having a hard time trying to decide which one to carry on with.

Ever the one for a spot of multi-tasking this wasn't an unusual state of affairs though, and as such he quite often found himself on the horns of one dilemma or another (or the demon that he'd accidentally brought forth from the depths of Hell that needed to be vanquished before it spread its infectious evil across the world in a bid to gain dominion over all of the earthbound creatures infesting the surface of the planet that Crumble managed to defeat by getting it in the eye with a squirt of lemon washing up liquid thus making it cry and flee the laboratory in shame with its forked tail tucked neatly between its hooves. Or something like that anyway).

That had happened a couple of weeks ago and said naughty creature from the bowels of the underworld was now plying his trade in far off Pentacle. He was quite good at making hats apparently.

The problem was, Crumble didn't know whether to finish perfecting his recipe for a new variety of herbal tea (a relaxing beverage containing a cunning fusion of youngerberries, barbecue sauce, fresh mint, and enough sedatives to put a Stegosaurus to sleep), or put the last touches to a dish that he reckoned could be rather fun.

He'd lined a large dish with pastry into which he'd placed some dominoes, Travel Scrabble, some succulent venison and Skullenian Monopoly. He'd then covered all of that with a crispy lid and popped it into the oven for an hour or so. And his name for this foul-tasting choking hazard? Game Pie. He figured it would perfectly combine the fine cuisine expected at any dinner party whilst incorporating all the entertainment that any guests could ever need. And let's face it, what gracious host could turn their nose up at that?

Of course, it was insane beyond words but that wasn't any great surprise coming from the chap who thought there wasn't any problem, anywhere in the universe that couldn't be solved with a cup of tea, a nice chat, and a bucket full of high explosives.

As he was pondering his decision, he became aware of a slow but steady change in the laboratory's atmosphere. It was subtle at first, but gradually built to the point that he began to look around to see if there was something in there with him.

And what made it even more perturbing was the fact he was absolutely, positively, and one hundred percenty sure it wasn't anything that he'd done.

Not that that was anything to go by.

You see, what with his capacity for causing the near death and almost total destruction of everyone and everything around him on a regular basis being as infinite as his lapses of memory, that particular assertion is as reliable as Henry VIII's marriage vows.

If questioned as to where the cup of tea that'd he'd just made had come from he'd genuinely claim not to have any knowledge of the incident, blame it on an itinerant badger, forget all about being asked in the first place, and blow something up.

Never the shrinking violet he'd been complicit in quite a few minor incidents over the years.

Take Tunguska, Russia in 1908, for example. The history books tell us that an asteroid some two hundred metres across exploded about five miles above the earth's surface, laying waste to a couple of thousand acres of forest. However, whilst satisfactory as an explanation, and eminently plausible given the evidence, that account isn't entirely accurate. There *was* an explosion over the area, and it *did* knock over about eighty million trees and turn them into toothpicks, but it was no chunk of rock that was responsible, oh no. It was actually a Screaming Siren, a highly volatile and very illegal firework that a young Rufus Crumble decided to pep up a smidge. Okay, so he didn't mean to boost its megatonnage to near extinction level capabilities, but his heart was in the right place (which was about thirty-five miles away with the rest of him).

Another incident of note was The Great Bloop. In 1997 a tremendous sound was detected on the floor of the Pacific Ocean. It was one of the loudest noises ever recorded and scientists have argued for years about what could have caused it. Some say earthquake, others proposed volcanic activity, and a few suggested an as yet undiscovered sea creature of gargantuan proportions.

Oh, how they'd be kicking themselves if they knew the truth (once they'd finished kicking Crumble into another dimension at any rate).

The Professor had come to the stunningly berserk conclusion that the oceans were a bit too dirty for his liking, and therefore in need of a spring clean. To that end he'd created a bath bomb roughly the size of a semi-detached house and let it go. On the way down it had popped, fizzled, and crackled, all the while soaking up enough sea water to put out Hiroshima ten seconds after it went pop.

When the submarine ball of destructive detergent had landed, it had split with such force that the sound waves had travelled round the planet three times, causing every item of marine detecting equipment ever deployed to overload. It also scared a Japanese whaling ship's crew so badly that they completely stopped what they were doing and weren't able to slaughter any cetaceans for almost twenty minutes.

But that's Crumble for you. He doesn't do things by halves, and I have absolutely no doubt that a spot of diligent research would raise some very interesting facts about how the Titanic actually sank.

The gleaming bulb hanging from his ceiling hummed furiously as its brightness increased to a level that far exceeded what it should have been able to produce. And then, just as swiftly, it started to dim and continued to do so until Crumble was standing in the midst of an eerie twilight, watching attentively as twisted shadows danced around the darkening, and increasingly claustrophobic room.

"How very bizarre," said the Prof, louder than he normally would when engaged in a conversation with himself. "I wonder what's going…"

Just than the light bulb exploded, sending a million stinging shards in every direction. Crumble barely made it out of the way in time, but some of the tiny fragments caught him on the hands and forehead. Luckily, he still had his glasses on, and if it wasn't for the fact they were so thick that it was a five-minute walk to go and clean the fronts, his eyes would have been cut to ribbons.

Strangely, it wasn't dark in spite of the only light source in the lab disappearing.

On the floor right in the centre of the room was a glow, a greeny/blue patch of luminescence that seemed to be increasing in size rather rapidly.

"I certainly don't remember doing that," said Crumble, backing up ever so slightly.

"*You didn't,*" said a soft, echoing voice that seemed to come from everywhere and nowhere at the same time. "*I sort of came to be by myself. It's a bit bloody minded I know, which is a constant failing of mine I'm afraid, but it certainly does have its practical uses.*"

"If I may," said Crumble, who, in spite of feeling rather disconcerted, and more than a tad apprehensive, maintained his impeccable manners. "Who are you? Or are you in fact a what? And if you are indeed a what, then what are you?"

The uncanny radiance expanded even more until it was almost as high as the ceiling.

Undulating tendrils snaked forth from its core and reached out to the Professor.

"*Let me explain,*" said the voice. "*It won't take more than a moment.*"

* * *

The next morning, Mrs. Strudel was busy in her kitchen, as was usual for Skullenia's premier provider of post-mortem provender. At present she was stirring a thick, bubbling mixture that was cooking in the vast cauldron on top of the stove. After a few more hefty swirls she tested it with her practised tongue and decided that it needed a pinch of salt. And a few more frogs' eyebrows. And maybe a soupçon of Hemlock's Mega Spice, a tangy concoction that made tongues cry, eyes scream, and hair grow on a chemotherapy patient.

Once she was happy that the blend would be to her customer's requirements, she gave it another vigorous stir and whacked the heat up to raging inferno (or, to put that into terms that an ordinary cook might understand, that's gas mark forty eight million, six hundred and seventy two thousand, five hundred and eighty six/as hot as the middle of a super morbidly obese blue whale's funeral pyre/a temperature roughly equivalent to the surface of the sun when it has a fever/or slightly cooler than the inside of a McDonald's apple pie).

She reckoned another five minutes would see it ready, a fact which was easily gauged by the amount of radiant heat coming from the food itself, the rivulets of condensation dripping down the walls, and the cast iron spoon that'd been resting in the liquid being considerably shorter, and distinctly less spoon like than when she'd started.

The chunky gloop roiled and effervesced thickly, producing coloured blisters that undulated, expanded, and then popped. It looked like a hot mud spring, only hotter, muddier, marginally springier, and a hell of a lot more dangerous.

It was Tumerian Stew, a piquant dish favoured by those ghouls in town who preferred their flesh and blood cooked.

Now, what with most ghouls preferring their meat on the raw side (thrashing about and screaming, "Please don't eat me"), and generally being as fussy over their food as a hungry tiger shark, this method of preparation is a bit unusual, but it's purpose is twofold.

Not only does it bring out the subtle flavours of the meat for the more discerning fiend, it also has the added benefit of softening the bones somewhat, which is a major boon to the older generation whose incisors and jaw muscles aren't as powerful as they'd once been. Cracked and broken teeth are a constant problem for the senior anthropophagi, and there aren't many places happy to make a person smoothie no matter how much you offer to pay, your assertion that you won't tell anyone, and that you're able to provide all of the requisite ingredients the drink requires, that being one human body (preferably deceased, but that's not mandatory).

Mrs. Strudel filled three large bowls and placed them carefully onto a tray. She didn't want to spill any because it played havoc with the stone floor.

"Eugene," she called out.

With a stomp, a red eyed glare, and an expression that changed less often than the surface of the moon, Eugene the golem, he of the silent demeanour, firmness of hand, and waiter extraordinaire, entered the kitchen.

"Here you go, love," she said, pointing to the tray. "Table six please. Mr. and Mrs. Stroker and their little one."

Before he picked up the gourmet autopsy, he handed Mrs. Strudel an order slip.

"Let's see," she read out loud. "Mug of tea with eight sugars and a slice of Inside Outy Coconutty Chocolatey cake."

She smiled and quickly put the order together. The tea went into a special mug (although mug wasn't the best word to describe the drinking vessel because you could have attached a slide to the side of it and had a pool party. It also took six teabags just to give the tea a modicum of colour, which is why she used nine) and the cake she didn't even bother slicing, that she just put onto a plate, whole.

She bustled into the front of house, spotted the waiting diner and made her way over.

"Hello, Doris. Quicker than ever today," said Constable Gullett, relieving her of her calorie laden load.

"You know me, Tobias," she said, sitting down opposite the policeman. "Always ready, willing, and able to keep my hungriest customers happy."

"Your fattest customers you mean." He patted his vast belly for emphasis.

"Oh, tish and pish. You're in fine shape for a man of your…"

"Weight?"

"Well, I was going to say age, but you do carry it rather grandly."

"I haven't got any choice," said Gullett, cutting himself a slice of cake that could've been hollowed out and used as a bus shelter. He took a substantial bite then fiddled with his belt.

"Problem?" said Mrs. Strudel.

"It's these damn uniform trousers. They've flipping well shrunk again."

Mrs. Strudel chuckled quietly as she wiped away some crumbs from Gullett's whiskers (which were so dense and bushy that the fallout from any meal could be swept up, put in a bag, and sent off to a third world country where it could be distributed amongst thousands of starving people, who would not only be grateful for a hearty meal, but also eternally thankful for the fact that it would prevent scruffy Irishman, crap musicians, and tenth rate celebrities visiting their huts whilst pretending to be upset).

"So, how's things been?" she asked. "Solved any big cases lately? Locked away any arch villains?"

"I found out who put all that graffiti on the fountain," Gullett said after a mouthful of tea.

"Oh yes."

"Mmm. Turns out it was Starry Biro. Mind you it didn't take a lot of working out to be honest. He's the only one round here who'd use the appropriate medical terms for parts of the body and spell them properly. He won't be doing it again though."

"Give him a good telling off, did you?"

"I most certainly did. And just to make sure he got the message I locked him up with Wendy."

"Well, that'll certainly teach him a lesson. He won't want to do that again in a hurry."

Wailing Wendy, a wistful, wandering, weirdly wacky, worrisome witch of a woman sadly went wildly wibble a few weeks ago (how's that for alliteration).

Fed up with being a bit socially awkward, she'd tried out a new spell on herself, one designed to make her more confident and relaxed around other people. Tragically, she hadn't got it quite right, and now spent ninety percent of the time screaming at the top of her not inconsiderable voice because she was now utterly terrified of everything and everyone. The other ten percent she spent screaming even louder.

When Gullett had released Starry the next morning, the good constable had needed to write down in large, and correctly spelled words, what he wanted to say because poor Mr Biro was having a spot of trouble with his hearing. This was given away by the fact that his ears were bleeding profusely, he had a haunted, vacant expression on his exhausted features, and had a ringing in his head to rival a concert by the Iron Thumpers of Zobaditzgoud, a thrash metal band of bell ringers who indulged in a form of musical destruction so heavy it not only woke the dead, it also gave them tinnitus, blurred vision, and a headache that would've floored an elephant wearing ear plugs.

(Even though you may not have heard of them, and believe me, if you had heard of them, you *would* have heard them, The Iron Thumpers were quite famous throughout Eastern Europe during the early eighties, and are still often in demand at festivals to this very day. You might know some of their songs. There's, 'Whack Me In The Clangers', 'Wrap Your Hands Around My Ding Dong', 'Polish My Throbbing Handle', 'Pull The Other One It's Got Bells On', 'Sally, Will You Hold My Mallet', 'Tailend Handstroke', and the ever popular romantic ballad, 'Can

I Stroke Your Muffler While You Poke Me In The Ringer?')

"Indeed, it did. But apart from that, and last night's weirdness there's really not much else to tell," said Gullett.

"Weirdness?" said Mrs. Strudel.

Constable Gullett told her about his incident on the road the night before and the accounts from the others.

"That doesn't sound at all like Noggin," she said. "Poor little thing." She paused for just a moment. "Actually, now that you mention it, he didn't come round last night."

"Come round?"

"Yes. He's been visiting me for ages, so much so that I've taken to leaving him a treat outside the back door. You know how he likes to have something to chew on in the early hours. This morning it was still there."

"What was it?" said Gullett.

"Oh, nothing much. Just a pig that I never got around to using. Something certainly must have scared the little dear for him to leave that. It's one of his favourites. Unless I've got a spare cow lying around of course."

"I'm surprised nothing else took it," said Gullett, taking another gulp of tea. "There's creatures a plenty round here that'd jump at the chance of a free meal."

"Nothing would dare. And even if they did, Noggin would definitely tear them off a strip or two."

"Once he'd finished with their limbs," added the policeman.

"True. It does sound a bit odd though doesn't it. Do you know what? I think there may be more to this than meets the eye, my dear Tobias. If there is something out there that can scare Noggin and put him off his food, I wouldn't want to bump into it."

Gullett finished his repast, made a show of offering to pay the bill, an offer that was declined as per usual, and went back outside.

'I wonder what's going on?' he thought.

He didn't have a clue, of course, but he'd find out soon enough.

And so, much like a cemetery operative suffering from a depth perception problem, he decided to do a little bit more digging.

\* \* \*

Deirdre had gotten rather lost. In spite of feeling pulled in a certain direction to locations unknown, the landscape that she was travelling through was bleak to the point of desolation, didn't appear to have any discernible landmarks and, as she had thought to herself on more than one occasion, all looked the bloody same.

She'd brought directions along of course, but after a while they'd became about as much use as the vegetarian option in a hyena's only restaurant.

After a certain amount of aimless wandering about like someone who didn't know where they were, she stopped and took stock of her situation (she didn't even know exactly how long she'd been lost. It seemed to have been dark for an age and her watch had decided to conk out).

It was whilst she was having a good look round that she saw something in the distance. A big something. A very big something. It was shrouded in dense fog and swirling mist and had a thunderstorm going on above it that didn't seem to want to move on. It looked a bit spooky and just gazing at it sent a frigid chill right up her neck and straight through her hat (the building was spooky by the way, not the storm. That was more…stormy).

But seeing as it was the only building that she'd seen for quite some time, it literally was the only port even if it was in a storm. Add to that the fact that her feet were aching like buggery and she was dying for a cup of tea and a biccie, Deirdre had no option but to start heading towards it, fervently hoping that the occupants, if there were any, would take pity on a poor old lady, lost and alone in the middle of nowhere, which she most certainly was.

*"Deirdre."*

"Hello."

*"It's Bumpy."*

"Yes, Bumpy, what is it, dear. I'm a little indisposed at the moment."

*"Oh, it's nothing really. I think I might have left the iron on. Do you think you can go and check for me?"*

"Bumpy."

*"Yes, Deirdre."*

"You died in 1896, love, remember? I think someone would have noticed and turned it off by now don't you? And if they haven't, I think an overheated item of domestic equipment may be the least of your worries."

*"Oh yes. Sorry, Deirdre. Bye."*

"Bye, Bumpy."

Deirdre began to make her way along a wide, cobbled path that eventually led her into a courtyard, on the other side of which was a front door that led into the massive edifice.

Being the cautious type, (obviously we'll have to ignore the fact that she'd set out on her own, on a mysterious quest to a strange and eerie place to determine the meaning of a cryptic message, and didn't have a clue what she'd be facing when she got there, and what dangers all the stuff she knew nothing about might actually pose to a woman who'd set out on her own, on a mysterious quest to a strange and eerie place to determine the meaning of a cryptic message, and didn't have a clue what she'd be facing when she got there, and what dangers all the stuff she knew nothing about might pose), and not wanting to head into the unknown without knowing something about the unknown that she was heading into (oh, the irony), Deirdre sent out her psychic feelers, something she always did when she was about to enter somewhere new, especially if that somewhere new was a bit on the creepy side.

(And that was a wise move, as I'm sure you'll agree, because judging by what she'd seen of the place so far, which wasn't much, it definitely had one foot firmly placed in the bizarre camp, right next to those adults who like scouting with young boys and helping them with their woggles, and the parents who actually think their children will enjoy spending a week in a muddy field where they have to sleep on ground that's lumpier than John Merrick's nose, use a toilet the size of a tin mug that's probably just a tin mug, eat nothing but cold beans, fatty bacon, and Smarties, and listen to couples called things like Merlin and Summer who love 'getting back to nature' so much that they keep everyone else up all night including the cows in the next field who start mooing in distress).

Without warning her extrasensory tendrils snapped back into her subconscious as if they were attached to rubber bands. Or had they been pushed? She certainly hadn't reined them in that was for sure. And not only had they not picked up anything, they were now hiding in the dark recesses of her mind along with her fear of spiders, cheese with fruit in it, and page seven of every book in the world.

(The cheese and spider phobias are obvious, of course, and common to many many people. Who amongst us hasn't gawped in slack jawed terror as some hideously glistening, darkly flecked monstrosity sits nonchalantly close by and stares into your very being with a soul crushing malevolence, as if daring you to approach it?

And spiders are just as bad. Even they flee in panic from a tangy Wensleydale that's got cranberries in it.

The number seven issue does need explaining though. When Deirdre was a young girl, she'd read a really scary book about a really scary monster, and it was on that dreaded page, the one between page six and page eight, that the really scary monster had done something really rather scary. And so, as a result of trying to tangle with the terrifying tome, Deirdre had developed a mind-numbing fear of that particular number, one that had affected her life ever since.

She'd learned to make adjustments, of course, but did so especially when it came to reading, which was still a favourite distraction of hers. She'd found that by skipping page seven, seventeen, twenty-seven etc. she was still able to follow a plot and doing so didn't really affect her overall enjoyment of a story. Much to her chagrin, though, it did mean that she'd never be able to enjoy the delights of literary classics such as, 'Great Sevens of Yesteryear' by Huxley Turnip, Oxford Jump's, 'Why I Love The Number

Seven', or Silvery Trade's, 'The Complete History of The Seven Times Table'.

Interestingly, she'd employed a version of the page elimination technique with The da Vinci Code. She'd found that by skipping every single page between the front and back covers, the novel had been rather enjoyable.

And don't moan about the explanation. I said it needed clarifying, I didn't say it was interesting).

It was then that she noticed some distinctly odd things (which is a woefully inadequate description given their distinct oddness).

A clutch of creeping, nebulous filaments that weren't there a moment ago were now snaking and writhing their insidious way around the courtyard (which is wonderfully adequate description given their distinct oddness).

At first, she didn't know what they were, but a crushing pressure in her head signified that some other paranormal presence was now with her, and it was powerful beyond anything she'd ever sensed before.

The slithering waves of ethereal energy approached and surrounded her, and unable to fend them off, they bored into her psyche and extracted information from the deepest vault therein. She tried to erect her mental barriers in an effort to stave off the assault, but it was of no use. She was utterly helpless against psychic powers of such magnitude.

Just as she thought of abandoning her trip right there and then for fear of what the encounter might do to her mental functions, the front door ever so slowly, and ever so surely, began to open, sounding for all the world like a crypt in a low budget horror film.

(You know the sort of thing. Despite several warnings that are dismissed as urban myth, a hapless, and rather stupid teenager enters an abandoned dwelling [insane asylum, hospital, etc], at night, [when else], because he's been dared to by his friends.

Then, after looking about for a bit [whilst being all cocky and dismissive], he ends up being confronted by some hideous, nether-worldly fiend [there's a shocker] who's hell bent on subjecting him and his friends to all manner of unimaginable and blood curdling horrors [usually involving ridiculously sized choppy things that are definitely over compensating for something or another] in reprisal for being bumped off by some of the locals because he was careless enough to butcher their kids ten years ago [i.e. parents who should have been on social services' radar from the moment the child was conceived].

If you don't know what I'm talking about go onto IMDB and search for films starring Neve Campbell, and if that fails, ones where the bad guy is a bell-end in a stupid jumper who's got a complexion like crispy bacon).

Quite unexpectedly, Deirdre found she was unable to move, not even so much as a muscle. Clearly, whatever resided in the castle found her intriguing enough to immobilise her.

By now she was genuinely frightened and wishing that she was safely at home and sitting at her kitchen table with nothing to think about other than which teapot went best with Oddleys Extra Strong.

Once the door had been opened a foot or so, a hand reached through the gap to help it along. She watched in rapt attention as a, well yes, a hideous and infernal region dwelling type fiend finally got the massive chunk of wood out of the way and stood there staring at her.

Then, in what was probably the most unnerving part of the whole episode thus far, it smiled.

"Hello," it said. "Do come inside. That mist will soak you through if you stand in it for too long. You'll catch your death."

In spite of its less than favourable choice of words, and not taking into account its outlandish appearance (she likened it to a giblet filled plastic bag that had been left on top of a hot plate), the overbearing and darkly menacing presence of the structure itself, and the fact that this was a situation that would have made the Grim Reaper himself think about hanging up his scythe and calling it an aeon, Deirdre suddenly felt strangely serene (well, maybe not quite as calm as that because that would be silly, but at least she wasn't wailing like a deranged Druid, pulling her hair out by the roots, and trying to throw herself off the nearest cliff in sheer terror like the milkman did every morning).

Finally, free of the force that had held her in place, Deirdre Clownpuncher walked steadfastly towards the unknown.

* * *

Ethan pulled open the enormous door that led to the storage area. It was an expansive, chilled environment situated at the rear of the werehouse, and it was within this frigid space that dozens upon dozens of carcasses, each one neatly butchered, bound, and hung up on a meat hook, were stored.

Don't be alarmed by that description, by the way. This flesh filled fridge does have a purpose and isn't as macabre and grisly as it may first appear. Well, it is a tad, I suppose, and all things considered it does sound a little bit like a serial killer's trophy room, but then it's hard to equate it to anything else really.

There're dead bodies in there for goodness sake.

You see, although hunting in and around the Skullenian forest is usually a plentiful pursuit for those creatures of a predatory nature, there are a few rare occasions when pickings can be a bit lean (especially after one of Mrs. Ladle's bake sales), and whilst inordinately tempting, it isn't considered very sporting to nonchalantly wander into town and start munching on the locals when you're feeling a bit peckish.

Not on the sly anyway.

Not that your average werewolf has any choice in the matter. As you can well imagine it's rather difficult to remain stealthy and camouflaged in an active residential area when you're seven feet long, covered in fur, and have claws like scimitars.

Although, if you live in the wilds of North Elmham, you'll fit in like a six fingered glove.

So, as you can see, being a lycanthrope does require an element of tactful diplomacy and a certain amount of planning, hence the well-stocked reposi-tory, an up to date list of who's in town (it wouldn't do to bite the head off a visiting dignitary), and the publication of a monthly time-table detailing who'll be out hunting and when. That way, if you got your-self all chewed up by Big Bailey, you only had your-self to blame.

There's also the added hazard of having to take your chances against Noggin.

As far as the mad moggy is concerned, it matters not one jot how many teeth you have or how big you are, if he thinks you're hunting on his turf, it's OUCH! time.

The friendly, neighbourhood vampire cat is a bit on the possessive side, you see and thus considers almost every piece of meat within a fifty mile ra-dius to be his personal property whether it's alive or dead, so a spot of night time forest foraging is best left to when he's having a kip.

And so, because the facility, or rather the prod-ucts residing within it, aren't used all that often, they have to be checked for deterioration on a reg-ular basis, and as one of the more senior members of the pack, it fell to Ethan to complete the task.

(Quality control is a very important undertak-ing when your diet consists primarily of meat, and whilst not the fussiest of diners by any means, even a werewolf at his hungriest would baulk at the idea of eating spoiled flesh.

Think of it like you or I consuming a blemished apple, although, in reality, your average Golden Delicious doesn't put up a fight, tell you get lost, and run off before you can sink your teeth into it.

Unless they're in one of Mrs. Ladle's pies, of course, in which case there's every possibility that said comestible might escape from its pastry topped cell, give you a damn good thrashing, and make a bid for freedom).

Now, the idea of a larder for shapeshifters may come as a bit of a surprise to some (usually simpering vegans who won't even tread on a lawn because they can hear the grass crying in pain), but as is the case with most supernatural beings, the feeding habits of lycanthropes is an aspect of their behaviour all too often misrepresented in popular culture, film, and literature.

Those mediums, as entertaining as they are, invariably portray the werewolf as a ravening, flesh craving psychopath, one who goes mental at the merest suggestion of a full moon and more than happy to feast upon anything with a pulse unfortunate enough to bump into it, be that a well to do lady of breeding wearing a dress so tight she can barely keep her boobs under control, a good looking chap backpacking, a middle aged office worker so boring he thinks an unscheduled cup of tea is taking a walk on the wild side, or some noisome hermit who hasn't been near a bar of soap for several increasingly fragrant and scabies ridden decades.

Now, in fairness, I will concede that the above observation is true, but only up to a point. I mean, let's face it, we're not talking about robots here are we. Quite naturally, any werewolf worth his/her fangs would have no problem whatsoever in sinking said dental extrusions into the soft, pliant flesh of some coquettishly innocent, stunningly beautiful, and reluctantly virginal, well to-do young lady (apparently they taste like chicken), or a firmly thighed, tightly buttocked, awesomely bearded fell-walker, (again, they taste like chicken, but with a hint of despair), but they'd draw a very, thick, and furry black line to feasting on brawn that's been marinated in filth for the last twenty five years.

And don't be thinking it's due to them being overly fussy either. It's simply because they're just as likely to get a gastrointestinal upset after eating something tainted as they would when in human form, and chowing down on the stinking corpse of a tramp who just happens to be living under a tree would be the equivalent of you or I partaking of a steak that'd been removed from its host a month previously and left to lie in the sun whilst playing host to every bacteria, scavenger, and egg laying insect within a two and a half mile radius.

So, if you imagine how sick that would make you, dear reader, picture the scene of a nauseous werewolf, one who decided to forego his usual fare related fastidiousness and feast on a hundred and twenty pounds of rancid human instead.

It's not a pretty sight trust me, and one far too grisly for the average person to witness, especially when eight out of ten of them can't handle their pet cat chucking up the occasional furball.

Anyway. The big fridge.

For ease, each slab of meat has a date stamped upon it signifying when it was killed and when it was stored. It's a clearly visible, and easily identifiable marker making it easy to tell whether it needs to be discarded or not, regardless of how fresh it may appear to be.

You, no doubt, employ the same 'use by date' system with the items in your own fridge. Except when it comes to celery, of course. That can go straight in the bin along with the utterly pointless and tasteless green rubbish called lettuce, those budget price sausages that have the same meat content as a 1993 Vauxhall Corsa, horseradish sauce (really! Have a look at a raw one and then see if you fancy it in your beef sarnie), the diabetic inducing wedge of satanic viciousness that is marzipan, kidneys because I will NEVER EVER eat anything I classify as a piss filter, the slimy and infected looking blob of snot that is the oyster, and prune yoghurt, which looks like the contents of a large and festering abscess circa 1436 (obviously your list of hated foodstuffs may be different to mine, but I very much doubt it.

Mind you, there are some weird folk about).

Ethan checked his list and counted off the items to his right, because they were the most recent additions. Once he was satisfied they were all in good order (in that they hadn't started to get a bit whiffy), he continued with those to his left and worked his way back along the line.

If he did discover any past their best, he'd take out a big black marker and draw a big black cross on them to indicate that they needed removing. These would then be placed in a trunk and discarded in the forest later, which was perfectly acceptable as it saved on waste by keeping the meat in the food chain.

And it *would* get eaten.

There's no end of less discerning creatures out in the wilds don't you know, and with many of them preferring to scavenge, they're always up for a free meal (especially one that isn't going to run off), and don't have any problems at all with eating spoiled protein.

(They also have no sense of taste, the ability to ignore the foetid and sickly-sweet stench of increasingly slushy and rapidly decomposing remains, and digestive systems like fourteenth century middens.

The hermits love it and have a veritable field day when it's chuck out time at the werehouse. All they usually get is a few acorns, a worm or two, and escaped pieces of fruit).

As he got about three quarters of the way down the line Ethan noticed that the bulb above the next section had blown.

He shook his head.

'Blast you, Phil', he thought.

Phil was in charge of maintenance, meaning he was supposed to deal with any issues that arose as and when they happened, not when he damn well felt like it.

Okay, so it wasn't a huge problem on the face of it but it might prove to be a bit of a nuisance when he got to the section in question as he needed to be sure about the dates he was checking.

Still, with the glow from the remaining lights and his enhanced eyesight he decided it shouldn't prove to be overly bothersome.

He'd certainly mention it to Phil once he'd finished, though.

As he wandered into the semi darkness, he thought he heard a faint whoosh behind him, the sort of soft exhalation you might hear when someone blows out cigarette smoke or extinguishes the candles on a birthday cake.

He stopped for a moment and let his senses wander.

Nothing.

The silence was absolute, and the air was as still as could be. Maybe he was hearing things.

Thinking no more of it, he carried on.

Ten feet further into the increasingly darkening room it happened again, only this time the rush of air was more insistent, and he felt its fluttering caress on the back of his muscular neck.

Ethan stopped where he was and froze in position. He was now more than positive that he wasn't entirely alone in the storeroom, although what exactly was in there with him wasn't immediately apparent.

A noise caught his attention. A scraping of sorts. It wasn't loud but it was constant, quietly insinuating itself into the silence filling the large open space.

Ethan turned a full one hundred and eighty degrees before he was able to identify where the noise was coming from.

He tutted and shook his head.

"Must be getting jumpy in my old age," he said to himself.

Two of the hanging carcasses were swinging gently back and forth as if someone or something had passed clumsily between them. The scraping he'd detected was the metal hooks rubbing against each other.

Relaxing, he decided it had to be some kind of practical joke, albeit a very weak one. That being the case, he allowed himself a wry smile and made a show of not being bothered by it. He didn't call out either because he didn't want to give the protagonist hiding in the shadows the satisfaction of knowing that their little stunt had succeeded in putting the willies up their intended target somewhat. And besides, it was childish, misguided, and most unbecoming for a full-grown member of the noble order of lycanthropes to engage in such behaviour, so there was no chance he was going to acknowledge it in any way. Not when he'd get his own back at some point, ha ha.

Ethan slipped the marker pen into his pocket and gingerly placed the clipboard onto the floor. Then, with a lightness of foot surprising for a man of his size, he crept over to the now slowed, but still swinging carcasses.

"They look like meaty pendulums," he mused.

When he got to them, he paused, closed his eyes, and listened. Again, there was nothing, not even so much as a...

Without warning, the carcass he was standing next to suddenly burst apart in a torrent of frigid flesh and coagulated blood that scattered dozens of feet in every direction. It was so completely decimated it was almost as if a hand grenade had been primed and then shoved into its very core.

Such was the intensity of the blast it knocked the startled Lycan clean off his feet and sent him sprawling to the floor at least half a dozen yards from where he'd been standing.

When he landed, he cracked his skull on the cold, unforgiving flagstone with such force it left him stunned and disorientated for a few moments.

But not many.

As quick as a flash he was on his feet.

He shook his throbbing head, then wished he hadn't.

When the carcass had exploded, he'd been showered with congealed blood and gelatinous, lumpy globules of fat, an oozing post-mortem exudate that was now in his eyes and blurring his vision.

He raised his hands to clear it away, but before he had a chance some unseen power launched him into the air once more. This time, though, he didn't come to rest on the floor. He was left suspended in mid-air as if he were nothing but a stringed marionette at the mercy of an evil and sadistic puppeteer.

He tried to move, but the more he struggled the stronger the unseen force holding him became.

All in all, it wasn't a good situation, but it was then made even worse by the fact that, for whatever reason, he realised he'd lost his ability to transform. Try as he might, he couldn't summon his alter ego.

For the first time since his inception, his rebirth if you will, Ethan's inner beast failed him.

Finally, thanks to the sweat pouring from his forehead, the gore cleared from his eyes allowing him to make out a hazy greenish blue glow before him.

"Sorry about being so rough," said a voice from somewhere. Was it in his head? He couldn't be sure. Now it seemed to be behind him. Now in front. "But I gather you can be a bit of a handful."

"Show yourself, you coward and you'll see a handful," said Ethan through gritted, ichor covered teeth.

"Mmm. Maybe not. I think I'll stick to my original plan if it's all the same to you."

"What do you want?"

"Funny you should ask, because I was just getting to that."

Ethan felt an intense, searing pain lance its way through his head and then he knew no more.

* * *

Back at the office and with very little to do, Ollie, much like a proctologist examining an elderly patient, had found himself at a bit of a loose end.

To combat this, he'd resorted to busying himself in well-practiced and time-honoured fashion.

"So, what did he do?" I hear you ask.

"Well, I'll tell you," you hear me reply.

"Why, thank you," I hear you say.

"You're welcome," you hear me respond. "Anything else?" you hear me add.

"You could get on with the story," I hear you exclaim. "My lunch-break finishes in ten minutes," I hear you plead.

"Sorry," you hear me retort, "but it gets a bit lonely here, tapping away to myself," you hear me plead.

"Stop making up conversations!" I hear you accuse. "Terry Pratchett never did that," I hear you conclude.

"Fine," you hear me huff. "*&^+%$@."

"What was that? I didn't hear," I hear you demand.

"Snigger snigger," you hear me snigger.

I hear your silence because your lunchbreak's over.

(Don't mess with us authors. We can write you out any time we want).

Anyway, to explain, Ollie had indulged in a spot of pottering, and as you might expect from such an endeavour he hadn't done anything in particular, hadn't been working to any specific agenda, and hadn't been pressed for time to get anything done so, like your grandfather in his shed polishing his tomatoes, your nan in her kitchen rearranging her cupboards yet again, or Michael Barrymore waiting for the swimming pool cleaner to arrive, Ollie had just pottered.

Put simply, he'd had some free time on his hands, and seeing as he had no truck with time wasting and those that indulged in such i.e. wasting time, he'd decided not to waste that free time by letting that time which had become free, go to waste.

And do you know what, he'd actually rather enjoyed the experience.

You see, what with one thing or another (the most prevalent being Crumble blowing something up, Stitches needing help sewing something back on, detoxing Ronnie, or Flug requiring assistance to remove something from his nose), it wasn't very often that he got any time to himself these days, so in the spirit of all things anti-social, he just got on with it by himself.

(As you can imagine that last example is the most frequent occurrence by far, the latest incident of which happened just the day before when Flug, in all his glorious stupidity, had managed to get an entire fork stuck up his expansive hooter.

Now, ordinarily it wasn't too much of a problem as he'd put various household objects up there before, not least of which was a sausage roll that's still in there somewhere. On this occasion, however, the situation was rendered slightly more awkward on account of the particular item of cutlery still being attached to the person using it to eat his dinner over at Mrs. Strudel's.

Needless to say, the dwarf in question wasn't very happy about it, but thankfully, it all got sorted out in the end.

After a little bit of gentle teasing, some tactful persuasion, and the promise that if he relented and let go he wouldn't get the granny kicked out of him, the chap relented and let go, the fork was removed, and Flug had eventually sneezed, reacquainting the diner in question with his leg of lamb, although he swore it hadn't had any mint sauce on it when it went in).

He'd tidied up his desk, rearranged the ornaments atop his fireplace, done a bit of dusting, and even cleared out a couple of items of paperwork that had been hanging around the office like a couple of items of paperwork that needed clearing out.

The first was an old note to the milkman stating, 'Please can you leave some actual milk today and not the gloopy purple stuff you've taken to depositing on the doorstep? PS. A bottle would be nice as well', and the second was a 'No thanks' reply he needed to send.

It was in response to an invitation from Skullenias self-proclaimed, foremost intellectual, Professor Tethered Shift who was giving a talk on, 'The Life and Times of Tethered Shift, Misunderstood Genius of the Era', an event Ollie fancied attending about as much as he had the urge to strip naked, cover himself in fresh blood, and giving Noggin a swift kick up the tail. The man was a famous arse and Ollie wasn't going anywhere to see some fathead waffle on about himself for a couple of hours, especially when he had to pay for a ticket.

Saying that, though, even if the event had been free, boasted a complimentary buffet, a magician, a blue comedian, a bag of party goodies, and hordes of topless, uninhibited, and highly accommodating waitresses willing to attend to ones every whim and desire without fear of recrimination or prosecution, he still would've said no.

Well, that's not strictly true. Ollie might be a bit on the shy side but he's not a complete prude.

I mean, who doesn't love a couple of rabbit jokes and a willy coming out of a hat?

Nota bene. I've just been informed that it should be the rabbits coming out of the hat.

No wonder I hated birthday parties at Gary Glitter's house).

So, all in all, he was having a lovely time.

That was until Stitches decided to pay him a visit and the phone rang.

Initially, Ollie thought about ignoring the whining, out of date, pain in the rear antique, but then changed his mind as he didn't want to hurt his feelings, so that being the case, he beckoned Stitches into the office and answered the wretched lump of Bakelite that was still clanging like an epileptic doorbell.

Although not likely to be anything important, and from past experience it very rarely was, you never knew when it might be, so it was best to be sure. And besides, if he was on the phone it meant he didn't have to listen to whatever inspired lunacy his zombie friend had come to enlighten him with for a few extra minutes.

As it turned out it was something, or rather someone important, proving that his decision to answer it was a good one.

On the line was none other than the Dark Lord of all Mischief and Wickedness himself, Count Jocular.

"Ah, good morning, Ollie," oozed the vampire, all dripping poison, evil intent, and far too much interest in flowery wallpaper.

"Greetings, My Lord. And how is your evil self to-day?" said Ollie, pleasantly.

He was much more comfortable talking to Jocular these days. Gone were the times that he'd sweat, get a bad stomach, and feel like curling up into a little ball in his coffin. The only time he did that now was when Flug asked him where babies came from.

"Oh, fine fine, sank you very much. I cannot complain. I leaf zat to ze guests in my dungeons, you see."

"Indeed, I do," said Ollie, knowing full well that the poor unfortunates locked away in the depths of Jocular's lair were as akin to 'guests' as wasps were welcome dining companions at a picnic. "So, what can I do for you?" he continued, hoping it wasn't anything too involved.

"I need you to come to ze castle. Zere is a person here zat needs some help. Yours to be precise. Vell, it is yours now... I am passing ze truck, yes."

"I see. Is it anyone in particular?"

"I do not know zat, Ollie, for I haff never seen zem before in all my born unnaturals."

"Okay, My Lord. Right, well, we'll see you very soon then. Oh, by the way."

"Yes."

"Are they still in one piece or do we need to bring some plastic bags?"

"No bags reqvired zis time." Jocular hung up.

"Jocular?" said Stitches, once Ollie had replaced the receiver.

"Yup," said Ollie.

"Shall I call Bill?" said Stitches.

"Yup," said Ollie.

"Great."

* * *

Upon their arrival at the imposing stone monstrosity that is castle Jocular, Ollie, as was usual, readied himself to getting his hands on the vampire lord's massive knocker and giving it an almighty thwack.

This time, though, he didn't get the chance.

You see, what with the interior of the building being so vast, and Egon being the only one who ever opened the front door, he needed to be able to hear it being knocked from every location within, which, up until recently, was a system that had worked perfectly well.

Lately, though, due to the onset of old age, the inevitable and gradual deterioration of the faculties, and the adoption of a hygiene regime a fourteenth century London muckraker would've considered a bit poor (the interior of the little servant's ear canal was so full of wax that he could keep Crayola going in the event of a shortage) Egon was going a little deaf.

To combat this, he'd first tried waiting at the front door in case anyone should arrive. Obviously rubbish and clearly impractical he thought it best to give it a go as it was Count Jocular that'd suggested it. The same Count Jocular who got a bit miffed if his ideas were poo pooed willy nilly. The same Count Jocular who forgot he'd suggested it and gave Egon a stern telling off for hanging around near the front door all day like a weirdo.

Next, Egon had tasked one of the flunky's to mind the door, a fruitless endeavour that led to strangers getting in, items being stolen, and Egon having to clear up several piles of steaming entrails.

Then there was the bell. Connected to all of the important rooms it had been loud enough to be heard from everywhere, a positive boon as you might expect. The problem was, every time it'd rung, the noise had driven The Children Of The Night into a fur curling, teeth gnashing, flesh ripping phalanx of ferocity that'd rampaged through the castle like a horde of annoyed Vikings attacking anyone who attempted to calm them down i.e. poor old Egon.

Suffice to say, at Egon's request, they didn't use the bell anymore. Not only did the batteries need replacing every fifty seven minutes, the last time the chiming little demon had been used Egon had wound up on the receiving end of a mauling not seen since the late Cretaceous period when a Tyrannosaurus Rex had stubbed his toe on a rock and took it out on a Triceratops who'd laughed because old Rexy couldn't reach his foot to rub it better.

It had taken Egon three weeks to recover from that, a further three days tidying up, and then three seconds to rip the bell out of the door frame and chuck it on a fire.

As Ollie and Stitches walked across the courtyard the door started to move, and by the time they'd reached what would have been considered knocking distance, it'd been opened wide. And there in the space that it'd previously occupied, stood Egon (although he didn't take up all of the available space, of course, on account of his being a bit on the short side. In fact, so compact was the shortened servant he would've had trouble stopping a determined hamster getting out of its cage).

"Ah, gentlemen. I'm so glad you could make it so quickly. If you'd like to follow me please, there is a certain situation that needs attending to."

"I see you've got a new system for opening the door," said Stitches. "So, what are you trying this time? Telepathy? Scrying? Prognostication? No wait. I've got it. Tarot cards."

"Not exactly no. I like to call it looking out of the window because I knew you were on your way," said Egon, without the faintest hint of sarcasm. "So much easier than all that mumbo jumbo."

"So, what are we doing here then, Egon?" said Ollie. "Jocular didn't give me too many details."

"Yeah, it was a bit vague. It almost sounded as if something's happened that Jocular can't cope with," said Stitches as he bent down to give Egon's humps a welcoming pat. "I see you've managed to come up with a system to identify them at last."

"Yes, indeed. And I have to say it's a lot easier now," said Egon, proudly admiring his two pets. "After all that messing about with colours it was the Master who suggested putting their names on their backs."

"I take it the gold, sparkly lettering was his idea?" said Ollie, who never would've thought that the two disembodied tumours could've possibly looked any stranger than they normally did. They already reminded him of a couple of tortoises that'd been carefully peeled (not that he'd ever seen a peeled tortoise of course, on account of his never having been to China for lunch).

Egon ushered the two pets away from the door and pushed it shut.

"To answer your initial enquiry," said the little servant, slamming home a bolt that could've been hollowed out and used as a train carriage, "yes, we do have a bit of a problem."

As they wandered through the castle, Stitches remarked to Ollie, "I swear we take a different route to the same place every time we come here you know."

"It does look that way doesn't it? Or should that be it doesn't, but it really does?" replied Ollie, "Anyway, that's a moot point because I do happen to know that it isn't?"

"Isn't what?" said Stitches. "I'm a bit confused now. Are we coming the same way as before or not?"

"Yes, because the corridors are the same, but the décor is different," explained Ollie.

"Ollie's right, and very observant to boot," said Egon. "The Master doesn't like his interiors to remain the same for any lengthy period of time, consequently nothing ever stays in place for more than a few days. In fact, it can be as short as a couple of hours, but that all depends on how fresh it is of course."

"Fresh?" said Stitches, warily.

"Indeed," said Egon. "You'd be amazed at the mess that one dripping creation can make, especially if the master's feeling particularly artistic and it's had various bits and pieces removed." (And by removed he meant hacked, sawn, yanked, severed, pulled, twisted, snapped, chopped, cleaved, and with one particularly conceptual piece, bitten off. Jocular was nothing if not experimental when it came to his designs, with the emphasis definitely on the mental).

Trying not to look at too much of the weirdness they were passing, they eventually arrived at wherever it was they were supposed to be.

"I know for sure that we haven't been here before," said Stitches looking around.

"That's true enough," said Egon. He pointed to a door. "This is The Standing Room. It's just like a sitting room, only instead of chairs there's just a..."

Egon was interrupted by the creak of the door as it opened by itself, revealing the interior.

"...seven-foot-tall iron spike in the middle of the floor?" Ollie finished with a shiver.

He'd meant it as a statement of fact, but couldn't help it coming out as a query, one not only questioning the logic of what he was looking at, but also the current state of Jocular's sanity. He'd never actually pose *that* question out loud, of course because that would be a bit rude, and all things considered, he didn't fancy being folded in half, stuffed with something squidgy, and used as an Ottoman.

"Qvite so," said Jocular, appearing out of nowhere like Mr. Benn's favourite tailor. "Persons who are infited to stay in zis room are zoes zat I deem in need off standing up for a vhile. If zey zen happen to become veary of ze standing, ze spike encourages zem to make more off an effort to remain upright of zeir own accord."

Although Ollie and Stitches knew exactly how the imposingly massive, and very pointy column of metal 'encouraged' someone to stay standing up, they determinedly tried *not* to think about exactly how the imposingly massive, and very pointy column of metal 'encouraged' someone to stay standing up. One thing was for sure, though. The imposingly massive, and very pointy column of metal would definitely encourage *them* to stay standing up come hell, high water, or the removal of both legs.

"Vould you like me to explain how my imposingly massif, and fery pointy column off metal encourages somevon to stay standing up?" offered Jocular.

"No no. That's fine, My Lord, thanks all the same," said Ollie, holding his hands up in supplication whilst a certain area of his anatomy clenched to the point that a triple helping of Montezuma's Ridiculously Hot Curry would have had trouble forcing its way out of his digestive system.

(Outside of anything harvested from the searing, iron clad inferno residing in Mrs. Ladle's kitchen, Montezuma's Ridiculously Hot Curry is the most dangerous food on, or indeed off, the planet. Since its creation in 1814 it's been responsible for more injuries and deaths than should be reasonably feasible for an item of food, and easily makes all the other dishes considered hot and spicy seem rather tame by comparison. For those of you in the know, it outstrips McCoy's Gypsy Hedgehog Stew, blows the lid off Bodiam's Rubber Dumplings, and knocks Ole Trumpington's Cocked Hat Casserole into an item of slightly askew headwear).

Ollie was just about to enquire as to why they had been asked to attend the castle, when a muffled murmur from a dark corner of the room gave him a hint exactly as to why they had been asked to attend the castle, handily negating the need for him to ask why they had been asked to attend the castle.

"Zo, do you know vhy I haff asked you to attend ze castle?" said Jocular, indicating with a nod of his head to the dark corner where the muffled murmur had come from.

"Well, I don't want to second guess as to the reason that we've been asked to attend the castle," said Stitches, taking a tentative step towards the dark corner where the muffled murmur was coming from. He thought it best if he voluntarily showed a bit of willing rather than be forced to show a bit of willing. It looked a lot better and would be far less painful. "But has it got something to do with whatever's in that dark corner, murmuring in a muffled sort of way?"

"Zat is correct," said Jocular. "Ze lady, did I mention it vas a lady? Maybe not. Anyvay, ze lady showed up here unannounced a short vhile ago. Ven Egon opened ze front door, he sought ve vere in for a pleasant visit, she does seem like ze friendly type after all, but her initial calm demeanour disappeared almost at vunce and she panicked effer such a little bit. And I'm sorry to say zat vhen she vas introduced to me she…vell, I'm not qvite sure how to put it, actually."

"Could she have fled in abject terror because she'd just laid eyes on a couple of supernatural creatures, and was maybe more than a little worried that she may be murdered without a by your leave and subjected to any number of excruciatingly painful tortures designed to cause her unimaginable anguish and soul destroying torment for all eternity, perhaps?" said Ollie, helpfully.

"I think he's saying she wet herself and ran in here," said Stitches. He lowered his voice and said to Ollie, "If that's the case, we're not going to be able to do any good. If she's in that much of a state, the sight of us two is liable to send her right over the edge."

"Is she frightened of informal gatherings then?" said Egon.

"That's a good point," said Ollie, ignoring the dwarf. He shook his head and sighed. "I wish we'd have known what was going on before we got here. At least we could have brought someone normal along to soften the blow a little bit."

"Normal! I think that's a commodity in very short supply round here," said Stitches.

"Oh, you know what I mean," said Ollie. "We could have invited Mrs. Strudel or Constable Gullett. At least they're human."

Suddenly the muffled murmur from the corner became slightly less muffled, although there was no doubt that it was still firmly entrenched in the corner and wasn't likely to be leaving its confines any time soon.

"H-h-hello," said a trembling voice.

"Um, hello there," said Ollie in as friendly and non-threatening a manner as he could manage.

"I've been t-told that I'm not in any d-danger?!" said the lady, questioning and pleading at the same time (hence the question mark and the exclamation mark. Clever huh).

Ollie now had a decision to make, one that was liable to have a major impact on the subsequent course of their interaction. Should he tell her the truth, in that she was as safe as any outsider who had strayed into the lair of a beast so ferocious that Vlad the Impaler would have considered his hobbies to be a bit over the top, or tell her a teensy weensy white lie implying that she couldn't be more inviolable in a safe-house run by the nuns of the Holy Order of St. Safety?

For practical purposes, and deciding there'd be far less crying, he went with the second option.

"You're perfectly free from any danger, my dear," he said, oozing so much smarmy charm that he might have been trying to sell her a second-hand car. "And whilst I can fully appreciate that the current situation and surroundings you find yourself in could be described as somewhat strange and disconcerting, please try not to let them bother you. Too much."

"Would they bother you?" she said.

He couldn't even begin to lie about that. Being economical with the truth was one thing, but there's some fibs so glaringly obvious even the most gullible person ever to have existed would have spotted them.

Examples include, 'Of course it doesn't make you look fat', 'I'll be ready in a minute', and anything that a politician says from the time he's elected to the moment he resigns after being caught fiddling his expenses, or discovered having an affair with an eighteen year old pole dancer called Aphrodite who's actually a burly hod-carrier called Dennis.

"Egon," said Stitches, "is there a chance we could have some light in here please?"

"Of course," said the little servant.

Moments later an elaborate seven-sticked candelabra burst into twinkling orange flame and illuminated the entire room, lending the dispiriting space a much-needed sense of comfort and warmth.

The flickering shadows it produced danced and shifted on the sleek, polished surface of the metal spike making it appear as if it were lit from within, an effect that distracted the casual observer from its grotesque aspect.

Ollie had to admit it was rather attractive in a glittery, silvery, spangly, I bet the point on that thing's been up a fair few backsides, thereby causing the poor unfortunate victims to be split in half over an unnecessarily long period of time way.

(Apologies for the lurid imagery but remember this is a room in Count Jocular's castle after all. It can't all be fluffy cushions, comfy sofas, and somewhere you'd want to take an elderly relative for a cup of tea and a slice of cake. Not unless you wanted rid of them anyway.

Actually, there's Under Dungeon number three if Nana fancies a day out. That's got an Iron Maiden sporting a beautifully crocheted sampler. It's on the inside).

"You can come out now, love" said Stitches, extending a welcoming hand. He'd already checked it. All the digits were intact and facing the right way. "Everything will be perfectly okay. We don't bite. Well, Egon and I don't at any rate."

"I do not sink zat comment is being fery helpful," said Jocular, quietly.

For some reason he was genuinely concerned about the old lady so, in an effort to assist, he was casually leaning against a wall and trying to make himself appear as unobtrusive and non-threatening as possible. And to be fair to him, he was giving it a good go, but on the whole, it was like trying to hide a top hat wearing, cigar smoking and bright green buffalo in the bottom of a tea cup (which clearly wouldn't work because there are no potable, hot beverage making facilities in the Wild Wild West. And besides, buffaloes prefer a pipe).

"Please come forward," continued the vampire lord, lowering his voice to more of a soft whisper rather than its usual ominous, head invading, I'm going to restring my cello with your innards even though I haven't got a cello, tone. "And please do not let our appearances distress you in any vay."

"Although that wouldn't be the case if you saw him after a night out," said Egon with an air of forced joviality. "He looks like an explosion in a cowshed."

"Right," said Ollie. "Do you think we could have less of the unpleasant comments now, please? I'm sure our visitor is having a hard-enough time as it is without being told that fifty percent of us are vampires who drink blood on a nightly basis. Oh, bugger! See, you've got me doing it now."

"Actually," said the lady, stepping into the light, "I'm feeling quite a bit calmer now."

And indeed, she did, her more relaxed attitude a direct consequence of her numerous and varied encounters with those that had shuffled off this mortal thingamabob.

Subconsciously, those experiences and interactions had helped her to acclimatise to her new surroundings, gently guiding her towards coming to terms with her current predicament.

On a practical level, of course, she knew there was more to this life, and what comes after, than anyone could ever imagine, so once she'd gotten over the initial shock of meeting up with a group of supernatural beings, her psyche very quickly adapted and allowed her to deal with the situation with the level headed rationality she was accustomed to.

Naturally, the welcome realisation that they appeared to be a load of floundering buffoons who seemed to have the collective intelligence of a bunch of bananas wasn't doing her stress levels any harm either.

"That's good," said Stitches. "Sorry about the silly comments by the way."

"Me too," said Egon. "Madam, may I offer you my most profound apologies."

"Oh, don't you worry," she said, keeping to herself that her initial fears had now evaporated to the point that they had now completely evaporated. All in all, she actually felt quite safe and come to the pleasant conclusion that she'd be in more grievous danger at a safe house with the nuns of the Holy Order of St. Safety.

Ten minutes later Ollie, Stitches, and Deirdre were sitting in one of the castle's many kitchens (they hadn't been in the original plans, of course as there's no call for them, and as you can imagine there's not many vampires who suddenly feel the urge to cobble together a chocolate truffle soufflé or whip up a quick mushroom stir fry because the neighbours had popped round. Such was the vastness of Jocular's dwelling, however, Egon had had a few surreptitiously added just in case he fancied a spot of lunch or a quick drink whilst on his long and tortuous rounds, rounds that could sometimes take days, especially if the radiators were playing up. Happily, they also served as handy bolt holes if he found himself being chased by The Children Of The Night, an occurrence that was happening so often now that just two more kitchens would see Wickes getting in touch enquiring as to why an unauthorised branch had been opened).

Egon, duty bound as always, had very kindly made a pot of tea before toddling off to tend to his master, who was getting ready for a session in one of his numerous subterranean torture rooms and needed some assistance getting his rubber waistcoat on.

After the introductions had been made, Deirdre told Ollie and Stitches about the incident in her kitchen and how it had led her to Skullenia.

"But why you?" asked Ollie, although he had a very small inkling that her visit and the recent occurrences reported from around the town were connected in some way. He decided to keep that thought to himself for the moment, though. It could be something or it might just as easily be a coincidence. Either that or the strange events were, as they had first surmised when they came to light, of entirely no consequence at all and this lady was just some random person who thought that Skullenia was an ideal spot for a bit of a holiday, although that hardly seemed viable on the face of it. That particular activity wasn't a likely candidate for inclusion on someone's bucket list no matter how much they were struggling to fill it.

(In fact, a recent survey has shown there's quite a few varied and diverse wishes more likely to be present on a person's bucket list above having a mini break in Skullenia because, one, they're far more enjoyable, and two, they're infinitely safer. Here's ten of them, in no particular order, for your perusal.

- Stand next to a group of soldiers, shout, "How many GCSE's have you got?" and kick as many of them in the grenades as possible.

- Get bitten by the most venomous spider in the world and wait for the superpowers to kick in.

- Same as above but with a mole.

- See what a frozen lake looks like from underneath.

- Have a tracheotomy so you can blow smoke rings through the hole and make a robot voice.

- Finish a book by Charles Dickens (possibly the toughest item on the list).

- Skydive using a giraffe as a parachute.

- Jump the Grand Canyon in a canoe.

- Climb Mount Everest wearing nothing but Crocs, and a pair of pants on your head.

- Buy a dog, call it Adolf, then, when it's running around the park shout out, "Heel Hitler.")

Deirdre took a sip of her tea to wash down the chocolate biscuit that Egon had very kindly provided (Ollie had furtively checked it first. As generous as the gesture was, he knew from experience that Castle Jocular was as well known for its fine dining as it was for its restful atmosphere, reposeful charm, and subtly assuasive ambience. Once accepted there was every possibility that said dunkable goody would not take kindly to being dipped and bite Deirdre somewhere painful. Near the sink for instance).

"I can only assume," she said, "that's it's got something to do with the fact that I'm a medium."

(Now, that statement, dear reader, might make you worry that I'm about to be less than pleasant about our lovely Deirdre.

'No', I say.

Whilst it might tempt lesser scribes to perambulate along certain playful pathways and dead-end promenades pertaining to portly ladies and their claims to be able to communicate with those that have departed this coil of mortality and who now re-side in the realm of the hallowed deceased, I would like to assure each and every one of you engaged in perusing this literary delicacy that there will be no occasion upon which I will stoop to using such cyni-cal and, quite frankly, obvious paronomasia relating to that subject.

Not while the fat old dollop can contact the dead and get them to haunt me.

I'm considerate, not stupid).

Stitches sucked his lips into his mouth, firmly closing the door on the wildly offensive, and sarcas-tic observation trying desperately to escape.

Sadly, he inhaled a bit too hard and ended up with his chin resting just under his nose.

"Is he alright?" said Deirdre.

"No, but you get used to it," said Ollie, pressing his foot onto the zombie's. "So, you're a medium." He pressed harder for added emphasis.

"Yes. I've always had the gift, which is why I can only assume the message has come from the great beyond."

Stitches repositioned his chin and wiggled his toes, which currently felt like sticks of vigorously chewed, extra chewy chewing gum.

"Well, you're in luck if you like talking to the dead," said the zombie. "There's loads of them in town. The streets are awash with them. So's the sky in fact, and The Bolt and Jugular's always full of spirits."

Ollie explained to Deirdre about the unique nature of their home, and then enlightened her as to recent events.

"Well, that certainly could explain things," she said, "but only up to a point. A chance scribbling on my kitchen window and a few strange sightings here are so far removed from each other it might very well be nothing. Although, that being said, I can't dismiss the possibility out of hand completely. I'd have to go into town and…"

*"Deirdre,"* said a voice in her head.

"Hello," she said.

"Hello," said Stitches, wondering why on earth the introductions were starting again.

*"It's Gladys."*

"Hello, Gladys," said Deirdre.

"Gladys?" said Ollie.

"I'm getting a message," said Deirdre.

*"Who from?"* said Gladys.

"From you, Gladys dear," said Deirdre.

"Oh, I see. Ooh, have you got company?" said Gladys.

"I do indeed. Ollie and Stitches," said Deirdre.

"Yes, Deirdre?" said Ollie and Stitches at the same time.

"I was talking to Gladys," said Deirdre.

"Who was?" said Gladys.

"I am. I'm talking to you," said Deirdre.

"Oh, I see. Have they come through at the same time as me then?" said Gladys.

"No, dear. They're sitting next to me," said Deirdre.

"Gosh! I wish I could do that," said Gladys. "I'd kill for a pork pie and a cigar."

"They're not dead, Gladys. Well, not really. It's more a sort of undeath. Anyway, what can I do for you?" said Deirdre.

"I thought you were coming to town with us," said Ollie.

"I am coming to town with you," said Deirdre.

"Shall I call back later then?" said Gladys.

"No, dear. You carry on. What was it you wanted to ask me?" said Deirdre.

"I can't remember now," said Gladys.

"Gladys," said Deirdre.

"Yes," said Gladys.

"You're hopeless," said Deirdre. "Take care."

"I take it that was Gladys," said Stitches.

"Yes. Memory like a sieve. She was just the same when she was alive. Couldn't remember a thing."

"How did she pass?" said Ollie, asking the most obvious of questions.

"She forgot she couldn't fly, which is quite a big no no when you're three quarters of your way through a bottle of gin and live on the seventeenth floor. She made such a mess they had to identify her using dental records."

"How does that work?" said Stitches.

"Her name was stamped on the gum," said Deirdre. "Well then, shall we head off into town? Someone or something is being very persistent. I can feel a force pulling at me and it's getting stronger by the moment."

That's probably gravity, thought Stitches.

He would have said it out loud, but that would have earned him a hearty slap from Ollie and left a dent in his head a panel beater would struggle with.

"I'll ask Egon to fetch Bill," he said instead.

* * *

Ollie, Stitches, and Deirdre stepped down from Bill's coach, bade him a weary farewell, then checked themselves over just to make sure that everything attached to their bodies was still attached to their bodies, and if such was the case, that it was in the right place and still working within normal parameters.

The return trip from Jocular's castle had been rather more hair raising than usual, you see, and the reasons for this were twofold.

Firstly, the skeletal driver had a new set of horses, a muscular quartet of rampant, frothing beasts if ever there was one (and there was, it was them), and they had a tendency to gallop as if they were being chased by the very hounds of hell, who were in turn being relentlessly pursued by the underworld's head castrator, a malignant monster of murderous miscreation who, whilst merrily miming the malicious maiming of malleable mammalian male matter with his mighty machete, can be heard to mournfully moan, "COME TO DADDY, IT'S SNIPPING TIME!"

Secondly, but equally firstly, was the route itself.

Previously, there'd been a healthy two inch gap between the wooden wheels of the coach and the infinitely black, certain death causing, nausea inducing, abyssal depths below the ancient rubble strewn path, but due to intermittent soil erosion, the inexorable degradation of the ancient rock face, the subsidence of the geological layers themselves, and The Children Of The Night thinking it would be a bit of a laugh if they chipped it off, the outside wheels now had fifty percent of their width peeking into the gaping chasm.

So, all in all it didn't make for a pleasurable ride.

(And just to clarify a point if I may, the head castrator isn't a castrator of heads, he's just in charge of all the other castrators and, like them, deals with spherical body parts much smaller, and rather more squidgy than a cranium.

What distinguishes the head castrator from all the normal castrators, though, an endowment leading to his being conferred with the title of head castrator in the first place, is he has a talent for, and specialises in the removal of spherical body parts from more prominent and upstanding victims.

And of course, the more prominent and upstanding the spherical body parts…oh, you get the idea.

Not that it really matters.

It's all a load of old bollocks, anyway).

So, where were we? Ah yes, the trip back from Jocular's castle.

"My God," said Stitches who, despite being deficient of a functioning nervous system to the tune of one, was shaking like a fat person on a waltzer. "I haven't been that scared for ages. I actually think I remember what nausea feels like."

Deirdre nodded in unquestioning agreement. As if meeting the skeletal, four eyed driver hadn't been strange enough for her, spending the entire journey flirting with death had scared her more than somewhat. More than any number seven that you'd care to mention certainly (which is one really isn't it).

"The last time I was that frightened," she said, adjusting her hat which had become ever so slightly askew, "was when my dear Bertram took me to see Attack of the Mutant Sock Puppets at The Monaco."

"A bit scary was it?" said Ollie, just beginning to calm down himself.

He'd attempted to remonstrate with Bill about the danger they'd been in during the ride home, and even made a half-hearted attempt at asking him to slow down a bit, but the only reply he got was, "Cor strike a banana me ole Richard. There's no dingin' meat flute darn there to give us the jibberin' cat flaps."

He hadn't bothered continuing the dialogue after that unintelligible retort, figuring that plummeting to a painful and extremely messy death was more preferable than trying to decipher what the psychotic skeleton was banging on about.

That was the interesting thing about interacting Bill. You didn't actually engage in conversation with him per se, it was just something that happened in your presence that left you floundering and wondering what the hell had just happened, much like slipping on a patch of ice, suffering a reasonably serious head injury, getting punched by an ogre, or sitting through a matinee performance of Les Misérables because your wife got the tickets for her birthday (thanks a lot, mum).

"I'll say it was," said Deirdre. "They were charging tuppence for a choc ice. I nearly had a heart attack."

"So, are you getting any vibes at all now that we've reached ghost central?" said Stitches.

"Not as yet I'm sorry to say, but that's no great surprise," said Deirdre. "I've learned from experience that a decent scare tends to put the kibosh on my psychic powers for a short while. It's almost as if intense emotions cause them to short circuit."

"Isn't that a little inconvenient considering your line of work? Not to mention a bit scary," said Ollie.

"Not really. And no, I don't find talking to the dead scary to be honest. I've been doing it for so long it's second nature to me now and no different to chatting to you."

"A five-minute conversation with Flug will soon change your mind about that," said Stitches. "You'll feel like joining them. All I'd say is be prepared."

And so, in the best traditions of The Boy Scouts and their unwavering willingness to help others, hardened soldiers readying themselves for battle, and Donald Trump formulating a pre-emptive apology before meeting the president of Nigeria (or any other African country that he couldn't point to on a map), she did indeed prepare herself for the sights she was about to see.

As you'd expect though, Deirdre's preparations didn't stop her from staring in wide eyed amazement as they made their way through the pseudo medieval backwater that was Skullenia, and she very quickly came to realise that a lifetime of communing with the choir invisible was no preparation for the visual images she was witnessing, and the palpable, almost magical vibration she felt as they strolled into the beating, undead heart of the phantasmal enclave.

(I know that by definition something that's undead shouldn't really beat, but it's a pleasantly worded phrase that's worthy of inclusion, and I had to describe it somehow. I can't say just it was nice).

Skullenia has an innominate, causative agent you see, an unidentifiable nimbus of supernaturally charged vigour that surrounds and imbues all the non-living creatures with the vitality they need to endure across two very different planes of existence.

It can't be analysed or quantified, studied, measured, or explained, it just is, always has been, and always will be, forever set in place and as unendingly endurable as the majestic mountains reaching for the heavens, the untamed, boundless depths of the oceans, the infinite and glorious wonder that is the universe, and, sadly, the acting career of Nicholas Cage.

Deirdre saw the assembled collection of itinerant dead flesh in Mrs. Strudel's café and the beings that were feasting on it.

She heard the shrill cacophony emanating from the forest, felt the crackling whoosh as the aeronautically mobile residents darted about the night sky, and, perhaps most disturbingly of all, smelt the rank and foetid odour that was the result of Flug flushing the toilet.

(Skullenia does have a functioning sewage system, but it does suffer from a rather severe case of halitosis and is currently about as much use as a rubber dinghy in the Sahara Desert.

Rather than being a collection of pipes that efficiently collects and then disposes of the town's effluent, it's a collection of pipes that efficiently stores up the town's effluent and allows it to rot to the point that an air freshener the size of the R101 shoved up its business end wouldn't have any noticeable effect. As a consequence of this basic lack of modern day plumbing facilities, the subterranean quagmire does need clearing out and disinfecting every few years, a noisome task if ever there was one, and as you'd expect not a single being volunteers to undertake the job so it's decided by drawn lots with the name of the chosen person pulled out of a hat. Obviously, to make it fair, that person's name isn't placed into the hat the next time the pungent project needs doing, because that would be unfair. Okay, so it's mostly because none of them are ever seen again, but you can't argue with an impartial system).

As they reached the office, they heard a friendly, "Yoo-hoo" from across the square.

"Hello, Mrs. Strudel," Ollie responded with a cheery wave.

"Have you seen Constable Gullett?" she asked. "I've got his second elevenses here."

"No, sorry. If I see him, I'll send him over."

"She looks human," said Deirdre in the vain hope she'd finally met another being not interested in what she tasted like.

"She is," said Stitches. "It's her food that's not. Be warned, Deirdre, even the most innocent looking dish in there has the ability to maim and slaughter on a ridiculously large scale."

"I see," she said. "The food from the hand that feeds you bites back by the sound of it."

Ollie opened the front door and showed Deirdre inside.

"Ronnie. Flug," he called out.

It didn't take long for the familiar, leaden footed stomp to start registering throughout the entire building.

"Here he comes," said Stitches. "Our very own mobile earthquake. Hiya, Flug."

"Hi, Stitches," said the massive misanthrope. "Who dat?" he added, pointing at Deirdre with a finger that looked like an acromegalic banana.

"This is Deirdre," said Ollie. "She's a new friend of ours."

"She no look right," said Flug.

In a remarkable coincidence, Deirdre had taken on the very same countenance as the creature she'd just been introduced to i.e. she'd adopted a droopy faced, terminally bewildered look not dissimilar to stroke victims, Alzheimer's sufferers, and members of The House of Lords.

Still, that was hardly surprising bearing in mind the countenance of the creature she'd just been introduced to i.e. Flug, who permanently wore a droopy faced, terminally bewildered look not dissimilar to stroke victims, Alzheimer's sufferers, and members of The House of Lords.

"Wh…wh…wh…" she blurted out, hanging onto her hat for comfort.

"Wh…wh…wh…" said Flug, smiling and thinking this was a brilliant new game to add to his list (amongst his current favourites were 'Spot the foot', 'Let's bury Mandeep in the garden', and 'Da toilet. How me use it again, Ronnie?')

Ollie placed a firm but comforting hand onto Deirdre's shoulder and whispered to her that everything was alright, and she wasn't going to be torn limb from limb by an eight feet tall, grinning column of meat, a consideration she hadn't actually considered until Ollie considered mentioning it just in case she *had* considered it. Which she hadn't, which was surprising considering her circumstances and taking everything into consideration.

Stitches did the same thing to Flug, only his whispered entreaty was more along the lines of, "Shut the hell up and try to act like a humanish being for a change, and not so much like a scary, pituitary challenged, haphazardly put together dinosaur."

(As well intentioned as it was though, the plea ultimately fell on deaf ears and would have no effect whatsoever, and had about as much chance of success as Heinrich Himmler's attempt to win Mastermind with his specialised subject of 'Why Jews are brilliant').

When she saw the stitched together behemoth's smile grow even wider, Deirdre's mood eased up a little (although said facial gesture looked more like a nasty axe wound than a grin, and would only normally be seen on someone who'd been hit in the face with a tractor), and when he held out his hand and offered her a sweet she relaxed a bit more.

"You probably don't want to eat one of those if I'm honest," said Ollie. "Flug's taste in confection tends to be a bit on the incendiary side. I suspect you'd be much better off, and far healthier if you had a nice cup of tea and a biscuit."

"I think you may be right," said Deirdre, looking at the orange, sticky, and fluffy item that, in all probability, may well have been in Flug's pocket for a month or two.

At least it was one of his, though. They were even worse if they came out of someone else's clothes. If he swapped sweets with the likes of Redemption Plinth, a forest dwelling hermity type who never washed, had an inch thick layer of dirt covering his skin, and kept his sweetie stash down his pants to stop the squirrels pinching them, you literally could be ingesting anything.

"Flug, mate, where's Ronnie?" said Stitches before the monster departed to tasks and destinations unknown.

"Dunno," said Flug. "Saw him s'mormin' and dat it."

"He's probably down the pub. We'll catch up with him later. Shall we?" said Ollie, indicating the way forward.

Three cups of Earl Grey and half a packet of triple choc, double choc chip, double choc, chocolate covered chocco chippo creams later, Deirdre felt as if she were finally getting over the initial shock of being immersed into the supernatural melting pot that was Skullenia.

To become *totally* used to it, though is a difficult and protracted process that can take many years, but her experience as a medium gave her a bit of a head-start, at least.

(This isn't always the case, however.

Take Noddy Dresden, local resident, who is so incredibly *not* used to his surroundings that even to this day he won't go out of his house if there's any supernatural beings lurking about, which, as you can imagine, is twenty four hours a day, seven days a week. In other words, he never goes out of his house ever in spite of living in Skullenia for over seventy years.

Now, many people will say, and quite rightly so, "Why doesn't he move?" to which they are told, equally as quitely rightly, "Didn't you hear what I just said, you cretin?" Of course, other people might then say, "Well why did he move here in the first place if he's so scared?" to which they are told, "Because he's a cretin, you cretin," which you have to admit is a very valid point.

What makes the whole Noddy scenario even more bizarre is the fact that he's a spectre and, strange as it may sound, it's this state of being that led to his affliction in the first place.

All ready for his first haunting assignment, he had no idea that he'd been set up by a couple of wags who thought it'd be fun to task him with putting certain willies up a certain vampire lord in a certain castle.

The details of what actually happened once he got inside are muddled at best, but no one will ever find out for sure because Noddy fled from Jocular's in abject terror, locked himself away in his house, and hasn't been seen since).

So, as you can see, and no doubt understand, Deirdre can easily be forgiven for finding the entire experience a little disconcerting at first.

(Which is fair enough. I write about it and I get scared stiff. Thinking on it though, that's probably got more to do with the fact my wife thinks I'm carving out a successful career in the logistics industry during the twelve hours I'm away each and every day.

The trouble I'll be in if she ever finds out all I do is sit in a swanky cafe, drink endless lattes, and pretend to be a tortured artist doesn't bear thinking about.

Suffice to say my final words will probably include "Ouch," "Please stop hitting me," "Not the poker," "Ooh my blobs," and "Aaaaaarrrrrgggggghh-hhh!")

"So, Deirdre, are you picking up anything yet?" said Stitches who, it has to be said, had always been a tiny bit sceptical about the whole living persons talking to dead persons business, which is a little paradoxical seeing as Deirdre was, at this precise point, talking to a two hundred year old zombie with the complexion of a corn husk, and a half human, half vampire who needs to ingest blood twice a day.

But hey, we're not here to discuss the relevancy of why something should or shouldn't happen just because someone has an opinion about it. If that were the case then Peter Andre would have been killed in a freak hang-gliding accident when he was four, and Sofia Vergara would be sunbathing in my garden.

Clearly, his slightly sceptical tone hinted at his nagging disbelief, and it didn't go unnoticed.

"Do I take it you're having a bit of an issue with my talent?" said Deirdre who, much like Christians, Devil worshippers, Scientologists, and England football managers, was well used to dealing with intransigent non-believers wherever she went.

"I suppose I am if I'm honest," responded the zombie, for once putting flippant and sarcastic remarks to one side. "But only because there's so many charlatans out there. I hate the way they prey on people who are clearly in emotional turmoil. You know the ones I mean. 'Is there anyone here called John Smith?' and 'Did you have a great great grandfather that's passed over?' It just seems a bit suspect to me that's all. No offence, Deirdre."

"Oh, none taken, dear," said Deirdre, smiling. She winked at Ollie. "I'm not fully functional at the moment but let me see." She leaned back into her chair and closed her eyes.

Stitches looked at Ollie and raised an eyebrow.

Then Deirdre nodded her head and let out a hushed giggle.

"I see," she said. "Thank you very much."

"Go on then," said the zombie, thinking this might be fun and he could mess around a bit, "what are you going to tell me? I've got a nose and I'm sitting down?"

"Oh no, better than that," said Deirdre, sitting up. "Who's Deborah?"

Stitches managed to keep his astonishment under wraps as Deirdre had correctly named his lady friend from his sojourn on Haiti.

They'd been happy times filled with laughter and love.

Until the unfortunate incident, of course.

The unfortunate incident that'd left him deader than a dead dodo and zombier than a zombified dead dodo that was, as we've already mentioned, dead.

"You'll have to tell me," he said, wondering if it was a lucky guess. "That's if I ever knew this lady of course."

"Right you are," said Deirdre, up for the challenge, as she relaxed into her chair once more.

Stitches and Ollie watched carefully, waiting and wondering if something was going to happen.

Which it did.

Deirdre commenced a conversation with someone who wasn't altogether there.

From their point of view, it was obviously a bit one sided, but it went thusly.

" "

"Did he?"

" "

"Whereabouts?"

" "

"I bet that made his eyes water."

" "

"Vaseline I would have thought."

" "

"Oh, my goodness. Well I hope you threw it away."

Ollie put a hand over his mouth to stop himself from laughing out loud. Not only was his imagination running wild wondering precisely what was being revealed in the half of the conversation he wasn't privy to, the shocked look on the zombie's face was now ingrained in his memory, and an image he would treasure forever.

" "

"Oh, you are joking?"

" "

"Didn't the goat mind?"

" "

"I must admit I thought that was illegal."

" "

"I'll keep that in mind. Bye, love."

The conversation over, Deirdre opened her eyes, picked up her teacup, casually took a dainty sip, and placed in gently back down onto the table. She had a very satisfied look on her face, but its intensity paled into insignificance when compared to the fangy crevice under Ollie's nose.

"Do you need to...?"

"No no," said Stitches, cutting her off before she could say anything else. "That'll be fine, thank you very much."

"Well, there doesn't seem to be anything wrong with your powers now," said Ollie, hoping against hope what he'd just witnessed was genuine. "Perhaps this would be a good time to try and find out why you're here."

"I couldn't agree more," she said.

* * *

The palpable, frigid darkness that would have struck fear into even the hardiest of creatures, was at best a minimally safe haven, but seeing as there was little choice in the matter, it was the nearest thing to sanctuary in this strange, almost alien environment.

Shifting figures stirred in the midst of the static gloom. Their movements were random, confused and shambolic, and they frequently bumped into each other causing scuffles to break out.

No major injuries were caused though, because the figures weren't able to coordinate themselves sufficiently to land any blows, so after a few moments of futile swinging they returned to their mindless wanderings.

As they shuffled along, they each emitted guttural, snarling, almost animalistic like ululations that forcefully hinted at their aggressive nature.

The only other sound that punctuated the intense black was the incessant scuffing of their feet as they were dragged along the damp, musty ground, and although they couldn't be seen, the floor was now home to a criss-cross of ever deepening and random furrows, no doubt the cause of many a stumbling.

After hours and hours of this monotonous behaviour, though none of the entities were aware of the passage of time, they all come to a sudden halt and stood as rigid and unwavering as marble statues. It was as if some unspoken command had managed to penetrate their primitive consciences all at once.

They stood silently and unthinkingly, unable to function of their own accord, other than to breathe and move their eyes in response to any vague noises coming out of the dark.

By design the figures had come to a stop in a rough circle facing each other, and despite the lack of light their attention was focused on one particular area, a smooth patch of ground right in the centre of the circle they had formed.

Although they couldn't see through the impenetrable and melancholy darkness, the figures closed together, joined hands, and began to chant. It was quiet at first but, as if by unspoken agreement, its pitch and volume rose until it culminated in voices raised to an almighty and exultant shout.

As they proclaimed this violent exhortation, another shadow, vague and discarnate in its construction, detached itself from the seemingly infinite Stygian iniquity and made its presence felt amid the group.

With an almost rapturous joy the once shambolic spectres revelled in wonder as the greenish blue glow emanating from the interloper washed over them.

A hushed quiet now filled the dark as the verbose chanting ceased, but all was not silent as a throaty chuckle filled the room.

* * *

As if by an incredible coincidence, Dr Zoltan, much like Deirdre Clownpuncher, was having something of a psychic episode of his own (that's if you believe in coincidences of course, and don't subscribe to the theory where everything that happens to a person throughout their entire life is purely down to being guided by some divine or mystical force called fate. For example, if you choose to get on a particular bus to work one morning and end up meeting the person with whom you're going to spend the rest of your days with, is it coincidence in that you may have caught a different bus, or walked, or chucked a sickie that day? Or is it fate? Meant to be. Written in the stars that the two were destined to come together because it's all part of a grand plan that's been in motion since the dawn of time.

There is a lot of conjecture on the subject, but despite exhaustive discussion, reasoned discourse, and a fair few academically inspired punch-ups, scientists, theologians, academics, and philosophers have never been able to provide an adequate answer.

Well, that's until now because I have a theory of my own. *I* am the person who met his future partner on the bus, *I* am the one who now spends every living moment with this person, so ultimately, it is *I* who can be objective and provide a considered answer to this, the most elusive of mystical dilemmas.

I can tell you all now, without a shadow of a doubt, that I don't consider coincidence, or fate, or the conjoining of heavenly bodies to have been a factor in any way, shape or form.

I'm just unlucky).

The eminent sawbones to the spooky was trying to determine precisely what was ailing his latest patient, and he'd had a premonition that he would shortly lose his temper in a big big way, use some rather fruity language, and shove a large needle so far up the idiots left nostril, only bone would stop it.

(I just need to qualify the use of the word 'eminent' to describe Dr Zoltan's curative expertise if I may, and to do that one has to resort to the medium of comparison, in that he is to the medical fraternity what the Nazis were to a fair days work and low cost housing).

The present incumbent of the bed before him was Lollipop Hammerbang, a dwarf from the northern mountains who had come into the hospital complaining.

He wasn't complaining about anything in particular, just complaining.

After a thorough examination (he got Lollipop to take his coat off), Dr Zoltan had still been still stumped as to what was wrong with the little chap, so he'd given him his big book of illnesses to look through, because after all there's nothing like a spot of self-diagnosis and looking at horrible pictures to convince yourself you're suffering from a whole raft of debilitating ailments.

(The exhaustive tome had been a gift from the faculty when he'd passed his final medical paper. He could have chosen a rather nice carriage clock, but seeing as how he'd forgotten ninety five percent of the course as soon as he'd walked out of the exam hall, he thought it was the wiser choice, especially as he didn't want to get sued by a hypochondriac vampire, of which there are plenty).

"So, Lollipop," said Dr Zoltan. "Have you come across any symptoms in the book that you're presently experiencing, because if I'm honest you seem perfectly fine to me."

Lollipop produced a sheet of paper from underneath his bed clothes and began to read.

"I've got the shakes," he said.

"Mmm. Could be Dwarven Flu," said Dr. Zoltan.

"And my vision is a little blurry."

"Right, that may be midget related myopia. It occurs from spending too much time staring at rocks."

"I've also got pins and needles in my nose."

"Okay, that might be high cholesterol."

"Really?"

"Certainly. You see, what with dwarfs' noses being so big in relation to the rest of their bodies…"

"Easy, Doc. Our noses aren't that big," interrupted Lollipop, assuming a rather indignant air as he touched the aforementioned fleshy appendage. "Mine's no bigger than yours."

"And you're completely right with that very astute observation, Lollipop, but whereas I'm a shade under six and a half feet tall and rather large of heft, you're a little under three feet tall and buy your clothes in the children's section. By that reckoning, if our facial features were to be of the same ratio, my olfactory instrument would be roughly the size of a fully grown butternut squash. May I continue?"

"Of course."

"Thank you. As I was saying, dwarf noses are so big in relation to their owner's bodies they pretty much act like any other vital organ in that they're excellent indicators of health and vitality, and a lot can be deduced from studying them. What's your diet like?"

"Beer, cheese, meat. You know, the usual stuff."

"Anything else?"

"Elevenses, lunch, dinner, tea, supper, or snacks?"

"Just give me a general overview."

"Beer, cheese, meat."

"Right, well I'd say that needs investigating for a start. That's a lot of fat and alcohol for such a sma…compact system. Any other symptoms?"

"I've got a strange, squidgy feeling in my tail."

Dr Zoltan instantly disregarded any and all treatments he'd been considering and directed a glance at the dwarf that intimated a phrase that rhymed with 'you trucking cat'.

"You haven't got a tail, Lollipop," he said.

"Well, I didn't bring it with me," said the dwarf, as if this were the most reasonable response in the world. "I keep tripping over it."

Dr Zoltan approached the bed.

"Take your helmet off would you, Lollipop, there's a good chap."

"I can't do that, Doctor."

"Why's that then?"

"It's too tight. I've had it on since October 1814."

Zoltan nodded his head knowingly.

From the time they become able to hold a pick-axe, dwarfs wear their helmets twenty-four hours a day. As you can imagine it's a necessary piece of protective gear when toiling away in the depths of the mountains, but after a long shift, the dwarf miners always go straight to the local tavern where the wearing of such an item of clothing is, if anything, even more important. Dwarfs can be a feisty lot at the best of times, and once an unhealthy amount of alcohol is added to the equation, a pub full of chaps in the terminal stages of little man syndrome can very quickly become a haven of testosterone fuelled and very extreme violence.

You'd have to get down onto your hands and knees to see it, but trust me, it's rough stuff.

And so, due mostly to their belligerent, short tempered attitude towards life, dwarfs always keep their helmets on as they never know when a stray axe, hammer, or rolling pin is going to come winging its way towards them.

The problem arises as they approach, and finally reach adulthood (or as adult as one can be with size three feet, an inside leg measurement of fourteen inches, and the ability to look through a letterbox without bending down).

With the passage of time comes growth, meaning said headgear is bound to get a little bit tight, a state of affairs which can lead to some rather nasty side effects including severe chafing of the ears, sticky out eyes, and every now and again, errant thoughts running through their squashed, little brains.

In one famous case, Cloudy Sweets, a member of the royal family who'd ruled over the subterranean kingdoms of the Far Far East, had worn a helmet so very tight that for three decades he'd believed himself to be a large rainforest deep within the Amazon basin containing undiscovered tribes, species thought lost to science for centuries, and untold mineral wealth.

So, why had his delusion lasted so long? Well, as a prince of the realm, he had a certain standing you see (not a very tall one, obviously), which, when combined with a bit of a temper and an executioner with an itchy axe arm, meant no one had possessed the guts to tell him he wasn't a lush swathe of greenery for fear of being put to death for being rude to a half-sovereign.

It wasn't until he'd been sitting in the garden one day, discussing the benefits of a new underground transport system and the possibility of making jam tarts illegal with a large rhododendron bush and a stand of nettles, that he'd been cured.

He'd spotted the royal gardener, who'd decided it was high time for a bit of heavy pruning.

Panicked at seeing the chap coming towards him with a pair of industrial sized shears, Cloudy ran off, exclaiming to one and all there was no way he was going to be cleared for logging.

A quick scramble up the larger of the gardens oak trees later, he turned to taunt those below, but lost his balance, fell backwards, knocked his helmet off, and came to wondering why everyone he knew had aged thirty years in the time it had taken him to go to the toilet.

With a sigh, Dr. Zoltan left Lollipop thinking about squidgy parts of his body he didn't possess and went down to the dispensary where he knew he had a jar of oil ideal for the job. He found it straight away and was about to return to his patient when he noticed something on the floor.

'That's strange' he thought as he bent over to retrieve it. The item was Nurse Parsnip's nursey hat, a frilly, white, lacy affair more usually found perched on top of her head. And what with her being so fastidious about the wearing of a correct uniform, to find it abandoned like this was odd to say the least.

He put it into his pocket to give to her later, which was not only his doctorly and friendly duty, but a nice excuse to see her outside of work hours.

Once he'd locked the dispensary door, he returned to Lollipop in order to divest the deranged dwarf of his overly tight lid.

Oddly though, said helmet was no longer perched upon Lollipop's head. Even more oddly, Lollipop's head seemed to have done a runner as well, as had the rest of his body. His bed was empty apart from his list of symptoms, Zoltan's book, and a three-foot-long, dwarf shaped groove.

* * *

After a couple of hours wandering about town, Deirdre had found herself feeling rather flummoxed. Or maybe overwhelmed was a better way to describe it.

Whichever way you'd looked at it, though, she'd certainly been feeling a little perplexed. Or maybe discombobulated was a better way to describe it.

Whichever way you'd looked at it, though…oh, you get the idea.

As we discovered earlier, when she'd first arrived in Skullenia with Ollie and Stitches, her natural psychic powers had been somewhat diminished, but that hadn't lasted long.

After a while she'd acclimatised and gotten used to things a bit, and with the careful application of another couple of cups of tea and a few more biccies, she'd been relaxed enough to fully open up and give her clairvoyant mastery free reign.

That had been about five minutes past three in the morning. By six minutes past three she'd had so many voices in her head clamouring for her attention it was all she could do to see straight.

And it had nothing to do with any of the various creatures they'd bumped into, either (or walked through, ducked under, side-stepped, stepped over, dodged, or plain avoided because they were hungry).

She could have spoken to them at any time, much as you would with anyone. This had more to do with those entities that had actually passed on in the fullest sense of the word, and seeing that Skullenia has a long and very colourful (mostly blood red) history, the number of them wanting to stop by for a bit of a chat numbered in the thousands. And the reason for this? Well, I'm glad you asked.

As is well known to those of a more spiritual bent, and what may come as a bit of a bombshell to those not quite so metaphysically but more religiously inclined, when mortal beings pass there's not much of a choice about what happens to their newly freed souls once they're liberated from the confines of the body.

Obviously, they'd love to be offered the option to transcend to whichever afterlife their religion currently believes in, but sadly that would only result in massive disappointment on a scale not seen since five thousand Galileans turned up expecting a banquet, only to end up with half a mouldy crust of bread each and the bill for a below par fish supper, wine not included (and let's be honest here, none of these supposed ecclesiastical domains exist anyway, be it joining a troupe of harp playing angels atop a fluffy white cloud and all the desserts you can eat, or descending down to red hot pokers, extremely sharp gardening implements, toilet roll made of sandpaper, and endless Kevin Hart films).

So, dismissing what might be referred to as a theological grey area (I think it's a cemetery just down the road from Canterbury Cathedral) all that's left for those spirits is to inhabit the non-corporeal netherworld, and have a bit of a laugh hiding their families keys, moaning a bit in the middle of the night, and slamming a door or two when everyone's downstairs.

(And yes, I'm well aware the existence of ghosts etc. is a controversial topic, but hey, it's my opinion. If you don't like it, you can go to He…oh bugger, I can't use that. I'll have to think of something else now. The Eastend of London will do. That's as close as you're going to get to hell on earth).

The problem with being a member of this non-secular, ethereal rambling club, and by association, what had given Deirdre such an overload, was that when those that have passed no longer have anyone still alive to remember them, they lose any tangible link they once had to the real world. Sadly, this causes their spectral energy to wane over time to the point it becomes totally spent and, as woeful as it is to say, they essentially die once more and pass forever into nothingness, and it's only the presence of a bona fide medium that affords them the chance to make themselves heard once more.

In most places, of course, this doesn't happen much of the time which is why you get overweight ladies on stage talking to themselves whilst passing on messages from absolutely no one and getting paid for it, but due to Skullenia being in a bit of a supernatural hotspot, the double dead have more than enough ethereal energy to feed off and make communication possible, which they were now doing very loudly and all at the same time.

And so, seeing that poor Deirdre was in a bit of a psychic pickle (there is such a phenomenon. Open up a jar of anything drowned in vinegar and you'll instantly know that it's going to taste revolting before it gets anywhere near your mouth, let alone give your gag reflex a damn good thrashing), Stitches had guided her to Mrs. Strudel's café for a sit down and a fortifying cuppa whilst Ollie returned to the office. Professor Crumble was bound to have something to help. And if he didn't he'd come up with an idea so outlandish, and no doubt liable to cause life changing injuries, that suffering with a headache nasty enough to make you want to stick a fork in your eye would be by far the better option.

He knocked on the door and called out but was met by silence.

"I bet he's listening to that heavy metal again," Ollie said to himself as he opened the door and walked in.

"Hi, Prof. I've..."

For the first time since he'd taken up residence in Skullenia, Ollie was amazed to find the lab was empty.

The professor, who is, by definition, virtually a hermit, was nowhere to be seen. He wasn't even hiding beneath the work benches, an oft used bolt-hole for the silly scientist, especially if he was mucking about with an item liable to go off bang at a moment's notice (which knowing the Professor could be anything from a suitcase full of nitro-glycerine to a teabag).

But, to Ollie's utter amazement the laboratory was bereft of idiotic inventors to the tune of one idiotic inventor.

After quickly checking the rest of the house, a search which didn't reveal Ronnie's presence either, Ollie made his way over to the café.

"So," said Stitches, "what have you got for us then? A hat made of silver foil to block out signals from beyond? A pair of built up shoes so they'll miss Deirdre's head? Or is it something weird?" He winked at Deirdre. Having explained to her whom Ollie was going to see she got what he meant.

"I haven't got a thing," said Ollie, sitting himself down.

"Well that's better than noth...What do you mean you haven't got a thing?" said the zombie.

"Crumble wasn't in his lab," explained Ollie.

"What, not even under a bench?" said an incredulous Stitches.

"Nope. Checked there. And the rest of the house. I couldn't find Ronnie either."

Mrs. Strudel appeared next to him like a vast, blue rinsed cloud and placed a steaming cup of Earl Grey on the table.

"Don't forget to send Tobias over when you see him, love," she said. With that she toddled back off to the glowing cavern that was her kitchen.

Stitches directed his gaze straight at Ollie. The zombie had a look on his pale, granular face not seen very often. Gone was the cheeky and ever-present grin to be replaced with the beginnings of mild concern.

"That's three people guaranteed to be in the same place at the same time every day, not being there," he said.

Before they had a chance to discuss the matter any further, Deirdre, for want of a better phrase, went a bit weird.

"Hey, it looks like Deirdre's gone a bit weird," said Stitches.

And indeed, a bit weird is precisely what she'd gone.

She'd flopped back into her chair like a relaxed mattress, her chins resting atop her chest like a pile of crumpets and her hat in such disarray, the ladies at her bridge club would have swooned at such a breach of millinery etiquette.

And the breathing.

Deirdre had commenced such forceful insufflation it can only be described as 'asthmatic wildebeest arriving at the top of a staircase because the escalator's broken down.'

(Naturally, you won't normally find an escalator on the African plain of course, but that's only because they all had to be removed in the 1930's due to the constantly terrified beasts weeing and pooing all over them.

You see, after the stress of traversing crocodile infested rivers, lion drenched savannah, and water holes teeming with fat arsed hippopotami looking for a chest bump, wildebeest do tend to relax a bit, and as unpalatable as it may sound, and indeed smell, this leads to certain biological functions happening unbidden and all at the same time.

Now, this might have been okay, but sadly, the wildebeest do tend to be a bit on the slobby, lazy, think of a teenagers bedroom and the festering pit of filth that is side, so it wasn't long before the escalators fell into disrepair as, not only are they not designed to have fifteen thousand wild animals emptying their bladders and bowels all over them on a regular basis, the maintenance costs involved in getting them unclogged was astronomical. As you can well imagine the call out fee to a barren patch of dirt in the middle of Swaziland is slightly more than Dave from Bermondsey driving his van to a shopping centre on a Friday morning because little Timmy has dropped his favourite cuddly toy halfway down.

So, remember, the next time you're watching a nature documentary and feel sorry for the wildebeest as he gets torn limb from limb, just remember this.

It's his own fault).

"She's not having a heart attack, is she?" said Ollie, worriedly as he gently shook Deirdre's shoulder.

"I hope not," said Stitches. "She hasn't paid for her tea."

Deirdre raised her head.

"Oh, my goodness that looks painful," said Ollie.

Her eyes had rolled back into their sockets leaving only the marble like, capillary strewn whites showing.

Thankfully though, and much to Ollie's relief, her breathing had become somewhat more even, and a smile had appeared on her face, although it wasn't a particularly pleasant facial movement as far as facial movements go. It wasn't so much the friendly smile of a loveable, grey haired, and lavender scented old granny, but more the crack faced leer of a serial killer who's just seen a lone female enter a dark alley at two in the morning.

"Are you feeling alright, Deirdre love?" said Stitches, easing his chair back ever so slightly.

*"Deirdre's not here,"* she said in a voice at least two octaves lower than the one they'd gotten used to.

Ollie looked at Stitches and mouthed 'What do we do?' to which the zombie, ever the helpful one, shrugged his shoulders and gave his best, I haven't got a clue look.

"Where is she then?" said Ollie, thinking that continuing the conversation was the only sensible course of action. It was either that or start an exorcism and he didn't have the time or the inclination for all that nonsense.

Besides, he'd just had his shoes polished.

*"She's having a bit if a rest at the moment,"* continued Deirdre/not Deirdre. *"I needed to borrow her brain pan for a while and this head isn't big enough for the both of us."* A phlegmy chuckle bubbled up from the old woman's throat. It sounded like she was choking on thick stew.

By now the other patrons of the café had stopped what they were doing (which was eating) and had turned their attention to the scene unfolding in their midst.

A nervous hush descended when they realised something rather unusual was occurring, so much so that several diners actually stopped eating, which when you consider their nature and where they live, is rather astonishing.

The last time anyone had stopped eating for anything was, um, let me see now, never, and the fact at least three of them were eating pieces of each other, thereby allowing their meals to escape, the incident needed to be something of a conversation stopper.

Not that any of this would put a dent in Mrs. Strudel's profits, of course. It didn't matter one whit whether her customers ate the food on their plates, the table it was resting on, or the leg of the person sitting opposite, she would still charge them for the privilege. Even though she hadn't technically provided some of them with a meal as such, on account of how they'd brought their own packed lunch so to speak, there were still services that had to be provided. Eugene still performed his waiting duties, the dining area had to kept at a comfortable temperature, and the area around the tables had to be cleaned as if there'd been an outbreak of The Black Death.

Ghouls in particular could be very messy eaters and still hadn't quite mastered how to use a knife and fork, figured out what a napkin was, or mastered eating with their mouths shut.

It was even worse if they hadn't completely subdued their lunch and it was still thrashing about a bit.

"Who are you?" said Ollie, quite astonished to be having a conversation such as this.

When he'd first met Deirdre, he hadn't let on to her that he was a little sceptical about the whole medium thing as well, especially as Stitches clearly felt the same way. She seemed like such a lovely person and he didn't want to hurt her feelings if he was honest.

The problem was, living in Skullenia kind of negated the necessity for believing in such things. It would be like going into a library and have someone read the books to you when you could quite easily do it for yourself.

(n.b. for anyone under twenty-five, a library is a big building that has lots of books in it. You can borrow them, take them home, read them, and then take them back. And guess what, it's free. If you're struggling with that concept, though, and can't quite get your head round what a book is, getting something for free, or going outside where the graphics are really good, imagine Google in paper form. Once you've finished with that, look up 'condescending', 'author' and 'who the hell does he think he is anyway telling me what to do?').

For research purposes Ollie had watched a couple of psychic type shows on the darknet, but they hadn't done anything to convince him, thus doing little to persuade him that it wasn't all thrown voices, sound effects, mood lighting, and some bloke hiding behind a curtain going 'Wooooooooh'.

One in particular had stood out. It's called 'This'll Make You Jump', and centres around a group of halfwits who travel to various locations where they indulge in a spot of ghost hunting. And not ordinary ghosts either, oh no, because there's tonnes of them knocking about. They concentrate on a particular type of manifestation, ones that prove much harder to find and, more importantly, have the capacity to capture the watcher's attention, and thus keep the viewing figures up.

They hunt the ghosts of famous people, and unlike past life regression, where everyone seems to have been either Henry the Eighth or Cleopatra and not some dung eating, medieval serf who died of the plague at the ripe old age of twenty three, the ghosts of the famous are extremely rare indeed, to the point that you're more likely to run into a polite Frenchman.

It's almost as if said celebrity had endured so much attention whilst they were alive and in the public eye, once they pass over, they take the opportunity to have a nice, long peaceful rest. The ghosts that is, not the French. They just carry on as per normal by way of eating amphibians, horses, snails, and anything else they can stick twenty seven garlic bulbs in, being derogatory about anything remotely British, using phrases like 'avoir le cul borde de nouilles', although how having your arse stuffed full of noodles is supposed to be lucky is anyone's guess, and making up excuses as to why no countryman of theirs has won the Tour de France since 1985 (though that might have something to do with the aforementioned food product and very tight shorts).

So, who are these people? (the ghost hunters that is, not the French. They just carry on...oops. Done that bit).

The fearless, nay brainless leaders, a husband and wife team commonly known as 'Quick, turn it over, those knobheads are on the telly again', adore being the centre of attention and take the opportunity to ham it up in front of the camera every chance they get.

They're ably assisted in their endeavours by a resident medium (or resident liar if you prefer.

He's constantly making up stories about how many ghosts he's seen, funnily enough all of them off camera) and has the side-splitting habit of becoming 'possessed' whenever a lens is pointed in his direction. It doesn't matter whether he's 'communicating' with a Victorian Lady, a medieval monk, or a cat, he always ends up shouting and screeching like he's having something long and blunt inserted into his ectoplasm.

The fourth member of the troupe is a sceptic who spends the whole show looking doubtful, waving pieces of electronic paraphernalia around, and trying to discredit everything from aberrations and apparitions to weird phenomena beginning with Z. After this he claims any 'suspicious activity' is caused by either the wind or a clumsy cameraman (and if that doesn't work, a windy cameraman).

And lastly, and by all means leastly, there's a female hanger on of no discernible value who does nothing other than scream, cry, flee in terror, and generally wail like a vegan in a slaughterhouse whenever she hears the slightest noise.

Don't watch it. It's a bit poo.

"WHO ARE YOU?" repeated Ollie, a bit more forcefully.

*"Non magnum est nomen meum, et tu simul desinunt ignorare satis,"* said Deirdre/not Deirdre.

"Forget the heart attack," said Stitches. "I think she's having a stroke."

*"Miser creatura. Nulla potestas terribilis ageretur in medio vestri. Sed quod mutatur in tempore."*

"It's clearly some kind of foreign language," said Ollie, ever the one for stating the obvious. "It's too regular and patterned to be just nonsense. I haven't a clue what it means, though."

Stitches would have admonished Ollie for stating the obvious, but that in turn would have been an obvious thing to state, so instead of stating the obvious in response to Ollie's stating of the obvious, Stitches went with the less obvious statement...

"It means I should have paid more attention in school. I have a feeling it's Latin."

"And you'd be right," said Mrs. Strudel, sidling up to the table. "Here, I've written it down for you. Phonetically of course because I don't know what it means either."

"Oh, hold onto your togas, she's off again," said Ollie.

*"Reliquum tempus frui parum diligenter. Si occurrat tibi meos, sympathiam."*

"Well, thanks all the same but I'm already spoken for," said Stitches.

Once the last word was out, Deirdre's body visibly relaxed, her breathing returned to normal, and her eyes returned to where they should be.

"Dearie me. Did I have an episode?" she said, her voice now returned to a more conventional octave. She took a sip of tea to clear her throat.

"I'll say," said Ollie, glad it was all over, and things had returned to their normal state of subdued weirdness. "I think the technical term for it is speaking in tongues. We don't know what exactly you were saying but Mrs. Strudel thinks it was in Latin."

"But I don't know any Latin," said Deirdre. "I did a term of Spanish at school, but I gave it up. All the lisping hurt my tongue."

"Do you remember anything at all?" asked Stitches, "because whatever took you over told us that you'd gone away."

"Not really," said Deirdre. "All I can recall is feeling a vague sense of being trapped, like someone had locked me in a pitch black, sound proofed room. There is one detail I do remember, though, a nebulous image that must have slipped through the psychic shroud confining me. I kept seeing a building."

"Which one?" said Ollie.

"That I don't know. But one thing's for sure, it's definitely here in Skullenia."

* * *

Flug didn't quite know what to do. Not an unusual state of affairs in itself, of course, but on this occasion, he was well and truly stumped.

Just before Stitches had left, Flug had asked him which of his sweets he should eat first, as he wasn't able to decide for himself (which, when you consider the last time he'd been entrusted with a choice to make on his own had resulted in the total destruction of three acres of forest, half a dozen scorched buildings, and the discovery of several heavily charred woodland creatures, one species of which would never be seen again unless Michael Crichton had got his sums right, it wasn't any great surprise that he was now, and for all eternity, discouraged from making any further attempts at decision making.

Still, on reflection, Ollie shouldn't have been very surprised, especially given the magnitude of the task he'd set the mentally challenged monster. When asked to make a piece of toast I'm sure many of us would be torn between using the toaster and setting fire to Mrs. Doom's garden shed in order to get the job done.

Ollie had vowed never to ask Flug to do anything bread related ever again.

Or anything else for that matter).

Anyway, back to the sweety dilemma.

Flug had three packets to choose from. Apricot Abscesses, an oozing, jelly filled treat that burst on the tongue, Rainbow Toenails, crunchy strips of nougat that even had a black rim along the bottom to represent a couple of months' worth of accumulated toe-jam, and Wandering Cherry Gonads which were round, sugary coated, toffee shells that had a live Steambug in each one.

(Apparently, the first two are actually quite palatable, but recent reports suggest the third one tastes like a sweaty gorilla's jockstrap and causes a urinary infection akin to, and I quote, 'pissing hornets'. Saying that though, they certainly have crunch. And legs, hence the name).

In order to help his friend, and to get out of his bedroom lest he be there for the next century and a half, Stitches had told him to take one of each and put them on his bedside table, which he duly did. He then closed his eyes while the zombie shuffled them about. When he was done Stitches told him to eat the one in the middle.

And so, after explaining in very simple terms what he meant by the one in the middle (he pointed to it and said, "It's that one, mate") Stitches had been able to escape.

When he shut the door, Stitches did so with rather more gusto than was usual for such an object, an action which caused the frame and the surrounding area to shake ever such a bit.

'So why did Stitches leave in a mood?' I hear you say. Well, he didn't. The reason for the overzealous shutting was because Flug's bedroom door was considerably more robust than any of the others in the house.

'So why is Flug's bedroom door...?'

Right, I'm going to stop you there, dear reader. We'll be here forever if you keep asking questions. Just keep reading. You'll find out everything. Eventually.

Right, where were we? Ah, yes. The door.

It needed to be heftier than your average instrument of ingress because Flug always woke up two or three times a night because something had scared him. Ollie had tried to make him feel less threatened by leaving the door open, but Flug just worried that something nasty would creep into his room while he was asleep.

It had come to a head a few months back when Flug had been startled from his sleep one night and done his usual of tearing out of his room as if the devil himself had been chasing after him (as it turned out it'd only been a mouse, and it wasn't carrying anything remotely like a farming implement, let alone a pitchfork. It was a small piece of cheese in the shape of a two-pronged plug).

Flug had then ran down the hall, burst into Ronnie's room, and begged to spend the rest of the night in with his friend. Now, that wasn't so bad on the face of it, but he'd arrived in Ronnie's place of slumber with the door handle, door, door frame, a hundred weight of brickwork and plaster, and followed by a very confused looking mouse who was wondering why his cheese had gone all dusty and crunchy.

And so, as a result of the mighty misanthrope's messy midnight misadventure, Ollie had had to have some repair work carried out, but to ensure there wasn't a repeat performance, he'd stipulated that Flug's new bedroom door be capable of taking a major pounding i.e. be able to withstand being rammed by a ticked off rhino who thought that Mrs. Rhino was on the other side of it and doing the horizontal shame shame with his best friend Bob, charged at by an out of control bull elephant wearing a concrete crash helmet and carrying a hippo as a battering ram or, as far as Flug was concerned normal, everyday use.

Anyway, due to its increased weight (it came in at four hundred pounds and in an emergency could be used as a flood barrier), Stitches had to shut the reinforced door with a hefty shove, which, as previously stated, caused the immediate area to shake, subsequently causing Flug's Apricot Abscess to roll off the table and onto the floor, leaving just the two sweets.

Now, the more perceptive of you out there, or those of you that are still awake at any rate, will no doubt now be aware of why Flug was in such a pickle. For those of you who aren't quite as astute, or who fell asleep when I started banging on about mice, fuses, overly heavy doors, and adulterous pachyderms, I'll tell you.

Poor Flug was now left without a middle sweet.

So, here's where we are.

1. It mattered not one jot that Stitches had pointed to Flug's Wandering Cherry Gonad and told him that it was the middle one.

2. It didn't enter Flug's thought process at all that even though it was previously the middle sweet, and as such should still be the first one to eat, he should eat it first.

3. It was utterly unfathomable to him that he could have retrieved the Apricot Abscess from the floor and returned it to the table, thereby returning all three sweets to their original positions.

4. And it was a sheer irrelevance he still had two sweets, he could find the other one at a later date, and that his Gonad was still sitting happily on the table (you can put your own joke in here).

According to Flug's addled brain, The Wandering Cherry Gonad wasn't in the middle anymore, and without a middle sweet, Flug didn't know what to do, and not knowing what to do meant someone would have to help, but seeing as there was no one here to offer that assistance he adopted his usual demeanour when faced with any tricky decision. In short, he'd stare at the wall until a solution presented itself, or to put it another way, he'd have to wait until someone dragged him back to reality, wiped the drool off his chin, and told him what to do.

So here he was, and it was here he would stay until the ice caps melted into the sea, The Himalayas were scoured from the face of the earth, and the glittering, viscous string of dribble descending from his slackened jaw reached his knee. (Oh yes. It was that thick).

Thankfully, it was then that his overtaxed brain got some much-needed aid.

"*Hello, Flug,*" said a voice.

"Hello," said Flug.

The fact the voice was in the air and not coming out of anything tangible didn't bother him at all, which was a turn up because he'd flee in terror if he overheard someone on the other end of the phone.

"*Are you okay?*"

"Yeah but no."

"*What seems to be the matter?*"

"Dunno what sweetie to 'ave."

"*Mmm, that is a tricky one. Tell you what, why don't you have both?*"

"Wot's bofe?"

"*Pick one of them up.*"

Flug picked one of them up.

"*Now the other one.*"

Flug picked up the other one. He stared at the two sweets resting on his palm and still didn't have any idea at all what was going on.

"*There you go. Now you don't have to decide. You can eat both of them you see.*"

Flug raised his arm but hesitated before popping the nuggets of yumminess into his mouth.

"Ronnie tell me off when me mix dem. He say it make me hydroattic."

"*Well, Ronnie's not here at the moment is he, so there's no need to worry is there?*"

"No."

"*There you go then.*"

"Okay. Wot?"

"*You can eat the sweets.*"

"Okay."

After he'd gobbled them down, a process that took slightly less time than the Higgs Boson particle exists, Flug decided he was tired and in need of a nap, so he lay down on his enormous bed.

Just before he closed his eyes, he noticed a greenish, blue sphere of light on the ceiling just above his head.

"Pretty," he said and nodded off.

* * *

Ollie knocked on the shed door, causing it, and the rickety wooden structure to wobble.

"I still don't see why we need this guy's help," said Stitches. "Surely there must be someone else we can ask."

"There is," said Ollie, "but without Henry and Mandeep he's the next best thing."

Hyde and Sikh's premises had been open but empty, and whilst not unusual for Henry Jekyll to be off somewhere doing whatever it is he and his alter ego get up to, for Mandeep Singh not to be present was rare. Very rare. In fact, it so extremely rare, I need a new paragraph.

Imagine, if you will, receiving a birthday present from a grandparent which, when opened, doesn't reveal a pair of multi coloured, hand knitted, seven toed socks made of wool harvested from the rear end of the dirtiest, ugliest sheep in the world and possessing the texture of a nutmeg grater, but the latest iPod, smartphone, tablet, 5G, wireless, e-reader, kindle, bendy, touchscreen, retina scanning, thumb reading thingamabob that does anything and everything you could ever want.

Well, apart from make bloody phone calls of course, but why would anyone want to do that? Ask for a phone that's just a phone these days and the vacant eyed, proto-human clad in the suit three sizes too small looks at you as if you've just stepped out of The Stone Age.

(I hope my disdain for modern technology hasn't come across as too vitriolic, but if I want to BBM, or instant message, or connect to Twitch, or WhatsApp, or watch the latest streaming Instagram, videoblog, or YouTube show then I'll ask for it. Obviously, I'll have to find out what all those things mean first, but on balance I don't want to and would rather place my left testicle into a garlic press).

When they'd left Mrs. Strudel's, Deirdre had noticed the town seemed rather more empty than it had been when she'd first arrived, and she'd only been there a matter of hours.

"Is it usually this quiet?" she'd said, as the three of them had walked along the eastern wall of the cemetery. Their position had been slightly elevated enabling them to clearly see the whole town.

"No, not at all," Ollie had remarked whilst gazing at the peaceful scene. He'd also pointed to the sky. Normally it was buzzing and full of all manner of flying things, even birds. It too was very, very serene.

Stitches had agreed and admitted to finding it all a bit creepy, saying, "I'm finding this all a bit creepy."

"Funny how you take things for granted isn't it," said Ollie.

And how right he is. It's amazing what becomes the norm, and how utterly bereft it can make you feel once it's no longer there.

The desolate emptiness of a house when the children have flown the nest.

The warm, life giving glow of the summer sun caressing your upturned face once the season changes and the chill winds are biting at your skin.

And the soft, silky feel of a chiffon negligee as it slides tantalisingly down your freshly shaved thighs and…

Oops. I think I've strayed into the realms of TMI there. Can you do me a favour, dear reader and disregard the last few bits of self-indulgent nonsense, please?

I don't want people getting the wrong idea.

I don't really like the hot weather.

With a wobbly clatter the shed door opened revealing the corpulent, mutton chopped hodgepodge that was Excalibur Cross.

"Well, good evening," he oozed as he beckoned them inside. He smiled broadly as he stepped away from the door. "I don't usually get visitors all the way out here, and I must admit you two wouldn't be at the top of that list even if there was one. And I see you've brought a guest."

He extended a pudgy hand towards Deirdre, an offer she accepted because she was starting to get to grips with recognising who was and who wasn't of the undead, supernatural persuasion.

And a good skill it was to acquire too because a shake of the wrong appendage could end up going really rather badly, really rather quickly, and in no time at all you could suddenly find yourself being slaughtered in cold blood and mutilated until there was nothing left but a few bite size chunks, half a pint of sticky goo, and a hat. Or at least getting a stern telling off anyway.

Still, if that had been, or was likely to be the case and things had, or were likely to go a little bit skewed, at least she was happy in the knowledge she had her two trusty guides with her to ensure her safety and well-being.

(Good job she didn't actually realise the folly of that assumption, though, because in reality, Ollie and Stitches were likely to provide about as much protection as a paper umbrella. Mind you, a paper umbrella might prove to be the better option anyway, because it was slightly more robust, was a damn sight sturdier, could put up a better fight than

Ollie, and had the added bonus of being able to last longer in a heavy downpour than Stitches should said altercation take place during a bit of inclement weather.

Now, I know it's unfair to have a pop at the aged zombie, but he does have skin like a three thousand year old Egyptian mummy who's lost her Avon catalogue, so standing about in a monsoon would only serve to turn him into a badly dressed, papier-mâché puddle. In fact, such is his dessicated state these days, if he wanders into a kitchen when a kettle's boiling, he tends to go a bit floppy and break out in algae, moss, and several varieties of toadstool three days later. Many's the time that a fluffy, green moustache has adorned his top lip that he's failed to notice, much to the pleasure of everyone he bumps into).

"Excalibur Cross," continued the crassly corpulent correspondent by way of introduction. "Lead reporter and editor in chief of The Skullenian Times."

"I'm very pleased to meet you, Mr. Cross. Deirdre Clownpuncher."

As he shut the door, Cross's imagination went into overdrive, his little grey cells having a field day thinking up headlines playing on Deirdre's surname.

As a reporter this was one of the more important facets of his profession and as such, he'd been responsible for some genuine crackers that had graced the front page of the paper during his tenure.

Some notable triumphs include this by-line detailing the occasion a stray dog got into the café and stole some food.

## 'Scandal As Doodles the Poodle Steals Oodles Of Noodles From Mrs. Strudel's'

Another came about as the result of a fight between Arsehat the dwarf and Jingles, the one-legged demon.

## 'Miniature Miner Comes A Cropper, Has Bell Firmly Rung By Netherworld Hopper'

One of his personal favourites had been about Count Jocular.

During one of the vampire lord's blood-filled benders a few years back, he'd chanced to sink his fangs into a rather smelly and well past its sell by date bit of meat (a malodorous homeless by the name of Mushroom).

Consequently, he'd gotten a bit of an upset tummy, produced an off red stream of coagulating vomit that looked and behaved like fresh lava, and fainted onto a chaise longe in very flamboyant fashion.

## 'Vicious Vampiric Viceroy Out For The Count After Dining On Fragrant Vagrant'

That last one had earned him a few accolades.

There was an honourable mention at the reporters annual dinner, a free subscription to the satirical magazine, WALLOP! and an overnight, upside down stay at Count Jocular's castle where His Lordship had very generously given him a severe talking to regarding respect, discretion, and his responsibilies as a journalist.

Sadly, come the morning Cross wasn't able to recall too much of the 'little chat' on account of excessive blood loss, but a handwritten note left in his pocket succinctly explained the vampire's position.

'Dear, Mr. Cross, if zis effer happens again zere von't be enough left off you to fill a small matchbox. Kind regards CJ'.

Ollie gave the reporter a quick rundown of what may, or may not be happening in town, although to be honest, it was more may not.

"Now that you mention it, I haven't seen Ramekin for a while," said Cross. "He went out a few hours ago to take some photos for a story but he hasn't come back yet. It shouldn't have taken him this long."

"Where did he go?" said Ollie.

"Over to Grendle's. For some reason his shop wasn't open this evening," Cross explained.

Stitches did a double take. Well, his neck did. His head gave up any attempt at movement after the first take, leaving him with a nice view of one wall of the shed.

He turned his body forty-five degrees and hoped no one noticed he was now speaking to them whilst doing a passable impression of the Jack of Spades.

"Well, surely that *has* to confirm something's going on," said the zombie who, due to the extreme torsion in his neck, now sounded like he was trying to swallow a recalcitrant bag of gravel. "That miserly old bugger never closes."

"A strange occurrence indeed, and one that I remarked upon. Ramekin and I discussed the matter at length before he left," said Cross. "You see, Miss

Clownpuncher, such is our local merchants' lust for commerce, he even stayed open for business during the Great Poltergeist Riots of '74. I even wrote an article about it. Excellent copy it was too."

(As you're no doubt aware, poltergeists are very rarely, if ever seen, and as a result of this a lot of their work is either dismissed, goes unrecognised, or attributed to other, more visible beings. And so, fed up with this lack of recognition, even though it was essentially their own fault for being so reclusive, they'd staged a protest.

On one terrible night they'd rampaged through the town moving chains ever so slightly, opening doors very slowly to make them creak a bit, uttering 'WOOOH' in an elevated whisper, and hiding things like bunches of keys, socks, and a tile off every third roof.

Once the residents had realised what was going on word had spread very quickly, and it wasn't long before the incident had acquired legendary status, and not much longer before they were all talking about the 'Great Things Moving About On Their Own, Maybe It Was A Ghost Incident' of '74.

As you can imagine this annoyed the poltergeists even more than before, and it wasn't until one particularly astute and enterprising member of the offended group of spectres made a few spooky noises, knocked over a stringed musical instrument, and wrote a message on someone's bathroom cabinet indicating the slight kerfuffle was attributed to them, that the slight kerfuffle was attributed to them.

On a side note that's why, to this day, any and all poltergeist activity involves certain tropes, actions, and signs designed to let people know it's them getting up to the mischief.

You'll no doubt be familiar with them as they've been incorporated into every bathroom scene of every spooky film ever made.

There's the creepy strains of a cello that only ever seems to play when the bathroom door's opened, a patch of mist that's strangely confined to the area just above the toilet, and an ominous scrawl that appears on a steamed up mirror the moment anyone's back is turned.

Obviously, this always takes place when a beautiful, uninhibited, and heftily endowed young lady is taking a shower, but that's the thing about poltergeists. They might be hard to see, but they're not stupid).

Ollie showed Cross the piece of paper that Mrs. Strudel had written Deirdre's coffee shop rantings on.

"I know you've got plenty of reference books here, Excalibur, so I was wondering if you'd be able to translate this for me? Deirdre had a visitation, and this is what she came out with."

"No need for books, my good man, reference or otherwise," said Cross, perusing the message. "I studied Latin at school, don't you know. Mater insisted. Mmm, let me see now. Right, well roughly translated we have, 'My name is not important, but you will come to know it soon enough.' Then, 'Pathetic creatures, you have no inkling of the power in your midst, however, that will soon change,' and, 'Take care and enjoy what time you have left for soon this will be over.' That's not a perfect translation, but I've given you the gist of it."

"Well, whoever it is has got tickets on himself," said Stitches. "And I think a certain psychotic vampire lord might have something to say on the matter. He won't take too kindly to someone trying to muscle in round here."

"Does it mean anything to you, Deirdre?" said Ollie. "Does it make any sense now we know what it says?"

"I'm afraid not, dear," she said distractedly. She was staring at a bookcase at the rear of the shed. It contained various journalistic accoutrements and a couple of rows of heavy looking binders.

"What are those may I ask, Mr. Cross?" she said.

"Oh those. That's every back issue of the newspaper ever printed. And yes, I know a lot of people have certain opinions about what we do here and question as to why should I bother collecting them," he looked pointedly at Ollie and Stitches just to let them know it was to them he was referring, "but Deadhouse and I are actually quite proud of what we've achieved here. And if nothing else it serves as an interesting historical record. There's reports of happenings in and around Skullenia going back, well, a very long time indeed. Would you like to have a look through them?"

"I wouldn't recommend it," said Stitches. "Not unless you want to read a week by week series of the greatest works of fiction ever written."

"That's a tad harsh isn't it?" said Cross, although he had to admit, the observation wasn't entirely unexpected.

"Oh, come off it, Excalibur," said the zombie, incredulously. "Even you have to admit there's a certain amount of embellishment that goes on. Even the weather forecasts are a bit suspect."

Cross shifted in his seat.

"You present your point very eloquently, and though I don't wholeheartedly agree with your assertion, I will say that perhaps, maybe, on occasion perchance, a few minor unsubstantiated facts may very well have crept into some of the stories I've been called to report upon. And whilst those particular snippets of information may not hold up to intense scrutiny or cross examination in a court of law, let it be noted for the record that I sometimes *have* to insert trivial yet unresearched details, but that's strictly to ensure the flow of the narrative and thus guarantee *all* of the pertinent and truthful details I *do* cover make for coherent reading. It's a cardinal lesson I learned very early on in my journalistic career, from my first editor in fact, and it perfectly highlights a fundamental rule, one I've stuck to every step of the way."

"Which is?" said Stitches.

"Every now and again you need to tell a little white lie or two to make things believable."

"Is that a very long-winded way of telling Stitches he's right?" said Ollie.

"Absolutely and categorically not," said Cross. "I was simply explaining some of the more subtle nuances of reporting to your curious colleague."

"I see," said the zombie. "So why did you report that Egon is a certified loon who can't sleep for more than three minutes at a time because he's allergic to the inside of his own eyelids, and keeps a collection of big toes in a box under his bed?" said Stitches, who now considered Jocular's servant to be more of a friend rather than a being to be avoided at all costs. Not a close friend, of course, because you didn't want someone of Egon's ilk being *too* familiar with you, especially with the amount of shedding he does.

For at least three million miles in every direction he's well known for being the only creature whose whole body is affected by dandruff.

If he stands outside in a high wind, he looks like a snow globe.

Cross raised his hands.

"Alright, fine. In the interests of transparency and a general entente cordiale, I will admit to not being totally infallible by any stretch of the imagination which, I'm sure you'll all agree, is a familiar and pervasive character flaw familiar to everyone, and one that may, very rarely, result in my getting the facts wrong here and there. I'm only human after all, and we all make mistakes don't we. But let's face it, no one's perfect. I do, however, constantly strive to maintain the highest of standards with regards to my journalistic integrity. And you have to agree I get it right most of the time."

"Well, that's okay then," said Stitches. "Just make sure you carry on getting stuff right. And just so you know for next time, Egon keeps his toes in a teapot."

"It is agreed then," said Cross. "Although I will add, if you ever tell anyone else about this conversation, I will one, categorically deny that it ever took place, and two, pen a damning story regarding your monstrous behaviour with a troll."

"That's two L's, don't forget," said Stitches.

"Any chance we can get on with what we came here for?" said Ollie, vowing to never, ever have a sneaky cup of tea with Egon ever again. He liked his Earl Grey with a bit of a kick but that was just disgusting.

"Of course," said Cross. "Now, where were we? Ah yes. Is there anything in particular you'd like to look at, my dear?"

"Would you have an issue with an aerial view of the town?" said Deirdre.

"Let me check for you," said Cross as he got up and went over to the paper laden shelf. "I've got them all alphabetised, cross referenced, and in date order. Shouldn't take more than a few minutes."

He selected the index volume and leafed through it.

"Ah, here we are," he said, replacing the binder and removing another one. "Mrs. Ladle captured an aerial shot for us a few years back when Flug went missing."

"Did he?" said Ollie, interested to know the details, but not at all surprised about the subject of the story. The overgrown idiot could get lost going from A to B in his head.

"Oh, he did indeed," said Stitches, nodding his head. It was back where it should be now. "It was the talk of the town for quite a while. Until something else happened, anyway."

"What was that?" said Deirdre.

"He got lost again. In the same place believe it or not."

In total, Flug had managed to get himself all AWOL for three whole days.

(AWOL stands for Absent Without Leave, of course, as opposed to Skateboard Scratch, an amputee who gets himself around on a three wheeled piece of wood. Not seen for months at a time, he goes Absent Without Legs.

Then there's Johnny the Worm, a painfully skinny wretch who often leaves home just before food, making him Absent Without Lunch.

And we mustn't forget Newport Pagnell's worst postman of all time, Altair Midnight, who, in the relentlessly hot summer of 1976, completely abandoned the above time-honoured acronym and went AWEL, Absent With Everyone's Letters.

Not seen since, his whereabouts remain a mystery, but his wife still gets a birthday card from him every year. It doesn't necessarily say happy birthday, and has someone else's name scribbled out, but he does have quite an extensive collection to get through).

Flug had had a dream that all of the sweets he could ever want, which was a lot, were kept secretly hidden down the bottom of a deep well on the outskirts of town, and Flug being his scatter brained self, had gone off in search of this amazing treasure.

And gotten lost.

The ensuing search had proved fruitless and revealed nothing, save for a new species of strangling ivy and the location of Professor Crumble's second favourite pair of glasses which he hadn't seen (through) since 1954 after they were stolen.

They'd been found on the thief who, in turn, was found throttled to death in the deadly and vast green oasis, a deadly and vast green oasis he obviously didn't notice, in spite of his newly acquired eyewear.

The theory was he'd been dispatched by the very same ivy that had been newly discovered during the search, ivy he must have stumbled into whilst making good his escape wearing Professor Crumble's glasses.

As Stitches had remarked, "Clearly, the glasses can't have been that good."

My, how everyone had laughed.

Anyway, it wasn't until Mrs. Ladle had taken Ramekin Deadhouse, a rather reluctant Ramekin Deadhouse it has to be said, on a broom ride to conduct an aerial search, that Flug had been found, although it was more luck than judgement that got them there.

Cross had told Ramekin to get plenty of pictures, and it was only when The Big Bang style explosion of light that was the photographers flash had reflected off Flug's bolt, had he been revealed.

Cross had requested the pictures as he'd wanted to put some of them in the paper. He'd thought they'd make for interesting viewing, especially for those residents unable to fly. It'd be a real eye opener for them to observe their town from an angle not often seen.

Unfortunately, though, only the first image had been useable. All the others had Deadhouse's dinner all over them thanks to him spraying the camera's lens in a series of colourful and rapidly congealing splats.

Still, they would have made an interesting flip book if you were that way inclined, which was funny because it was being inclined a couple of hundred feet in the air that had caused his meal to make a reappearance in the first place.

"Here we go," said Cross, laying the hefty tome on the table open to the correct page. "That shows just about every building in town. The only one's missing are Jocular's castle because it's too far away, Hyde and Sikh's because Mandeep has it camouflaged to protect against an aerial attack, and Mr. Curtain's, whose house exploded when he flushed his toilet a week earlier."

"How can flushing a toilet make a house explode?" said Ollie.

"Professor Crumble tweaked his plumbing," said Stitches.

"Oh right."

"They found a third of him on top of the pub," said Cross.

"What about the rest of him?" said Deirdre as she studied the photo.

"We never found out," said Stitches, "although Noggin was ferociously guarding something behind the police station for a few days afterwards. No one could get near the place. He was chasing everyone and everything away. In fact, he put on quite a few pounds as I recall."

"I've found it," Deirdre announced. "The building I saw in my vision is here."

"Which one is it, my dear?" said Cross, leaning over to get a better view.

Ollie leaned back slightly as the reporter's expansive belly pressed against his shoulder.

Deirdre placed a confident finger next to the portion of the image that she recognised.

The three Skullenian residents looked at each other and nodded in agreement.

It was the hospital.

\* \* \*

Bradawl, the current landlord of The Bolt and Jugular, looked around his half empty establishment and sighed.

'If this is how things are going to be', he thought, 'I think I might call it a night and head off to bed'.

Still, at least it was quiet, and he was still alive, which was always a bonus.

Being the custodian of Skullenia's one and only inn was a position best described using one word. Dangerous.

The local pack of drinkers, a dedicated bunch of staggering inebriates who'd sell their own grannies for a pint or fourteen (and at least three who'd sell her just because they felt like it), were religiously, zealously, and fervently keen on their alcohol, pretty much to the point of obsession, and that being the case (or barrel) it had to be just right i.e. a specific colour, a specific temperature, a specific amount and, in the case of some of the more ethereal patrons, a specific gravity.

It was no good giving your average ghost a pint of light and frothy ale, for instance. All that'd happen is he'd go all fizzy, float to the ceiling, and spread out like a pool of particularly unruly mercury, a position he'd stay in until he dried out and returned to the floor where he'd land like a splat of semi putrid cottage cheese, not very nice if it happens while you're enjoying a quiet little drinkie as I'm sure you'll agree.

No one wants to be sipping their favourite beverage only to find what appears to be the contents of a freshly lanced and infected cyst floating in their glass.

Not that that would bother everyone in the pub, of course. A fair percentage of the clientele would just assume they'd been served a new and exotic cocktail.

So basically, the landlord of this incredibly unique establishment had the onerous task of getting everything one hundred percent right, for one hundred percent of the patrons, one hundred percent of the time. If he didn't, he could be one hundred percent sure he'd become one hundred percent dead in very short order.

The previous occupier of the role (a job considered by many to be more dangerous than traversing an active minefield on a seventeen pronged pogo stick, and coming with a life expectancy slightly shorter than a determined suicide bomber who's got very little to live for) had been a fellow by the name of Hangnail, who'd been forced to hand in his notice when he got an order wrong and presented Arthur Twonecks with a white wine spritzer.

(I say handed his notice in, but that probably needs a little clarification. The head of the brewery had a package delivered to his office the next day in which rested Hangnail's right hand. On the back of said extremity was scrawled, I QUIT. No one was quite sure what happened to the rest of him, not that they'd admit to anyway, but suffice it to say the pub menu contained rather more protein than usual the following week).

The chap before that, a flamboyant character called Gabriel, had actually lasted quite a while, but he'd ended up in various parts of the forest after he'd suggested that 'gaily coloured cushions and lacy doilies' would make a 'fabulous' addition to the seating area, and replaced the traditional pub games with pastimes such as musical quiz nights, themed evenings involving costumes guaranteed to make the wearer question their sexuality, and amusing diversions such as Which Corset? Pin The Pompadour On The Popinjay, and Spot the Flower.

Needless to say, those were all terrible lapses of judgement, ones that made Noah's decision to have woodpeckers on the ark seem rather sensible.

Pub games, as is well known and documented, are the most important and quintessential pastimes that take place in every drinking establishment (apart from drinking, of course, which is quite important on the face of it, and sort of quintessential) and there was no way in the world that anyone would convince the Skullenian regulars to pass up the chance to play a game of OUCH!, or refrain from indulging in a couple of rounds of How Many Fingers?

So, as you can see, it's not a job to be taken lightly (or for very long).

Bradawl pulled another pint of Speckled Thump and put it on the bar in front of Tam Sprout, semi-retired warlock and chairman of the 'Sitting About On Your Fat Arse All Day' society. It wasn't actually an official title, or an actual club for that matter, but his long-suffering wife needed something to shout at him when he staggered home from the pub.

"There you go, Tam," said Bradawl.

He glanced around the bar and furrowed his brow. He was sure there were more customers the last time he looked. He shrugged his shoulders and resigned himself to the fact he was probably suffering from extreme boredom and not paying proper attention, because there was no way any of the drinkers could sneak out of the building quietly. Not unless quietly meant bumping into everything in sight, swearing profusely in three different dialects, and trying to pick a fight with a hat stand.

"Cheers, mate," said Tam, before taking a long, slurping draft of the gloopy beverage. He chewed on the frothy head until it was less like hardened concrete and more like slightly softer concrete and swallowed it down.

(Most of the drinks on offer at The Bolt and Jugular do have a tendency to contain solid parts by nature. In fact, some of them are so dense the glasses have to be specially reinforced, and in the case of Tolstoy's Bloody Peculiar, you're advised not to drink it without first donning a pair of steel toe capped boots and attending a manual handling course).

"Quiet in here tonight," said Tam, with the searing insight of the perennially drunk. Another couple of pints and he'd know exactly how to manage a football team, the dynamics of which he would ably demonstrate by moving sodden beer mats around the bar, be certain in the knowledge that the moon landings were faked and were actually filmed in his uncle's garage, the dynamics of which he would ably demonstrate by moving sodden beer mats around the bar, and feel amorous enough to make a blubberingly romantic pass at anything vaguely vertical, including a tall stack of sodden beer mats that had spent the entire evening being moved around the bar, and the hat stand, which has a rough time of it on an hourly basis.

"I know," said Bradawl as he tried to chip something off the bar top. He didn't know what it was, but he was on his second knife. "It's normally a lot busier than this. I'd have more luck down the mortuary with a packet of scratchings and a six pack." (The scratchings were abstract in origin which is why they're not assigned a species. Even the manufacturer couldn't be a hundred percent sure where the meat had come from so it was best not to speculate).

"Must be the greeny/blue," said Tam.

"Excuse me."

"The greeny/blue. Been all over town lately."

"I haven't got a clue what you're going on about, Tam me old mate," said Bradawl, wondering where this latest, bibulous ramble was heading. "Where did you hear about this greeny/blue?"

"Bloke down the pub told me," said Tam.

An idea suddenly flashed through Bradawl's mind, but he was diverted from thrusting a broken glass into Tam's flaccid throat by a shout from the other end of the bar.

" 'Nother flagon o' Rabbit if yer please, vetinry."

"How many times do I have to tell you this isn't the vets?" said Bradawl as he approached Ticktock Powell, livestock producer, tiller of the soil, and drunk of immense proportions.

God alone knew what he got up to when he actually paid a visit to the vets, but word had it his cows were permanently sloshed, and his bacon came pre marinated. "This is the pub remember?"

"Course I remember, vetinry. I ain't bein' no simple-minded bumpkin. Now wash yer 'ands before ye pours me drink. Don't want no innards floatin' about in it."

(Obviously, that was a ridiculous statement to make. As if the drink he requested would be laden with chunks of unidentifiable meat.

He'd have to order Steamboat's Foggy Water for that particular delight. The colour of terminal cancer and tasting like a cross between utter despair and a fully laden cess pit, it's the only ale in the world that has a cholesterol level).

Bradawl took Ticktock's empty glass, put it under the nozzle and pulled the dark, well-worn handle, but instead of the steady flow of alcohol, all he got was a throaty gurgle and a spray of foam. It was like the pipe had contracted rabies.

"Give us a minute, Ticktock," he said, putting the glass down. "I need to change the barrel."

"Righto, vetinry. I'll be in the top field checkin' me bullocks."

You'll have more luck checking between your ears for those, thought Bradawl as he opened the cellar door and descended the rickety wooden steps that led down into the bowels of The Bolt and Jugular.

(And bowels is a very apt description of the gloomy and damp subterranean pit.

Containing all the various barrels, casks, crates, and vats one might expect to find under a public house, the cellar has a certain fragrant ambience.

It's a subtly alcoholic and occasionally violent climate, one not only liable to cause even the hardiest of drinkers a mild dose of merry inebriation, but one capable of dealing the uninitiated a coma inducing, ninety percent proof left hook.

But then there's the pipes.

Ah, the pipes.

An ancient and turgid collection of leaden arteries, they deliver whichever beverage a patron requires. Be it Mother Levenson's Bubonic Gin, Saxon's Sausagey Ale, or Willow's Garlic Furball, the throbbing vessels provide the thirsty with their mostly liquid refreshment.

So, it's thanks to this primitive potpourri of putrid potables that the aforementioned bouquet is so utterly unique, and so very pervasive. That and the squidgy floor, the sagging ceiling, the spongy bricks, and the various fungal growths on every available surface.

The eclectic mix also means they do get a tad clogged up from time to time, of course, but that's easily remedied by way of a high pressure flush, an extremely vigorous irrigation of a profoundly incendiary nature, and the introduction of several rather potent chemicals even the Byzantines would have considered a bit harsh.

In fact, so destructively corrosive is the toxic brew, several of the regulars can only drink a pint of it at a time.

Anyway, that's a task best related when I'm sure that you, dear reader, aren't eating, although the resulting effluent emanating from the constipated system has been described as being similar in colour, texture, and odour to what comes spraying out the rear end of a warthog suffering from irritable bowel syndrome.

The liquor itself is far worse, though. Even the rats, who due to the nature of Skullenia are used to ingesting organic matter that wouldn't have looked out of place on the field of Agincourt half an hour after the English and the French had stopped messing about, had abandoned the cellar due to being disgusted at the dining arrangements and an increasing incidence of cirrhosis).

Because Ticktock was the only patron left who supped Valiant's Addled Myxomatosis (a peculiar and aromatic beverage boasting the jellied consistency of luke-warm sludge, the post-mortem hue of a mass war grave, and the vague glow of a potato grown just outside Chernobyl), Bradawl hadn't ever had to change the lead-lined, concrete barrel so, unsure exactly where it was, he stood on the bottom step and scanned the dank cellar.

(Of the other customers who'd favoured a pint of Rabbit, one had died of extreme alcohol poisoning, a second had died of extreme alcohol poisoning, and the last had died of extreme alcohol poisoning. It was for this reason that Ticktock had all of his affairs in order, had made preparation for his animals to be adopted, and filled out his death certificate and given it to Dr. Zoltan).

After a few minutes, Bradawl shook his head.

"Typical," he muttered.

Right at the back of the cellar, in possibly the darkest corner ever to have been discovered (it wasn't the darkest corner per se, though. That was so *very* dark it had yet to be discovered), he located the barrel, and judging from the state of things, no one had been over there since some knuckle dragging primitive had gazed at a round bit of stone and thought it'd be handy for moving things about (Bagthorpe, Norfolk, June 1979).

As he made his way across the cellar he sighed.

The barrel, dusty, aged, and cobweb ridden, was hidden behind a whole array of publy items, an odd assortment of necessities essential to the smooth running of the establishment.

There was a second aid kit for afterhours lock ins (someone had stolen the first one and eaten it), a mighty scythe (for when patrons needed a bit of gentle persuasion to leave after a lock in), several stretchers (for when patrons needed temporary assistance to leave after a lock in because they'd ignored the gentle persuasion provided by the mighty scythe and so met with the robust handle of the mighty scythe), half a dozen coffins (for when patrons needed a firmer, and rather more permanent reminder to leave after a lock in because they'd ignored the gentle persuasion provided by the mighty scythe, and disregarded meeting the robust handle of the mighty scythe), and a semi-automatic, heavy-shot firing blunderbuss (even when they've been chopped in half some people just don't listen).

As he started clearing the detritus out of the way he had the sudden, and worrying feeling that he wasn't alone, and not in the usual 'finding that Hector Lozenge had snuck down to get to the alcohol at source' way. It was more a creeping uneasiness that snaked up his spine, nestled on his shoulder, and whispered tales of doom into his ear.

He was about to dismiss it and carry on when he heard a loud pop and a rush of liquid as a cask to his left burst open, flooding the cellar floor with seventy percent proof booze.

*"This stuff isn't very good for you, you know,"* said a voice, as the dark room was slowly filled with a greenish blue light.

Bradawl, taken by surprise, was instantly far too frightened to offer any sort of a reply which, when you consider he regularly serves trolls, ogres, demons, ghouls, flesh-eaters, witches, wizards, evil dwarves, imps, semi-sentient ectoplasm, wraiths, djinns, warlocks, poltergeists, spectres, chimeras, and the occasional Jehovah's Witness, is ample testament to how scared he really was.

The landlord staggered backwards, tripped over an empty crate of bottles, and landed on his backside with a resounding thud.

As the glow encompassed him the voice said, *"Let me tell you about something that's far better for you."*

Bradawl howled and slipped into unconsciousness.

* * *

What with Ollie and Stitches being as adept at the detailed research of relevant, historical data as the Nazi's had been to the preservation of Europe's cultural diversity, Excalibur Cross had spent the last half an hour going through even more back editions of his paper. He was only scanning them, though, otherwise they'd be there all night.

Once finished with an issue he handed it to Deirdre who put it on the table so they didn't get mixed up, a table that was getting increasingly shorter volume by volume.

(Can something get 'increasingly shorter'? No, of course it can't, it's just another example of some of the nonsense produced by England's mother tongue. Think of, 'You youngsters don't know you're born', which is ludicrous and suggests that people are walking around wondering why their mum's womb has got cars and buildings in it.

'As safe as houses', not very apt if you happen to live near the San Andreas Fault, and, 'Don't teach your granny to suck eggs'.

Now, I may be old fashioned, but I never saw any of my beloved grans, non-great, great or otherwise, pop a shelled ovum into her mouth and give it a damn good slurping.

Then again, I wasn't around during the 1940's and things were a bit different back then. The egg was powdered for a start, so it probably needed a decent suck before you put it between a couple of slices of cardboard bread, had a cup of weak tea, and bombed Dresden.

Such simple times).

"You can't deny the fact it's a riveting read," said Ollie, glancing at a copy and reeling off a headline at random. " 'We Lift The Lid On Able Fluid's Collection Of Flip Flops.' "

"Fascinating," said Deirdre, perusing her own copy of journalistic tomfoolery.

"Indeed, it is," continued Ollie. "Apparently, he keeps them in a rack."

"That's a long way to go if you fancy slipping on some holiday footwear," said Stitches, registering a magnificent 8.6 on The Somper Scale.

(For those who've never heard of it, this interesting unit of measurement quantifies the level of a person's misunderstanding of a statement or situation.

It came into common use during the early eighteenth century when Genesis Somper, after being coerced by his older brothers to indulge in a bit of shoplifting, attempted to pick up his local branch of 'Hair Today, Gone Tomorrow, Wigmakers of Distinction' via its side wall.

Stupid? Obviously, but what with every cloud having a silver lining and all that stuff and whatnot, the fact he'd suffered a double hernia and a prolapsed disc the size of a dinner plate paled into insignificance when informed he'd been the catalyst for the invention of a new system for measuring linguistic misinterpretation, an accolade that, not only made him very proud, but took the edge off being told he was a massive twat.

Other examples include Lee Harvey Oswald who was meant to take out the Dallas branch of KFC, Leonardo da Vinci misreading his commission to paint his neighbour's wife Moaning Lisa, and, on the occasion of choosing a drummer for his band and becoming bored with the entire process, John Lennon saying, 'Right, that's it. I've had enough of these losers. What about bingo?').

"Here we go," said Cross, at last joining them at the table. "It's an edition from, my goodness, over a hundred years ago. That's when Melody Gears was at the helm." He handed the old paper to Ollie.

The headline read, **'Horror Haunts Hospital. Wards Awash With Blood.'**

"I'm guessing it's not a cheery, human interest piece then?" said Stitches.

Ollie read the article out.

"Last night our august medical institution became a scene of slaughter as at least seventeen patients were brutally murdered in their beds. Although, as yet, the authorities have no clue who could have perpetrated such a vicious and sadistic massacre, they say it is a fast-moving investigation and that an arrest would follow swiftly. When attending the scene, Constable Fortitude vomited profusely and said, 'Bloody hell, it looks like half a dozen ogres have exploded.'

One can only speculate as to how this gory tapestry came about. We'll have pictures in the next issue once they've been drawn.

Cross went back to the shelf to get the next edition.

"Just a couple of points if I may," said Stitches. "Firstly, I think they could have solved the case in about three and a half seconds if they'd bothered to find out what Count Jocular had been up to that night, and secondly, and in direct contradiction to my firstly rendering it pretty much redundant, no one *would* have thought of that because Skullenia's policing record is on a par with anything that's absolute rubbish."

"I see what you're getting at," said Ollie, "but only up to a point. As bloodthirsty as is he I'm not convinced even Count Jocular would stoop so low as to kill a load of sick people in their beds."

"Is he quite a sympathetic sort of a chap then?" said Deirdre.

"It's not so much that," explained Ollie, taking a moment to choose his words carefully.

Not only was Cross liable to print anything he said, or didn't say for that matter, walls, as is well known, do tend to have ears (and as the result of one unfortunate experiment in Crumble's lab, a nose, half an ear, and two suspiciously round objects in a small, recognisably wrinkly pouch.

No one knows precisely where they came from, least of all Crumble himself, but there is a teensy weensy suspicion they may have once belonged to Frankie 'No nose, half an ear, squeaky voiced' Moppet, but on that, the jury is still out, as is his singing voice, the angle of his spectacles, and the cut of his trousers).

"It's...?" said Cross, notebook open and pen at the ready.

"More to do with the fact he likes a bit of a challenge," said Ollie.

"Oh," said Cross, notebook closed, and pen returned to pocket.

"What he's saying is Jocular likes his food to put up a bit of a fight," said Stitches.

They carried on.

"Found it," said Cross ten minutes later.

He put the paper onto the table, already open to the right page.

Depicted on it were half a dozen artists' renderings showing the scene of the grisly massacre from differing angles and perspectives. There wasn't much more detail print wise, but then how could there be? People had been slaughtered; it was as simple as that.

There were some gaudy and lurid headlines, though, with.

**BED-BATH BECOMES BLOOD-BATH!**
**WHO MOVED THE MORGUE?**
and
**GRISLY PERFORMANCE IN THE THEATRE**
**OF DEATH**

being three of the grimmest.

"Is there any other information there that can help us?" said Ollie.

"Nope," said Stitches.

"There is one thing I've noticed," said Deirdre as she studied the images. "If you look, you'll notice this symbol has been daubed on the walls. It's shown in all of the pictures."

"It's sort of hard to make out properly isn't it?" said Cross. "Is it some kind of a knife?"

"That's not a knife," said Stitches who, despite having eyeballs that were as dry as sun baked prunes, had reasonably good vision. "That's a scalpel."

"So it is. Do you suppose it means anything?" said Cross.

"Nothing I can think of," said Deirdre, pushing the paper to one side. She'd had quite enough of staring at its gory content for one day. "Apart from knowing that surgeons use them. Maybe it's a clue of some sort."

"Or perhaps it's a calling card," said Ollie.

"What do you mean?" said Cross.

"Oh, you know. When someone commits multiple murders, they like to leave something behind linking them to the deed. Or it may be they arrange the body in a certain fashion, or leave it in a specific surrounding, something like that. Serial killers are notorious for it. Obviously, they don't want to get caught, I mean, who would, but their egos won't allow anyone else to take the credit for what they've done. That's why the police always hold back on giving out all the information about a murder, especially if it's linked to others. They always keep some details to themselves to weed out the hoax calls."

"I see what you mean," said Deirdre. "It's like an artist signing his paintings."

"Exactly," said Ollie. "Only more anonymous. If he didn't sign it people would still be able to tell who it was by the brush strokes, or how the composition was put together."

"So, we're looking for a mad painter who was in hospital and decided to swap his brush for a scalpel the size of a machete? Shouldn't be too hard to find," said Stitches.

(Despite the zombie's scepticism, Ollie had actually made a very good point. The bloody and brutal history of mass, and in particular, serial, and or, multiple killings is littered with examples of what he was alluding to.

In 1654 BC, Phartenofften, a malodorous Egyptian task master who'd attracted more flies than there's bricks in the pyramids, went on a blood drenched rampage during the course of which he slaughtered one hundred and eighteen slaves, four chickens, a selection of small rodents, and an elderly donkey that had stopped for rest. Sadly, for him, though, his joy was short lived, and he was captured almost straight away. What with those being the early days of such murderous larks, he hadn't quite fully grasped how vitally important the concept of anonymity was to a burgeoning psychopathic killer. Instead of leaving behind something subtle and mysterious, he had carved 'Phartenofften woz 'ere,' into his last victim.

By 127AD, the idea of leaving a calling card had become quite the norm, and, as is the case with these inveterate show-offs, the more outlandish said token the better.

Osric the Undecided, for instance, a low-ranking British nobleman of no discernible merit, developed the messy and very unsociable habit of dispatching Roman dignitaries. His particular signature was to paint the big toenails of his victims' bright green and leave a freshly made loaf of bread shoved up their private place.

Obviously, he had to kill them first, which he achieved by slitting their throats and tearing out their hearts. It was no good trying to bake a crusty manchet if the victim was still wriggling.

Anyway, although suspected of the nefarious deeds, he was never caught and got away with his crimes for years until finally, on his death bed, he gleefully confessed to the murder of nearly six dozen Romans.

Unfortunately for Osric, however, he wasn't quite as stricken with the lurgies as he'd first suspected, and after a good night's sleep and a spot of breakfast he was up and about and feeling much better. Quite naturally word spread quickly about the naughty noble and his ill-timed admission, and by that afternoon the list of people wanting to torture him had gotten so large, the participants had to take it in turns, and the entire spectacle more or less turned into a competition.

Osric ended his days crucified upside down by his buttocks and stoned, after which he was boiled in honey, giving a serious telling off, then chopped up into bite sized chunks and fed to the local consul's pet cat, Softimus Fluffimus.

One of the most ostentatious of the life ending lunatics has to have been one Griswald Estuary, a nutter who terrorised London in the 1880's with his murder/makeover spree.

Once a successful clown, he'd been relieved of his harlequin duties when it was discovered he'd been fraternising with a suspiciously fake bearded lady, one Edward Loquacious Tripod.

A bit miffed, Griswald's subsequent, and quite frankly, childish rampage left forty-two people dead, each sporting a squeaky red nose, a pair of big floppy shoes, and hair that went up at the side when a little string was pulled.

Never caught, Griswald bypassed being punished by the authorities, but the case was finally solved after he hanged himself underneath Putney Bridge.

In a final zany act, he'd hung himself with his braces instead of a rope, so rather than a broken neck, the coroner determined that poor old

Griswald had succumbed to one hundred and seventy two blows to the head, a fact the investigators, and the crowd that had gathered upon hearing a series of increasingly squishy thwacks, found wonderfully hilarious, a state of affairs which would have pleased the deceased clown no end, to be honest.

And was it guilt that forced his hand? Remorse? Nope.

He'd decided to end it all after he found out the government were going to put a tax on oversized trousers, honking horns, custard pies, flowers that sprayed water, and bow ties that twirled round.

As is common, he was found next to a suicide note, a tidily written and poignant missive that contained his confession, although it took a while to decipher because it had been written on shiny paper, torn into thousands of little pieces, and placed into a bucket labelled 'WATER.'

The only other item at the scene had been his carriage, but that wasn't any use because it fell to pieces when a constable tried to open the door).

"So, what now?" said Stitches.

"I suggest we go and have a chat with Mrs. Ladle if she's still about," said Ollie. "Maybe she'll have an idea or two."

"Then what?" said Cross.

"The hospital," said Deirdre.

* * *

Mrs. Ladle, that delightful doyen of all things witchy, burny, and cigarettey in Skullenia, was blissfully unaware of what had been going on in town, the arrival of Deirdre, or much of anything else outside her front door for that matter.

At present she was languishing in self-imposed exile in her kitchen, a place she'd been for the last eighteen hours up to her elbows in muck, filth, grease, cogs, oil, squidgy bits of something the colour of poo, and a bag of sugar the size of a triple duvet.

Surprisingly, or maybe not so surprisingly if you know anything about her at all, she wasn't putting an engine back together, working on a particularly difficult spell, or creating an elaborate torture device designed to get to grips with the softer parts of the male anatomy. No, she was attempting to formulate a recipe for a new kind of biscuit, one she could take along to the next coven meeting of The Witches Institute to dazzle her friends with.

(Actually, given her dubious past record with all things culinary, and seeing as I already mentioned torture devices, pretty much anything she dragged kicking and screaming from her oven could be used to inflict severe pain, to wit, one bite of her kidney and strawberry flan is more than enough to ensure suffering on a scale not seen since Pol Pot told the Khmer Rouge to have a bit of a tidy up).

Anyway, back to the WI.

For a little while now, each member of the club had taken along some sort of fancy delicacy for everyone else to try, after which they have a discussion how yummy they are, share the recipes, and determine which ones can be sold to raise vital funds, monies used to pay for things such as guest speakers, monthly activity workshops, occasional days out, and other institutional sundries such as fresh potions, a new broom stand because Mrs. Nutella forgot to turn her broom off again, some reinforced crockery, and a new pair of boxing gloves (things could get quite heated when it came time to elect a new Chairwitch).

Mrs. Ladle had come up with the idea for the bake sale about six months previously, and despite a few teething problems (several elderly patrons losing items of dental furniture to Mrs. Flanks' Lime Cement Meringue, and Mrs. Cloggs belting Mrs. Parasol in the mouth with a scone possessing the texture and density of a cannonball) it was proving to be something of a hit (although it wasn't for the quality of the cakes, of course. Don't get me wrong, word had spread quickly, but that was actually thanks to Mr. Doom who'd attended the first sale whilst suffering the worst bout of constipation since that endured by Henry VIII after he'd consumed seventeen swan burgers, two sugared badgers, and a stoat on a stick.

Looking rather like a bloated hot air balloon and feeling as if he'd swallowed a bollard, Mr. Doom had partaken of Mrs. Ladle's Prune and Candied Wallop Surprise, the consequence of which saw him rushing to the lavatory four seconds later where he preceded to perform his finest impression of an exploding chocolate soufflé.

Naturally, he'd been more than pleased with the unexpected result, and when he got out of surgery, he made sure he told everyone he knew).

Anyway, all that silliness aside, it was going fine and dandy, which was just as well because the calendar the ladies had put together hadn't sold very well at all.

Obviously, and more importantly, thankfully, the witches hadn't gone the whole hog and completely divested themselves of their garments because that would have been rather unseemly for persons of their maturity, as well as being more upsetting than a train crash involving puppies, fluffy bunnies, and kittens (although what a kitten is doing driving a train is anyone's guess).

Lord alone knew what Mrs. Bonk was thinking when she'd suggested the idea because let's face it, the sight of a group of witches posing seductively for the camera wasn't ever going to be the most appealing of visions. In fact, it was so disturbing at least three people had gone insane when they'd seen it, one had gone mad just hearing about it, whilst another unfortunate viewer had been so terribly upset he'd gone intentionally blind (well, I say that. He'd closed his eyes and run away).

Now, no doubt most of you will have guessed why it sold as well as a Braille steering wheel and caused more ocular outrage than walking in on your parents because there's funny noises coming from their bedroom, but for those of you that haven't, it was because most of the ladies have figures resembling hessian bin bags stuffed full of rice pudding that have been left out in the midday sun to set, kicked down a flight of stairs, and then haphazardly punched by a troop of outraged baboons.

The others just look like outraged baboons.

Thankfully though, they'd kept the publication classy and had the photos taken whilst demurely raising their skirts, lowering their socks (thank goodness it wasn't the other way around), and showing a bit of ankle.

In spite of these sartorial restraints, though, it still wasn't entirely pleasant, and the whole spectacle looked more like a health booklet detailing the signs and symptoms of a dozen or so highly infectious, terminally malignant, and catastrophically disfiguring diseases rather than a bit of fun for charity.

And so, with the calendars consigned to the bin (and quite a few farmers' fields) the age of the bake sale had come to pass.

So, where were we? Ah yes, Mrs. Ladle.

As is increasingly (un)usual these days, Mrs. Ladle wasn't following any particular recipe because she likes to give her culinary imagination its head. She also believes that those cheffy types who publish books about how to cook, and how great they are at cooking because they've published a book about how to cook, are nothing more than a bunch of overpaid fat-heads who think they're clever simply because they know which end of a spatula to use and can manage to make a raspberry blancmange that doesn't require locking up.

To that end, her current method of production, one that had proved moderately successful in the past, involves chucking a load of ingredients into a bowl, mixing them up a bit, removing the lumps, stringy bits, and any remaining signs of life, slamming it into an oven hotter than the surface of the sun, and hoping for the best.

So far it was going alright, but there was one little fly in the ointment (as well as a moth in the batter, a woodlouse in the cream, and a rather confused wasp in the anchovy jam).

To describe the enterprise as going alright, was only alright if going alright was defined as not going very right at all and going all wrong.

Two batches had exploded on contact with anything warmer than an ice cube, one had been so incredibly and irretrievably dense that the biscuits had gone supernova and had to be broken up into minute particles before they could be removed from the oven, and another had disappeared completely leaving nothing but a terrible stench and ten blackened outlines. It was as if the biscuity corpses had been removed from the baking tray for post-mortems, and chalk outlines had been drawn round them whilst the crime was investigated.

She stepped back from the unadulterated carnage that was her work surface (it looked like Omaha Beach on D-Day), wiped her hands on one of her more robust tea towels, and sat at the kitchen table.

"Time for a break I think," she said to herself.

She lit a cigarette (unhealthy I know, but at least it would freshen the air), took a long, satisfying drag and blew the smoke out, where it got lost in the smog that her culinary efforts had produced.

'Come on, Evelyn,' she thought to herself. 'What can I do to impress the ladies?'

The cause of her consternation was that one of the rules of the venerable organisation that is The Witches Institute, a rule proving to be more and more of a pain in the dumplings as time went on, is that all baked goods brought to meetings have to be cooked without recourse to magic of any sort, so every cake, biscuit, flan, sponge, or any other sugary whatsitsface that counts as a baked item has to be made in the traditional manner.

As with all cooking, though, the ingredients nestling within said yummies are a matter of individual choice (or in the case of Mrs. Womp's spleen and apricot fool, need referring to the authorities as evidence), but as long as they've been mixed by hand and cooked in an oven, they're deemed acceptable, although that word can't always be ascribed to how they look and taste.

At the last meeting, for instance, the delicacies on offer included a Victoria Sponge (incorporating some carefully selected body parts from a lady by the same name, a Mrs. Hilary Sponge, formerly a resident of Scapularis), Pungent Chocolate Fingers (not too much explanation needed for this one other than think about what happens when you buy cheap toilet paper. If you don't understand that reference then you're either very lucky, extremely privileged, or live in a forest), and Groaning Artichoke Wafers (so named because they have a tendency to upset ones tummy to the point they're best eaten within a stiff legged, clenched cheek walk of the nearest water closet.

Ironically, it was after sampling one of these bowel busters that the recipe for Pungent Chocolate Fingers was invented. Well, discovered anyway).

So, in short, what Mrs. Ladle was after was something spectacular. Something headline grabbing. Something monumental and something with a bit of a WOW! factor. She didn't particularly mind, or care, what sort of a WOW! it was, of course, but then she wasn't a fussy woman. Naturally, she'd be delighted with a, 'WOW! that tastes wonderful, Evelyn,' but would quite happily settle for a, 'WOW! that tas…is that cement? Excuse me I need to go to the hospital.'

She stubbed her cigarette out and was about to scrape the oven clean, again, when she noticed a greeny/blue glow above it.

"Oh no," she said out loud. "What have I done this time?"

*"You've done nothing. I was just admiring your handiwork."*

"Really?"

Being a lady of experience, Mrs. Ladle wasn't overly concerned that a voice was coming from the strange light. Over the years her dabbling in the kitchen had produced some quite startling results, ranging from the melting of a portion of her roof, to the total obliteration of a fishing village in seventeenth century, southern Finland. Therefore, it was of no great surprise to her when the nebulous fallout, apt because that's exactly what it looked like, engaged her in a conversation.

*"Yes indeed,"* continued the voice, *"and if you have a moment, I can show you a way to make the best biscuits in the world. And if you'll pardon the pun, they'll be so tasty, the ladies at the Institute will be literally green with envy."*

"Go on then," said Mrs. Ladle, relaxing and lighting up another Black Lung Superking. "Thrill me."

*"Excellent. Challenge accepted."*

The greeny/blue mist expanded and began to take up more of the kitchen, and as its snaking tendrils got closer, Mrs. Ladle had the sudden realisation that maybe not all was as it should be.

Suddenly, she started to feel sleepy and noticed that her eyelids were beginning to droop. Then her whole body went limp as if she'd been overcome by a very abrupt and overwhelming tiredness.

Her head nodded as if the muscles in her neck no longer had any power left in them, and as she began to succumb to the irresistible pull of unconsciousness, her hands fell to her sides and her lit cigarette slipped from her fingers and fell to the floor.

"W-what's going o-o-n?" she mumbled as she hovered on the brink of torpidity.

*"Nothing for you to concern yourself about. Just sit back and enjoy the ride."*

By now she was totally immersed in the greeny/blue glow and struggling to stay alert. She felt as if she'd been drugged, but just as she was about to pass out completely...

"Mrs. Ladle. MRS. LADLE!"

She felt her shoulders being tightly gripped and vaguely realised that she was being shaken, and not gently either.

"Wake up. Come one now."

A sudden and heart stopping, frigid cold snapped her back to the land of the living. As she blinked and the kitchen came back into focus, she felt rivulets of freezing water running down her face.

"Ollie. Stitches. What on earth are you doing here? Is that you, Excalibur? And who's that? And what the bloody hell is going on? And why are you in my kitchen? Not that you're not welcome of course. And how did you get in? Ollie. Stitches. What on earth are you doing here? Is that you Excalibur? And who's…bugger me my head hurts."

Stitches handed her a glass of something brown and claggy.

"What's that?" she asked.

"I poured it out of a bottle from your medicine shelf," said the zombie. "It's labelled Magellan's Fortifier. You look like you could do with a liquid kick in the pants and it sounded just right."

She chugged it down like a seasoned pro, shook her head, and breathed out heavily.

"Right. Who's going to fill me in?" she asked.

Ollie stepped up, introduce Deirdre, and proceeded to acquaint the witch with events thus far.

"So, we decided to come and see you," said Ollie.

"The trip over here was weird as well," said Stitches. "The town's virtually empty. The only people we saw were Hector and Noggin. Not that Hector strictly counts as people of course. Anyway, neither of them was behaving normally, although it's hard to tell to be honest. Again, I'm referring to Hector primarily."

"And you seem to think it's got something to do with the hospital. Or a presence within it to be more precise?" said Mrs. Ladle.

"Yes, I do," said Deirdre. "I saw it in the vision Ollie mentioned."

"Interesting."

"We didn't try you first because I know it's your cooking night, but we very quickly ran out of options and people to ask, so in the end we came over," said Ollie. "But when we knocked and there was no answer, knowing you were definitely in made me think that what's happened to everyone else had happened to you."

"Aw, you were worried about me. That's nice, dear," Mrs. Ladle said.

"Well, we do have to look after the elderly and in-firm in the community," said Stitches. "It's our civic duty, after all."

"Oh, is it? So, tell me, which one of those categories do you think I fall under then? Or is it both?" she said, her eyes turning to granite. "I'd be really interested to know."

Stitches, realising that his mouth had gotten him into trouble again, sensibly allowed Ollie to continue, which was a wise move because he'd look rather silly with his feet and his ears swapped over.

"Anyway, we were about to leave when Cross noticed the smoke coming from underneath your front door," Ollie continued.

(Although the sight of Mrs. Ladle's home awash with smoke isn't an entirely unusual occurrence as you can well imagine.

Her house is the scene of more accidental conflagrations than a meeting of The Parkinson's Disease Society Fire Eating Troop. Mind you, they're safer to watch than their darts team. The last time they played a match they'd used a board the size of a barn door and still managed to injure seven people standing behind them. They're not hopeless at everything, though. Very good at mixing cocktails).

"And so, thinking that all was not well," said Cross, "I applied my not inconsiderable tread to your portal of ingress."

"Come again," said the witch.

"I kicked your door in."

"Oh, right."

"And when we got in, we saw the strangest thing," continued Ollie. "You were slumped back in the chair, more or less out for the count, and had dropped a cigarette on the floor, no doubt the source of the smoke that Cross saw."

"Well, that does happen from time to time to be honest," said Mrs. Ladle. "Especially after a coven outing. They can get pretty wild don't you know."

"I'm sure they can," said Stitches, "but I suspect those don't routinely end up with you almost disappearing in a cloud of greeny/blue smoke."

Mrs. Ladle thought about that for a moment. Although she had got up to some rather ridiculous shenanigans in the past, she couldn't recall a time when she'd been attacked by a wandering, and talkative, fluffy cloud. (She'd obviously forgotten about the time she made a batch of marshmallow that decided to flee the shackles of its oppressor and strike out on its own. It left her a very polite note, though).

"Fair enough. And thank you. All of you," she said.

"Righto, gang. Let's get going, shall we?" said Ollie.

"Where are you off to?" said Mrs. Ladle.

"To the hospital, of course," said Ollie. "All indications seem to pointing that way."

"Okey doke. I think I'll come with you if that's alright."

"Are you sure that's wise?" said Stitches. "You do look a little frazzled."

"I'll be fine," she said, getting to her feet and straightening out her skirts. "The day I can't go out on a jolly to kick someone's butt because of a fainting spell, you can put one between my eyes and call the undertaker."

The five of them left for the hospital and whatever waited therein.

* * *

Egon, it has to be said, was not in a very good mood.

At present, he was slap bang in the middle of a major clean-up operation, one that was taking much longer, and proving to be far messier than expected.

What really galled him, however, was that he didn't really think he should be doing it in the first place.

(Technically, he should be thus engaged, of course, as it's his job, but hey, we all like to have a moan about certain tasks from time to time don't we. Mrs. Author does, although, in my defence, I did have a ferociously squitty tummy, and had no idea she even had a favourite towel).

Egon was currently in sub dungeon number three, or as it's more commonly known, the resting place of The Children Of The Night.

(It's even more commonly known as the 'stinky poo poo pit', but the staff keep that to themselves on account of them all having ever such a tiny aversion to being hung, drawn, quartered, and eighthed, a particularly nasty form of treatment very similar to the traditional method of execution except, as is obvious from the name, the corpse is split into eight sloppy, twitching chunks rather than four.

According to Jocular it makes them easier to dispose of, but they all knew that was a massive fib and he just got a kick out of chopping things up.

He'd have moved onto sixteenths if Egon hadn't hidden his fruit knife).

It's essentially their lair, their sanctuary if you will, and when the little cherubs from hell aren't out and about in the forest doing whatever it is that insane, flesh hungry, murdering beasts get up to when they're not sitting about licking themselves clean, it serves as their place of rest, a safe haven in which to recharge and recuperate.

And the reason for Egon's ire?

In between bouts of licking and napping, The Children Of The Night, despite being overly muscular, fully grown, and extremely heavily equipped threshing machines, like to have a play with what they've brought in, the result of which is a bit of an untidy room.

The problem is, The Children Of The Night possess all the tidying up skills of a sixteen year old boy, and the bathroom habits of a new born hippopotamus, one that's ingested way too much food, fallen foul to an aggressive case of dysentery, and succumbed to the urge to produce as much bodily waste and room based disarray as is feasibly possible in a very short space of time.

And hippopotami are just as bad.

The room frequently looks as if it's been invaded by three quarters of a ton of mutant frankfurters that have run out of energy, collapsed to the hay strewn floor, and been scattered haphazardly about the place, making it look as if a cess pit the size of an Olympic swimming pool has exploded.

Also, due to their meat rich diet, the stench in the room was frequently almost beyond description, being a cloying and tangible amalgam of poo, rotten meat, poo, decaying cabbages, poo, unwashed intimate areas, poo, putrefying organic matter, poo, poo, and more poo.

In fact, such was the severe, radioactive-like toxicity of the atmosphere, several servants had actually died due to inhaling the gas accumulated within the room, and it was also wise, as a couple of others had found out to their cost, never to enter the place with a naked flame.

(It's interesting to note that the bathroom issue is yet another aspect of supernatural life not mentioned in literature or alluded to in any film or TV programme. You see, whenever there's a plethora of carnivorous beasties, many with the cerebral aptitude of a verruca, living in the one space, and who all view a toilet as something grassy underfoot and containing trees, there's going to be a problem with waste. In other words, effluent that makes sulphuric acid look like spring water builds up rather quickly and the resultant fallout is, more often than not, quite staggering in its potency. That's the reason why you won't ever have seen Bela Lugosi or Christopher Lee popping down to the dungeons with a dustpan and brush, a bag of cat litter, and an air freshener. Not only would it have been demeaning to them as actors, it would have taken some of the otherworldly and evil allure from that most venerable of fictional characters, Count Dracula. As well as the shine off their shoes, the white off their fangs, and at least an eyebrow or three).

And don't be thinking that Egon's a whinging shirker, a bit precious about nasty niffs, or squeamish about waste related matters, either, because he isn't, so there.

Over the many, many years that Egon had been in Jocular's service, he'd grown accustomed to all manner of incidents and situations, you see, ranging from the state of the Master's clothes after a night out frolicking, to seeing exactly what the minions got up to on their days off, but clearing up after the Count's assorted pets was a task he had never gotten used to. And never would.

He'd tried delegating the onerous job a few times, of course, but that had only resulted in the aforementioned deaths and him needing to clear the drains again.

Also, such was the length of the undertaking, those that had given cleaning the room a go and survived for long enough had used the room as, would you believe it, a toilet, figuring if it was good enough for The Children Of The Night then it was good enough for them, proving once and for all there's creatures in the world, supernatural or otherwise, that really are as thick as shit.

And so here he was once again, dressed in a biohazard suit that would have seen him alright on Mercury, wearing a helmet and visor slightly smaller than the Statue of Liberty's head, and halfway through filling up his ninth bag of semi solid nastiness.

A bead of sweat rolled down his forehead making it itch, and he noticed that in spite of the protective clothing, half a dozen soiled fragments of sawdust had infiltrated his helmet and stuck to the inside of his face plate.

Not wanting to breathe in the befouled motes and succumb to a chest infection that'd leave him sounding like an asthmatic bison and coughing up cancer coloured custard for a couple of weeks, he decided it was time for a well-deserved break.

He stepped from the room into the clearer and more fragrant air of the corridor (although that wasn't saying an awful lot as far as improvements went seeing as the whole castle in general smelled like a land fill site in down-town Delhi), and poured himself a refreshing cup of tea from his flask.

As he drank, he wondered if he should gently and politely remind his Lordship that his beloved furry companions were a bunch of barely broken in savages who wouldn't know what a toilet was if they sat on one.

He doubted if it was worth the effort, though. As far as Jocular was concerned the horrible things could do no wrong and he probably wouldn't have a word said against them.

It hadn't always been like this, though.

When Egon had started working for the Dark Lord there hadn't been any Children Of The Night, Toddlers Of The Evening, Infants Of The Noon, or any other creatures of an arbitrary time of day.

(They did toy with, 'The Babies Of That Bit Of The Day, The One That Usually Falls Between Breakfast And Lunch, Commonly Known As Elevenses, But Often Referred To As Brunch', but by the time the sign for their door was finished the babies in question were shaving, having kids of their own, and flat refusing to sleep in a cot because their feet stuck out the end).

There were flunkys, servants, thralls, and scream-ing victims galore, of course, but that had been it.

Then, one fateful night, after returning home from a particularly rambunctious excursion to a lo-cal village (an evening of debauched gluttony and mass bloody slaughter bordering on a Crusades type genocide) in a rather jolly mood (in the throes of a blood high equivalent to a normal person smok-ing a three foot long joint the width of a rolling pin), Jocular had decided to go out for a walk before retiring, and it was whilst he was mid promenade somewhere in the castle grounds that he'd stumbled across a cute, fluffy bundle of fluffy cuteness that appeared to have sustained some kind of injury (as I said, he stumbled across it). One of its legs was bro-ken, it had several older wounds, and not a few cuts and scratches, some of which had become infected.

Now, on any normal day, the good Count Jocular was about as sympathetic to the plight of his fellow beings as a fifteenth century torturer who'd got up late, had a row with Mrs. Torturer, and dropped his best thumbscrews in horse manure on his way into work was to a very naughty heretic, but something about the little creature had melted the blackened and malignant lump of flesh that was his heart, and he'd taken it indoors and vowed to look after it until it was recovered.

Over the following few weeks Jocular had tended to its every need and delighted in seeing it get better day by day. And bigger. Much bigger. And bigger still to the point that it wouldn't fit through the back door anymore, and was eating the equivalent of four or five flunky's a day (or four or five actual flunky's if there wasn't anything else suitable to hand like a coach party of old people, a flock of sheep, or a displaced rhino).

One morning, Egon, who by that time had already come to the inevitable conclusion it would be easier for Count Jocular to get a sun tan than it would be to castle train such an overgrown and fragrant beast, entered sub dungeon number three to find that the furry, marauding degenerate had brought home several of his 'friends.' And not only that. Much to his disdain, they were all fast asleep, had clearly been engaged in some sort of sordid nonsense, and covered in so much filth that Egon couldn't immediately determine how many of them there actually were.

Seeing such disregard and, it had to be said, disrespect for the interior of the castle, this had become only the second ever incident to cause Egon such upset that his rage very quickly reached supernova like incandescence, a state of temper that meant he was duty bound, nay, compelled to speak out (the other time had been when he'd stumbled somewhat over the leg of a chair that a domestic flunky hadn't placed correctly, ruffled a curtain a tiny bit as he'd grabbed a hold of it to stay upright, and knocked a painting slightly askew with a stray elbow. Oh, and fallen through the open window hiding behind the curtain and plummeted four stories to the cobbled yard below. As you can imagine that had gotten him all riled up good and proper, so he'd made his position very clear and in no uncertain terms. Once he'd got out of traction that is. It's all very well being annoyed, but you can't really make your position clear when you're stuck in a full body-cast, being fed through a straw, and having to wee into a little bag).

And so, with a confidence bolstered by outright anger, Egon had marched determinedly to his Master's quarters and demanded that he come at once and deal with the havoc his atrocious pet and its reeking companions had wrought downstairs, lest he take up arms and slaughter them in cold blood, all hail the revolution and death to the tyrannical overlords who impose their infantile wills on those whom they think are less worthy.

(Or, to put it another way, he'd sidled up to his Master with such obsequiousness that his chin was nearly on the floor, and muttered humbly, "Would you mind coming with me to sub dungeon number three, please, oh Avenging Demon To The House Of The Splayed Buttocks, and Baleful Slayer Of Those Who Fold The Corner Of A Page Down Rather Than Use A Bookmark. There seems to be a bit of an issue with regards to the housekeeping."

Quite rightly, Egon had decided to put his incandescence on the back burner. He was angry, not stupid).

On arrival at the door to the festering, fly ridden, pseudo prehistoric swamp the room had become, Egon had warned Jocular that what he was about to see would likely cause him a terrible anguish he'd not felt since Throppington's, 'Carpet Makers of Distinction to the Well Heeled', had delivered unto him a rug that was just the wrong shade of puce to match his new curtains. Oh, how he'd gnashed and wailed, my, how he'd howled with lament, cried with anguish, wallowed in despair, moaned forlornly, and indulged in various other types of over the top histrionics, which, quite frankly, were a bit pathetic and more suited to an upper class, Victorian lady who'd seen a gentleman in his undergarments, rather than a vampire lord who had to return a length of fabric to the shop because it was the wrong colour.

Ooh, he can be such a big baby sometimes that Jocular.

Oh, and just in case you're wondering, he did return it, and got a replacement. He killed the shopkeeper of course, but then, as they say, the customer is always right. And going to murder you if he's a vampire lord.

Right, where were we. Ah, yes. Outside sub dungeon number three, long ago.

After pausing for dramatic effect, and to take a deep breath because he knew how badly it stank, Egon threw open the door.

He hadn't said anything to the count, figuring the wretched tableau would speak for itself, and what with a picture being able to speak a thousand words and all that pretentious, over hyped twaddle, he figured the job had pretty much been done the moment he'd opened the door.

Seeing the unholy mess, Jocular had put his hands to his face and gazed stony faced at the spectacle in wide eyed wonderment, a reaction that'd pleased Egon no end, and confirmed that he wasn't being overly precious about a second rate dungeon.

In fact, the little servant had got all excited, already relishing the prospect of wielding the electric cattle prod that he'd had on charge for just such an occasion.

His hopes, however, had been dashed like a raft against jagged rocks when Jocular had exclaimed, "Ah, look at ze little fellows. Are zey not sveet?"

And that, as they say, was that.

From that day onward, The Children Of The Night, every stinking, snarling, sneering one of them, had taken up permanent residence at the castle, and short of having them all killed and disposed of, there was nothing that Egon could do about it.

He drained his cup and went back into the dungeon looking at the remaining piles of excrement with scorn.

*"You don't have to do this you know,"* said a voice coming from a particularly large and oddly greeny/blue heap.

"Who's that?" said Egon, picking up his shovel in preparation to deliver a firm thwack to anything that came at him.

The lack of an immediate answer got the hackles up on the back of his knees and set his latent servant sense to tingling.

(Like spider sense, it lets him know when things are about to happen, acting like a biological warning system apprising him of imminent danger. Or it should have done if it worked properly.

Unlike the unerring, near sentience of an arachnid's talent for spotting trouble, Egon's is just a bit less reliable, and doesn't seem to have much of an understanding as to what constitutes a perilous situation. On the one hand it might warn him that he's going to run out of sugar at some point the next day, but then be noticeably absent just as he's about to be molested by some hairy, snarling cryptid that intends to use him as a chew toy.

So now, whenever his alarm bells start ringing, he just assumes the worst, which is why he was fully expecting to be waylaid, accosted, mauled, subject to some other type of disabling physical injury, or come to the horrifying realisation that he'd forget to empty the bins tomorrow, and his favourite mug was about to be pooed in again).

In spite of this unerring talent for spotting trouble he wasn't a nervous sort of chap, though. I mean, how could he be when you consider where he plies his trade and with whom he shares the castle but hearing the strange voice and seeing the oddly glowing pile of straw put him a bit on edge.

"But why?" I hear you ask. "He must see all sorts of horrible things every day."

And you'd be right (as well as being a bit picky for wanting to know the ins and outs of a witch's cauldron), but the horrors aren't always what you might expect.

As you'll have surmised, there's lots of creatures of every description living in the castle, and whilst many of them could get lost in a chair, are scared of the toilet, and think cutlery far too complicated to use, there's quite a few that are consummate practical jokers and see Egon as an easy target.

Many's the time he's been the victim of some childish prank or another and ended up having to be released from somewhere, put out before burning to death, cut down from something, let out of somewhere else, scrubbed clean of some type of muck, or rushed into emergency surgery.

Needless to say, he was wary.

*"I am no one and everyone,"* the voice continued as the greeny/blue haze began to spread, *"but to you, Egon, I am salvation from this den of filth and putrefaction."*

Egon was slightly worried now and wishing if this was a prank, it would end tout de suite so he could toddle off to the infirmary and get his wounds looked at before the pub shut.

As tangible as the concern for his somatic welfare was, though, the threat of impending physical torment was beginning to become overshadowed by the fleeting, yet potently nagging apprehension he was experiencing with regards to the owner of the voice.

Outside of himself and his Lord and Master, there was nary another being in the castle capable of putting such a coherent sentence together. The only one that came close was Smirnoff the thrall, who had once pointed at the moon, concentrated really hard, and said, "Biccit."

Compared to this veritable genius of god like stature, the rest were an uneducated and barely evolved bunch of misfiring synapses that relied on grunts, shrieks, howls, rudimentary weapons, chucking things about, and extreme violence to get their point across.

It was like a state school in Lewisham only with more fur.

"No one can give me salvation from that which I endure but Count Jocular, and I endure it gladly and wholeheartedly. Whatever you are, you have no sway over me. Only the Dark Lord himself, my one true Master has that privilege. Now bugger off or I'll get the exorcist in, and I'd imagine you know how much that hurts," said Egon, robustly.

The greeny/blue entity receded into the pile of dirty straw until it was no more.

"Egon one, weird thingamabob nil," he said, making a mental note to have the lower floors checked for interlopers.

As be bent over, the shovel was ripped from his grasp by a tremendous force and sent spinning toward the ceiling. There, it hovered for a few seconds before flying towards him and crashing down onto his skull.

Egon was unconscious before he hit the floor, which was just as well because his landing was soft, warm, and extremely unpleasant.

* * *

"I think I can honestly say, without a shadow of a doubt, fear of contradiction, and with absolutely no pun intended, that I have never, ever seen Skullenia this dead before. Has there been a mass exodus we haven't been told about?" said Stitches.

Upon leaving Mrs. Ladle's and venturing outside they'd been struck by the lack of noise in the area.

On any normal night Skullenia sounded like an overpopulated jungle in which the apex predators were making a concerted effort to kill as many inhabitants of the lower food chain as possible. Tonight though, it was as peaceful as a deserted church. Not only would you be able to hear a pin drop, you'd detect the clatter of the dust motes it'd kicked up returning to earth as well.

"I can actually hear birds," said Ollie. "That is definitely a first for me round here."

"I must concur. It is a most disconcerting scene," said Cross, who was so amazed he hadn't even got his notebook out.

"Come on," said Mrs. Ladle, already recovered from her encounter with the greeny/blue. "If Deirdre's right about the hospital being the focus of all this nonsense, I suggest we get there as soon as possible. Who knows how much time we have left."?

"I don't think it's much," said Deirdre. "The voices have been disappearing at an alarming rate. They're only coming sporadically now at best."

They made their way past Grendle's shop, which looked forgotten and forlorn, to the outskirts of town where the road divided into two separate paths. The one to the right would take them to Jocular's castle, whilst the second would lead them west alongside the cemetery, past the abandoned mill, and onto the hospital.

(Apologies for having an abandoned mill in the story, but it's a requirement of every tale involving anything remotely horror related. It's an industry standard you see, and one of many you'll no doubt recognise once they're pointed out. So... spoiler alert...

If the scene is vaguely Gothic there'll always be an attractive Edwardian lady with a mystifying shortness of breath, a readiness to faint at any given moment, and a large, heaving bosom. Resting about three inches under her chin it constantly looks as if it's trying break free from the confines of her corset and make a bid for freedom.

If someone gets separated from their group whilst on a camping trip, within seventeen seconds they'll become hopelessly lost in the woods, won't be heard shouting even though their friends can't possibly be any more than fifty yards away, then get very messily slaughtered in a rather inventive manner usually involving things such as rusty hunting paraphernalia, sharp kitchen implements, ancient gardening equipment, or a combination all three.

If someone is being chased by a monster, it doesn't matter how slowly said creature moves, or how quickly the person sprints, there will never be more than ten feet between them, and the monster will always get them in the end.

If a murderer is hiding in a building, be it a haunted block of flats, a dilapidated mental home, or a tree house with a creaky floor, one of the victims will always locate, and think it's a good idea, to hide in an air conditioning system, a wardrobe, or a bathroom with a flimsy door. Obviously, they get killed.

If, after a chase, the intended victim finds a car, it doesn't matter if it's brand new, has a full-service history, is full of fuel, and has the keys in it, it won't start.

Perhaps the most recognisable vignette happens about a third of the way into the story and involves a lone female. She's probably called Dana or Cindy, is usually blond, very pretty, wearing a t-shirt that would have been too small for her when she was seven, and a pair of denim shorts that have less material in them than a potato.

After wandering into the darkest and most forbidding part of the forest because she's desperate for a wee and couldn't possibly do it while her friends are within a mile and a half of her, she ends up being spied upon by a rapacious slasher who's decided the best way to get to know her is to rearrange her intestines and chop off her head.

Then, thanks to the killer grunting with drooling lust because he's seen a bit of thigh, our heroine realises she's being watched and takes flight, instantly coming to the obvious conclusion that running further away from her friends and deeper into the trees is her best option.

And so, she spends the next couple of terrifying minutes attempting to flee from the stabby item wielding lunatic who's now fallen in love with her and developed separation anxiety.

And is her escape from certain death easy? Of course not. It's hindered by whipping branches, muddy hollows, and a ridiculous number of obstacles that she's forced to vault over. There's fallen tree trunks, of which there are many, abandoned vehicles that have no business being in a forest in the first place, and at least one lethal trap she's just happened to notice, despite the chances of her running that way in the first place being astronomical.

Despite all this, however, she continues to bravely forge ahead, and even though she's traversing through rapidly encroaching darkness, fighting her heightened panic, and trying to ignore the slobbering grunts of the inbred maniac behind her, she manages to stay looking absolutely gorgeous, so much so that all the male viewers now don't really care whether she lives or dies, as all they want to see is the outline of her chest because, would you believe it, it's started raining.

Anyway, in spite of all these problems, she's really doing rather well by this point, and even though she's lost a shoe, can't see anything because of the monsoon, and is now so far from civilisation that she might as well be in North Wales, she sees a light in the distance that can only mean her salvation is at hand. Sadly though, and with a soul crushing inevitability, just as she's about to reach the aforementioned safe haven, she trips over a leaf, twists an ankle, and can't get up. Yup, you've got it. It's game over.

You'll also notice these incidents only ever happen to people under the age of twenty-one.

Now it could be argued that persons in this particular demographic are unfairly portrayed in these tales, in that they all come across as hopeless wastes of space that deserve everything they get, and to be fair, based upon their maturity, current skill sets, lack of relevant life experience, preoccupation with alcohol and the opposite sex, and their general outlook on life, this might very well be the case, but I think it's got more to do with the fact that they're all really annoying and when we're watching we want them to die in as horrific a way as possible.

What's also bizarre, especially in light of the ineptness of the assembled gaggle of youngsters, is that the ravening murderer/slasher/cannibal/savage/resident of The Isle of Sheppey ((supremely, dedicated individuals who've spent years honing their slicing and dicing techniques to the point they could take out a Roman legion single handed)), suddenly have trouble killing off the members of the group, to wit; even though they're invariably wearing dungarees covered in blood and viscera from a recent killing spree shown at the beginning of the film, have a selection heads nailed to the walls of their cabin, a chair made of bones and covered in skin, and a kitchen that looks like a medieval torture chamber, all of a sudden they behave as if they couldn't handle a plastic spoon, and act as if they'd have trouble subduing a truculent kitten.

And speaking of the group, usually numbering five, let's meet them shall we.

Firstly, there's a couple who head straight into their tent as soon as it's up who then proceed to indulge in some very noisy and very obvious naughties.

Then there's the boy and girl who've fancied each other for ages, a timid pair who haven't had the confidence to get together yet. About two thirds of the way through the film, though, safe in the knowledge they won't be caught because their friends are off canoodling, exploring, or getting their hair cut with a Viking war hammer, they finally take the plunge and have a kiss and a cuddle, aww, a romantic clinch that only lasts about three and a half seconds because Mr. Party Pooper has decided that's the optimum time to chop her in half, and hang him upside down and gut with a lawnmower or something.

Lastly, and very leastly, there's a lone, geeky male who's a computer whizz, always seems to be ill, and has no real idea what a girl is.

And don't think they've arrived unprepared, either. They'll be packing a whole raft of items guaranteed to ensure their safety, because one of them has read 'How Not To Survive A Slasher Movie' by Bear Grylls.

There's mobile phones that can make a call to Jupiter on a normal day that now can't get a signal three feet into the woods, batteries for said communication devices that run out of charge as soon as a button is pressed, several pairs of inappropriate footwear that make flip flops look sturdy, enough alcohol to fill a lake, copious amounts of drugs, and a guitar.

There, I think that's everything. And I'm sorry if I've ruined the slasher movie genre for you, but it was about time it was killed off).

As the group traversed the perimeter of the cemetery Deirdre stopped. She rested her hands against the ancient stone wall and stared into the darkness. Her eyes darted from one moss covered tombstone to another.

"This isn't right," she said.

"Is everything okay?" said Ollie, moving closer. He put a comforting hand on her shoulder.

"It's so quiet," she continued. "I'm hardly getting anything from the other side. There's a vague trace but it's so indistinct it's hard to make anything out. It's like someone's shouting at me from a great distance."

"Oh, I wouldn't go worrying yourself about it too much, dear. Take advantage of the peace and quiet, I say. You'll miss it when it's gone," said Mrs. Ladle, who could put a positive spin on anything.

If you lost both of your legs, she would extol the virtues of being able to have a nice, long sit down whilst saving money on shoes.

Suffering from a crippling stomach bug that has you squirting out of both ends like a mad hosepipe? She'll congratulate you on how much weight you've lost.

And if you live in Scotland, she'll cheerily point out that…no, scratch that one. No one could possibly find the silver lining on that particular storm cloud.

Probably because it's raining.

Let's face it, released by Somali pirates after two years in captivity you'd think twice about returning home north of the border.

Maybe even thrice.

As they left the graveyard behind and continued along the lane they were again struck by the lack of sound and activity. There wasn't even much going on above them, apart from the odd bird or bat flapping about and taking advantage of the clear, predator free skies.

As they passed the abandoned mill two things became apparent. One, a faint greeny/blue light was coming into view in the distance. It seemed to be emanating from a dome of ethereal luminescence hovering above where they knew the hospital to be.

The other thing was Deirdre.

She'd started to feel…something.

What it was she didn't know, but it was becoming increasingly tangible and more pervasive, seeming to flow into her very core unbidden. And yet, as mysterious as it was, she knew it wasn't altogether friendly. It was as if a malevolent presence were probing the ramparts of her psychic defences and laying siege to her inner being, and she somehow knew that it wouldn't cease its onslaught until it had conquered her spirit and destroyed her essence entirely.

And then she recognised the psychic signature of the renegade invader. It was the same sinister interloper that had come upon her in the café.

She immediately marshalled her mental forces in an attempt to keep it at bay. If she let her guard down…

"I hope that's a circus," said Stitches as they continued onwards. "Although, I've got a horrible feeling it isn't. Not one I'd want to see anyway."

Deirdre stopped again, once more prompting concern for her well-being. She rubbed her temples gently.

"Whatever's in there it knows we're coming, and it isn't very happy that I'm a part of the group. I'll be fine, but from here on in we need to watch every step. We're all in terrible danger," she said.

"That's good advice," said Ollie, wishing the situation didn't warrant such advice, no matter how appropriate that advice may be. "Let's take extra care and watch out for each other."

"Ollie," said Mrs. Ladle. "Look."

Ollie suddenly regretted his words and wished he hadn't tempted fate so blatantly.

Excalibur Cross was gone.

*  *  *

The town of Skullenia, home to supernatural beings of any and every description, and those that defied any sort of description completely, had become that which it was by default when awash with ectoplasmic goo, shimmering, ethereal bed sheets, and ghastly, flesh hungry fiends that would make James Herbert turn in his grave. It had turned into a ghost town in every sense, devoid of any and all life be it human or otherwise.

Mrs. Strudel's café, always a hive of activity as ravenous creatures tucked into their meals, stood empty and silent. Chairs and tables had been knocked over, condiments littered the floor, and nary the subtle chime of cup against saucer, nor the gentle rap of fork against plate sounded within. From the recesses of the industrial furnace that was the kitchen, there came only silence, its once bright and fiery heart now extinguished, leaving it a frigid and impotent void. The shop door, always open to welcome the next hungry customer, swung gently on its hinges, lightly buffeted by a sallow, whispering breeze that traversed the forsaken streets.

The Bolt and Jugular was a muted shell. Bereft of drinkers it was dejected and eerie, a dispirited tomb of shadows that reflected the despair of the town itself. Glasses had been left on the counter, rudely abandoned by those who were present no more, the remaining liquid within them rapidly warming, a previously unheard-of occurrence in the tavern. Behind the bar a tap trickled, the wooden handle above it left half open as if whoever had been using it had suddenly gone. Within the pipes, those creaking, metallic arteries that never stopped pumping, intoxicating, gilded fluid fought to continue its journey. Almost an entity in itself, it was the lifeblood sustaining the building, an embodiment of the vigour and activity that went on when it was in its pomp, It's energy was waning, though, and as time marched irrevocably onwards, the already debilitated stream from the icy spout became slower and slower, growing ever more lethargic in momentum as it struggled to achieve release, until drop by tear shaped drop, it finally ceased and flowed no more. A large puddle of alcohol spread across the aged floorboards and seeped through the planks into the cellar below where it formed grotesque and fantastical, yet vaguely recognisable shapes in the pallid dust, elusive signifiers that perhaps represented the ghosts of patrons long since gone. Outside, the weather-beaten sign rocked back and forth above the door like a tattooed pendulum, but no one was present to see it, or to hear the amorphous creak as its centuries old hinges rocked in their mountings.

The only appreciable sound that perforated the all-pervading silence to any degree was the steady and ever flowing gush of the fountain. Its timeless and rhythmic incantation was usually drowned out amidst the heady cacophony that was the thriving village centre, but now its gently muted, cadenced refrain had become the only indication that any sort of life, however multifarious in its diversity, had once existed here. It was all that remained, a liquid, scarlet heart beating its rhythm to deserted streets and abandoned buildings.

Skullenia, secluded vestige of the paranormal, welcoming oasis to the dispossessed, the misunderstood, the outcast, and the unwanted, and sanctuary to those that would normally be shunned and mocked by everyday society, was dying.

* * *

Count Jocular, much like Egon before him, was annoyed.

Incredibly annoyed.

Actually, and to give his current frame of mind its proper status, he was way beyond incredibly annoyed, becoming increasingly annoyed by the nanosecond, and quickly reaching a level of rage that usually resulted in prolonged, painful, and extremely messy deaths, cruelty and maiming to anything that drew breath, and sitting in his favourite chair and having a bit of a sulk whilst flicking rolled up pieces of paper into a bin.

So, why was the all-powerful vampire lord having a bit of a paddy? No takers? Okay then. Let's go back about half an hour and find out shall we. That'll be fun.

Suddenly overcome with a creative gush that simply wouldn't relent, and thus finding himself bursting with an all-consuming and gloriously inventive enthusiasm that needed release right then, he'd immediately gotten to work in his study, the room that his flash of inspiration had guided him to.

Twenty minutes later he was flying (ha ha), but it was whilst in the throes of making some fancifully ornamental adjustments to a flamboyant pelmet, that his efforts had been rudely brought to a screeching halt by a pair of very awkward curtains, a dapper duo of decorative drapes he'd thought would look rather smashing at the main window, and seeing as how he'd grown tired of the current pair, now had seemed as good a time as any to get the job done (well, seeing as this has already happened it was then rather than now, but who says that? Or is it said? Oh, who cares? It's all made up anyway. Or is it?).

Anyhoo, seeing as the old ones had been hanging there for quite a while (about a week and a half) he'd decided it was high time for a change, not to mention the fact they'd become overtly drab in hue and somewhat dreary of aspect, subtle, yet important environmental factors that rather spoiled the reposeful ambience he so very much craved whilst resting in his private chamber.

The other reason (or main one, depending on your point of view, sense of smell, and the results of your latest psychological evaluation) was that they were made of human skin, and seeing as that made them a bit tricky to keep moist, they'd dried out somewhat making them rather difficult to draw, although ironically, they now had no problems whatsoever in drawing a voracious, noisy, and increasingly large population of flies.

And so, he'd decided to replace the offending drapery with a rather fancy pair of puce, velvet curtains, but due to an oversight re folding, the left one had developed a crease the size of a small canyon that was proving more difficult to shift than an overweight pachyderm that'd been glued to the floor.

"Vot to do?" he'd said to himself as he'd stared at the crease, a negligible blip that, to his eyes, was now the size of the San Andreas Fault.

What he needed, of course, was Egon to deal with the problem, or more specifically, whatever it was that he did with some steam, a foldaway length of wood, and a flat piece of iron that goes hiss.

(As you've no doubt surmised over the course of these tales, and if you haven't, go and read the previous five you Philistine, Count Jocular isn't particularly au fait with domestic undertakings which is why he only ever refers to them by description. Those that he's aware of at any rate.

As far as he's concerned clothes wash themselves then hang themselves up to dry, furniture is self-dusting, and the remains of the guest that he'd entertained in one of the dungeons were cleared away by the innards fairy.

Still, why should a high-ranking vampire Lord be bothered with such menial tasks when he has his own stuff to be getting on with? That's what servants are for after all. Sounds like a teenager with fangs doesn't it).

And so, with his curtains in a bit of a tizz, Jocular had sent out his psychic calling card instructing the little dwarf to attend to him at once.

(Apologies for blatantly using 'little dwarf,' a phrase as redundant as a Thomas Cook employee, but it sounds so right and gives such added emphasis, it just has to go in).

Much to Jocular's chagrin though, Egon had failed to avail himself of his master's presence at once, which was a very very peculiar occurrence, indeed (although, how something *not* happening qualifies as an occurrence is anybody's guess).

Normally, the little fellow arrived quicker than a reporter to a royal birth, and such was his alacrity and devotion to his master's beck and call he sometimes managed to attend before Jocular had finished the actual summoning.

Trying not to let it to bother him too much (he'd still been concerned about his curtains, of course, but don't overly concern yourselves. He'd pull himself together eventually. Ouch. That hurt. I better call the bad joke police. That one needs locking up) he'd cast his mental net once more, but again his servant hadn't arrived.

Therefore, for the first time in all the hundreds of years that Egon had been indentured, Jocular had had to go looking for him, and as one can imagine, this didn't sit very well with his Lordship, and the longer the search went on, the more uncomfortable that subconscious recliner became.

As he'd stormed from room to room, corridor to corridor, and floor to Egon free floor, something else had become apparent to the darkest of the dark lords.

The castle was strangely, confusingly, and deafeningly quiet.

The normal flurry of panicked activity, stampeding hustle, scattergun bustle, and general 'let's look busy the boss is coming' that occurred whenever he went a wandering, was absent, as were the creatures that caused said rumpus.

As a rule the dozens of flunky's that he kept in service out of the goodness of the pitiless, black void where his heart should have been, were scattered around the interior of the castle like strategically placed and well intentioned boils, ready and willing to burst into action and execute his bidding at a moment's notice.

But not tonight, though.

In the hour or so that he'd been traipsing up and down like an annoyed vampire he'd only come across one other creature, that being a fourth level domestic by the name of Meat.

(The Count hadn't recalled seeing him before, but he was no doubt nothing of importance in the grand scheme of things, and probably served in a menial capacity as a purely functional dogsbody whose sole responsibility was something like...oh hell, Jocular didn't know, and to be honest, he didn't really care).

When Jocular had enquired of the little half-wit re the whereabouts of Egon, everybody else, what was going on in general, and did he know anything about getting the creases out of curtains, Meat had looked up at him with a vacant, far away gaze, eaten something that he'd dug out of the deepest recesses of his nasal cavity, and said, "Blep!"

(As is clear, Meat wasn't the brightest of souls by any biological standard, resting idly on the evolutionary scale somewhere between a daffodil and a Bourbon biscuit).

I'm not going to go into too much detail of what took place in the twenty seven seconds following Meat's highly articulate and informative outburst, suffice to say that once he was found, Egon would need two buckets, a wallpaper scraper, a change of clothes, and a gallon of industrial strength stain-remover that worked on ceilings as well as carpets.

And walls, paintings, woodwork, silverware, soft furnishings, jewellery, furniture, and the lawn outside.

(Now, I know it may seem like I'm stating the overtly manifest making reference to a lawn outside, but you have to remember this is His Royal Fussiness, Count Jocular, decorator extraordinaire we're talking about, so you won't be surprised to learn that dotted about the castle there's at least half a dozen rooms that are awash with various horticultural displays of one sort or another, including, as alluded to, several grassy bits.

One of them, a small annex off torture chamber number six, actually has a fully grown tree residing within.

"Pourquoi?" I hear you opine.

Well, Jocular, the little scamp, likes to hang people from time to time, you see, especially at Christmas as it gives the place a happy, festive atmosphere.

Well, it does as long as you're not the poor bugger having your neck stretched, obviously. That sort of thing does tend to put a bit of a damper on things for the person concerned.

It's hard to keep your paper hat on with your head at a forty-five-degree angle).

Finally coming to the conclusion that, for the very first time since taking up his position, he was totally and utterly alone, Jocular decided there was only one thing left to do. He'd have to flipping well go out and flipping well find out what the flipping hell was going on with his flipping servants and flipping well give them a flipping good telling off that they'd flipping well remember for a flipping long time.

"First sings first sough," he said to himself, turning tails and heading back to his study. "I'll just haff anuzzer crack at zose flipping curtains.

\* \* \*

"I don't like this," said Stitches.

"And which bit in particular would that be then?" said Ollie. "The deathly quiet? The eerie stillness? The desolate emptiness? The destitute, barren wasteland our town has become, or the disappearance of Cross?"

"The fact they changed Opal Fruits to Starburst. It's all those things, you clown," said the zombie, "but Cross going missing is definitely the front runner. He was here one second and gone the next. Literally."

"Still, if nothing else, it's given us a real idea of the malevolent power we're up against," said Mrs. Ladle.

"Please don't use words and phrases like that, Mrs. Ladle. Especially, 'malevolent'. I know things are horribly bad, but you saying things like that makes me think they're…horribly badder, especially when they're probably an awful lot worse," said Stitches in a vain effort to completely disregard his ever-growing fear. "Hey. Maybe there's a massive game of hide and seek going on, and everyone from town is in a cupboard waiting for us to find them."

"Although that's a lovely thought, dear, I do happen to agree with Mrs. Ladle," said Deirdre. "And whilst I don't want to be the one to spread doom and gloom, I'm sure when Cross was taken, I sensed a hint of satisfaction in the ether. Whatever this is it was very pleased with itself."

"Marvellous," said Stitches.

"As well as malevolent," Deirdre added.

Suddenly, as if by silent agreement, all conversation between them came to a halt. They were about to make their way passed the abandoned mill and it wasn't the sort of place that you wanted to be advertising your proximity to.

It was a strange and fantastical place, an otherworldly realm housing an undetermined number of loathsome, cantankerous, and downright odious spirits who'd been sealed within to keep them from wreaking havoc in the outside world.

However, like the Sirens of legend who'd tried to lure sailors onto the rocks, these abhorrent entities took every opportunity to do the same to any unwary traveller who neared their ghostly abode.

Only without the rocks.

The mill is made of bricks.

And a bit of wood.

Insidious, yet enticing whispers emanated from within the very bosom of its crumbling walls and mouldy beams, hushed musings uttered by silver tongued phantoms who dripped poisoned honey into the ears of those passing nearby in the hope of beckoning them inside by promising them everything their hearts could possibly desire.

Then, once ensnared, the pact was broken leaving the poor victim facing certain death and nothing to look forward to but an eternity drifting amongst the ranks of those unblessed and outcast wastrels.

It was for this very reason that a post box had been placed about ten yards from the outskirts of the grounds. It was the type often seen outside American houses, but no letters or parcels were left inside this one. It was home to a tin box that contained dozens of packets of ear plugs, and it was here that they paused to ready themselves.

(For the more observant reader, and there's always a few, wondering why there isn't another path to the hospital, or why Ollie and Mrs. Ladle didn't just fly there, let me explain. The mill is surrounded by a thick, dense wood of indeterminate age that's kept in place to minimise how many access points there are to the area. It covers a massive amount of ground that stretches all the way to the hospital itself.

As to the flying issue, the magic sealing the assorted spectres in the mill is of such potency that it drains the efficacy of any other spells cast in its vicinity. And as for Ollie, who when in bat mode is rather small, the ear plugs would have been bigger than his head rendering them as useful as a radiator in an igloo. There, that's that particular bone of contention sorted out. If there's any other plot issues you can get stuffed).

Ollie retrieved four packets of the yellow ear defenders and handed them out.

They opened them carefully because even the rustling of the packaging could be enough to rouse the denizens of the mill.

Deirdre bounced the plugs up and down on the palm of her hand as if she was unsure what to do with them.

"You need to put those in, dear," Mrs. Ladle said as she dislodged a clod of wax from her right ear that could have been used as a hockey puck. It hit the ground and flattened an unsuspecting ant. "They won't work there."

"I'm afraid they're not going to work at all," said Deirdre forlornly.

"What do you mean?" said Ollie, shoving his in.

"I hear voices in my head, don't I? I could stuff my ears with reinforced concrete, and it wouldn't make a blind bit of difference. The spirits would still get through. Is it a major problem?"

"Kind of," said Stitches, being careful with his own plugs. If he pushed too hard there was every chance he'd cave in the side of his head or end up scrabbling around in a stand of Bubo Nettles looking for an eye.

(The Bubo Nettle is a horrible plant kept in place to deter people from sneaking through the undergrowth in the general vicinity of the mill. It works as well, but, if you're unlucky enough, and by unlucky I mean completely stupid, to get stung by one of its knitting needle like barbs, lumps the size of oranges will very soon appear in the affected area, lumps that very quickly become quivering bags of congealing, foul smelling pus, that make the unfortunate, and by unfortunate I mean completely stupid, sufferer to resemble the Elephant Man with a hefty dose of the mumps.

Or if you got it really bad, Anne Widdicombe).

"Once those voices get inside your head that's your lot," Stitches continued. "The only person that's ever gotten away with it is Flug, but that's only because there isn't enough going on inside his head to be influenced, so he was fine."

"Didn't he use the ear plugs then?" said Mrs. Ladle.

"Kind of," said Ollie. "He ate them. He thought they were sweets. Sixteen times we had to stop him coming back for more. We had to tie him up in the end."

"It is going to pose a problem, though," said the witch, removing an even bigger lump of wax from her left ear. This one would have been suitable for a shot putter. "She won't get more than a few feet before she's taken over."

"Would putting her to sleep help at all?" said Ollie.

"Maybe, but we haven't got time for you to tell her about your coaster collection, mate," said Stitches.

One of the things Ollie hates more than anything else is mug, cup, or glass rings left on surfaces. It doesn't matter if it's a table, the arm of a chair; his desk, or even the floor, there has to be something underneath it (the vessel that is, not the floor).

To that end he has a collection of coasters. He keeps them close to hand wherever someone might avail themselves of a drink and will reprimand anyone who doesn't adhere to his strict policy of coaster usage.

If anyone puts any sort of drink container on an unprotected surface he usually reacts as if someone's used his coffin as a toilet, after which he'll administer a stern lecture about the horrors of 'the ring', and proffer the offending heathen an appropriate, circular protection device.

Except for Count Jocular, of course, who could have seared a golden, smoking halo onto the surface of Ollie's finest, vintage table with a cup of molten lava without so much as a word being uttered. Which is fair enough. I made him up and *I'm* terrified of him.

The trouble was, Ollie's desire to protect his furniture had transcended necessity and turned into something of a hobby, and over a relatively short space of time he'd already amassed a collection close to seven hundred.

Unlike most other collectors, though, and as you've no doubt already gathered from the thrust of the previous remarks, Ollie likes to make use of his acquired items, which is fair enough if you think about it, logically. I mean, who wants a load of old tat gathering dust in a cupboard that's only ever going to see the light of day once you've died and The Antiques Roadshow comes to town.

Anyway, as nice as that is, the coasters being put to their intended use did pose a problem of sorts, in that he didn't want his treasured possessions marked by any spilled liquids.

'Mmm', I hear you mutter. 'That's a tricky one'.

And yes. Yes, it is.

Or at least it was.

To combat this potentially disastrous occurrence, Ollie has also accumulated an equal number of bog standard coasters, ones that can be placed on top of the collectables so they can be protected from the drinking vessel they're protecting the surface of whatever they're on from.

Problem solved?

Oh no.

Far from this solution making things all hunky-dory, another issue arose when he realised he could never guarantee the cleanliness of the actual surface itself.

Ronnie is notoriously sloppy with his tea, you see, and Flug can spill just about anything and is more than capable of producing a post-apocalyptic type disaster zone armed with a teaspoon, a boiled egg, and half a dozen buttered soldiers (which he now knows to be made of bread, after Stitches noticed that the silly buggers toy box was slowly being depleted of items from his 'Third Foot and Mouth Regiment, Battle Action Set'.

The clues were there for all to see. There were traces of butter on the lid of the toy box, Flug was complaining of a bad stomach, there was bit of a stench following him around, and he'd suffered a whopping vomiting fit that produced three cannons, six light infantry divisions, four and a half armoured vehicles, an assortment of tanks, and a squadron of cavalry on horseback).

So, how was he going to protect the underside of his fancy coasters? Oh, yes, you've got it.

Ollie, whom the others had concluded was getting a tad obsessed re all things drinky and coastery, was now well prepared for any drink related eventuality having purchased *another* seven hundred run of the mill coasters to go underneath the special ones to protect them from the potentially dirty surface they were supposed to be protecting from any spills from the drinks.

Blimey, what a palaver. Tell you what, it's all a bit mad this collecting lark isn't it. And even though it's an activity I don't have any interest in, and certainly don't understand, it does bring up one interesting question. Why on earth do people collect things in the first place? Surely, it's pointless to have a couple of thousand of the same type of object dotted around all over the place and taking up so much room that there's nowhere to sit.

Unless it's chairs of course.

Or books come to that, of which no collection would be complete without this one or the previous five).

"Very amusing," said Ollie, deciding not to let Stitches know that whilst inserting an ear plug, the zombie had moved his bottom jaw out of line. It looked like the lower portion of his face had been removed and replaced by its Hall of Mirrors reflection. "What I meant was…"

"Cast a spell on her and put her to sleep?" said Mrs. Ladle, pre-empting Ollie's suggestion.

"Yup," said the half vampire.

"Can't use magic here remember?" said the witch.

"Oh yeah. Damn."

"Knock me out," said Deirdre.

"But Mrs. Ladle just said that won't work," said Stitches.

"I meant the old-fashioned way," said Deirdre, pointing to her chin.

"We couldn't possibly do that," said Ollie, who was frankly horrified at the very idea of punching a lady, let alone one as mature and refined as Deirdre. "No gentleman would ever stoop so low as to use violence against…"

In a flash, Mrs. Ladle's clenched fist shot out like a bony piston and caught Deirdre a blow on the jaw that a heavyweight boxer would have been proud of, one more than capable of turning his opponent into a dribbling, stuttering, and ever so confused member of the vegetable family. I think most of them work for the local council.

The crack of knuckles against bone echoed up and down the lane as Deirdre hit the dirt like a pole-axed pensioner punched by a second, partly potty pensioner.

Ollie and Stitches stared incredulously at the witch, neither of them able to come up with a suitable comment to express their opinion about what they'd just witnessed.

But Mrs. Ladle, ever the paragon of patience and understanding, deftly, diplomatically, and subtly explained her thought processes in as gentle a way as possible so as to allay their alarm at the shocking event.

"Oh, stop looking at me like that you pair of girls. It was her idea. Now wipe the goggle-eyed expression off your dozy faces and help me get her up. She won't be out for long. I didn't hit her that hard."

Both secretly vowing never to anger the mad old bat to the point that a hard punch would come pile driving its way towards them, they got Deirdre up off the ground.

"I wasn't expecting that," said Stitches.

"Me either," said Mrs. Ladle as she threw the comatose clairvoyant over her shoulder.

Despite Deirdre's grandmotherly bulk, she was surprisingly light, so the witch had no problems whatsoever hoisting her up.

(Not that she had any choice in the matter. Stitches couldn't do it because any weight on his frame heavier than a frock-coat would cause him to collapse quicker than a bridge constructed entirely of bread, and Ollie said he would've been delighted to help, but sadly couldn't, on account of having a bit of a bad back. Apparently, he'd slept awkwardly in his coffin).

As they made their way past the mill, earplugs securely in place, and unconscious medium hoisted atop Mrs. Ladle's sturdy shoulder, their collective gazes were drawn towards the dilapidated structure.

It was swathed in dark, green ivy that covered the decaying bricks like a second skin, but through it the windows could still be seen, many of them smashed, staring outwards like misted, cataract shrouded eyes.

And it was via these fractured portals that they could see the figures within. They were ghostly in aspect yet seemed curiously solid, pale but resonating wastrels that looked to be festooned in opaque, pallidly shimmering jewels, vague and barely coruscant reminders of an otherworldly power that was on the wane.

Open mouthed and staring, the tremulous features of the spectres were wasted and distant. And yet, however pathetic in their soulless angst, they presented as a forlornly hopeful army of undead impenitence, one whose sole purpose was the entrapment of others.

If not for the ear plugs, their plaintive wails of longing would burrow into the subconscious and plant their desperate seed, a beseeching prayer that would very quickly persuade the unlucky or the ignorant that their only recourse was to join the baleful legions of the forgotten and the disavowed.

It was either that or the most flagrant case of attention seeking since a second rate carpenter, fed up with the nine to five routine and sick to death of getting splinters, decided to tell everyone that God was his dad and that he was the light, the truth, and the way.

(No wonder they nailed him up, which was ironic bearing in mind his obvious aversion to wood-based injuries and a hard day's work hanging around hammers and nails. It just goes to show that being a bit of a show-off can make you very unpopular, so if you keep the bragging to a minimum, everything should be alright.

Now, back to this stunning and, quite frankly, un-surpassed work of literary genius).

As they finally passed the threshold and the spec-tral figures receded back into their pallid domain, Mrs. Ladle lowered Deirdre to the ground, removed her earplugs, and lit herself a cigarette.

"Just need to jump start the old lungs," she said, once the other two were divested of their own ear defenders. She patted her chest and breathed out heavily. "Now I know why I love my broomstick so much. This walking lark is definitely bad for my health." She coughed and launched a gelatinous, slightly brown missile into the undergrowth. A siz-zle and a puff of steam issued forth from where it landed. Nothing would grow there for quite a few years.

"Do the honours would you, Ollie love," she said, pointing at the recumbent medium. "I don't want to get smoke in her face."

"As opposed to a bunch of fives which is perfectly acceptable, I suppose?" said Stitches, proffering a fist that couldn't have made a dent in a candy floss cloud.

"Oh, stop moaning. It got us here didn't it? Honestly, you two. I've never known such squeamish undeads."

Ollie had kneeled down and was now gently shaking Deirdre by the shoulders. As she started to come round, he noticed a burgeoning bruise on her chin. He and Stitches helped her to her feet and held her steady as she dusted herself down.

"That was quite a blow," she said, rubbing her jaw. "I didn't even see it coming. Who was it?"

"That would be me, my love," said Mrs. Ladle.

"Oh right," she responded, somewhat surprised.

"It wouldn't have been Ollie or me, of course" explained Stitches. "We're far too polite. You know, chivalry, the gentlemen's code and all that."

"Plus, they both hit like pantomime dames," said Mrs. Ladle, who, as well as having bones like granite and a left hook that could take down a mammoth, had boxed for her nursery school.

"At least I don't look like one," said Stitches, cheekily winking at the witch. "And Ollie is far too feminine."

"Oi! Don't tie me to the tracks in front of the verbal train wreck that's heading your way," protested

Ollie, eyeing Mrs. Ladle's fist. "And I am not in any way feminine. It's the twenty first century for goodness sake. Lots of chaps use moistu…which has nothing to do with anything. So. What's next?"

"Well, we can't be too far away," said Deirdre. "I'm feeling quite a pull now. There's a powerful force in there."

They crested a small rise in the path, passed through a secluded copse, and exited into a large clearing. Thirty yards ahead was a set of steel gates beyond which lay their destination.

"Well, here goes nothing," said Ollie.

"Indeed. And we'll talk about the moisturiser later," said Stitches, smirking.

Cautiously, they approached.

* * *

With purpose and intent, the presence within the hospital gathered those it had summoned to attend to it. And attend they did, destitute wraiths, lurching with a graceless motility, devoid of all intelligence, and lacking any semblance of awareness or sentience as they came. They trudged through the silent halls unaware of their purpose but drawn inexorably onwards by an impetus beyond their com-prehension.

The time was close at hand, a moment long waited for, one that would redeem the conjurer from banishment in purgatory, a wretched and tawdry existence in which it had languished these many years.

"Hello," it whispered, almost tenderly. "It's almost time."

\* \* \*

"My goodness," said Stitches, staring up at the massive looming building looming over them like a massive looming building. "And there was me thinking the abandoned mill was the creepiest place round here. I certainly don't now." He pointed at the hospital. "Because that takes the biscuit. And the rest of the packet, the wrapper, the barrel you put them in, and all the crumbs left over."

"I know," said Ollie as a tweak of fear nudged his muscles. His survival instinct was kicking in and his body was getting ready for action (although, that's not as grandiose as it's sounds. Rather than the traditional 'fight or flight' response, Ollie's was more 'hide or run away like buggery and then hide').

"There's a definite vibe coming off it and not a good one either. It's usually a bustling, jolly sort of a place, but not anymore."

(Which is essentially true because Dr. Zoltan very much believes in laughter being the best medicine, which is just as well because when it comes to real medicine he's a bit rubbish, and about as much use as a homophobic zebra trying to infiltrate and covertly disrupt a gay pride march for giraffes.

And on that very topic, and if I may be permitted the indulgence for just a moment, I'd like to take issue with the phrase, 'laughter being the best medicine'.

Now, clearly I'm speaking as a layman, and as such possess about as much medical knowledge as a packet of Flumps, but I have to say that I'm not entirely convinced about the effectiveness of that particular form of treatment if I'm being brutally honest.

When a friend of mine got run over by a van leaving him with several broken bones, a ruptured spleen, and in need of a skin graft the size of Luxembourg, I'm not completely sure his recovery would have been as rapid if the doctor had dispensed with things such as heavy sedation, emergency surgery, and resetting his fractures, and told him a hilarious knock knock joke instead.

Mind you, the way the NHS is going these days that could very well be the future of medicine. I can see it all now. You make an appointment with your GP when you're feeling a bit poo, get diagnosed with, let's face it it's going to be a virus, it always is, but instead of being given a prescription for some antibiotics, you get an Amazon voucher. "There you go, Mr. Sick Person. Take fifteen minutes of Micky Flanagan three times a day for a fortnight and you'll be right as rain.")

Once they'd passed through the gates and were walking along the path to the main door, they saw not a single light in the place. The only source of illumination was the ever present greeny/blue glow that seemed to be growing in intensity by the minute.

"So, what's the plan then, boys?" said Mrs. Ladle.

Ollie looked at Stitches.

Stitches looked at Ollie.

Then Ollie and Stitches looked at Mrs. Ladle.

Mrs. Ladle then returned the favour and looked right back at the both of them, only with double the intensity which, seeing as there was two of them, made it four times as much.

"You don't have a plan at all do you?" she said with a certain hint of inescapable inevitability and a knowing lilt to her tone, one that is naturally inherent when the asker of a question knows precisely what the answer to the question being asked is going to be almost before they've asked the question that they've asked.

Ollie looked at Stitches.

Stitches looked at...oh, you know the rest.

"Um. No. If I'm honest we don't really have a plan, no," said Ollie.

"We sort of just came here," said Stitches, making that the worst ever excuse for an action since AD43 when Emperor Claudius claimed that he'd invaded Great Britain because he fancied a Cornish pasty.

"Well isn't that marvellous," said Mrs. Ladle, shaking her head and taking on the demeanour of a moderately outraged mountain gorilla. "Absolutely useless the pair of you." She turned to their travelling companion. "Deirdre, seeing as The Brothers Dim here aren't proving to be much help, it looks like it's down to us to come up with a plan. So, what do you think we should do, dear?"

"I think it's quite straight forward," said the medium. "The problem is in there and we're out here, so the only way we're going to get to the bottom of it is to head on in and face whatever it is."

"Sounds good to me," said the witch.

"I could have said that," mumbled a disgruntled Ollie.

The path to the hospital wasn't overly long but it was swathed in such tacit darkness that, despite the presence of the eerie greeny/blue light, it seemed further away than it actually was.

As they got closer to the shadowed building the air cooled to such a frigid intensity it caused their skin to tighten and glisten as if they'd suddenly strayed into the midst of an early morning frost.

As they edged ever closer their footsteps echoed back to them through the becalmed atmosphere. The sound was almost mocking in tone as if the very structure itself were tapping out a warning to the approaching interlopers to stay away.

(In fact, the combination of their steps *did* spell out a message, although it wasn't anything in particular. It went along the lines of either, 'brudhsd 2&^+% mnjdhhdg quac231def', 'fismuth keishdyc 21z octopod', or, 'please come now the trousered otter is stuck to the gentleman's upper left ventricle', which, though absolute nonsense, will at least give all the abstract philosophers and conceptual thinkers out there the chance to start banging on again about a rather large amount of time, some curiously well behaved monkeys, a few robust typewriters, and the complete works of Shakespeare.

Now, clearly that conjecture is a topic of furious debate, and one completely dependent on whether you believe in the idea of an infinite universe or not, but as far as I'm concerned, if that scenario was ever likely to arise, the only things those primates would ever be likely to produce is either an infinite amount of drivel, or an Eastenders script, which is wonderfully ironic because that rubbish seems to go on forever.

On a side note, Eastenders is massively popular with philosophers and theoretical physicists because they haven't got time to watch it).

About six feet from the wooden door they passed from the confines of the natural night air and into the clutches of the greeny/blue aura that held the building in its colourful embrace.

The surroundings popped and crackled as they broke through the barrier, but it caused them no harm, well, no apparent harm anyway.

"Goodness me," said Deirdre, waving a hand in front of her face. "That's quite an abrupt temperature change isn't it. If anything, I would have expected it to drop not increase."

Mrs. Ladle undid the topmost button of her outer cardigan in silent agreement. Luckily, she was only wearing seven of them tonight so didn't have to take anything off.

Ollie, obviously, felt the increased heat, but then he is a half vampire, after all, and as such possesses a core temperature just above that of frozen methane, but it was Stitches who was going to have to be ultra-careful. He has little enough moisture in his system at the best of times and to lose anymore would rapidly turn him into a walking sack of rolled oats.

Ollie reached out a tentative hand and rested his fingertips against the door.

"I wonder if it's open," said Stitches.

Ollie wasn't wondering anything of the sort.

He was more...hoping. Hoping...

1. That it wasn't.

2. There wouldn't be another way in, and

3. he'd have no option but to go home, have a cup of tea, hide in his coffin, and chat to his

mum until all this greeny/blue silliness blew over and everything went back to abnormal.

Ollie gave the door a little push.

It swung open.

"It's open," said Stitches.

A few wary glances later, they stepped inside.

"My goodness, this light is so weird," said Mrs. Ladle.

Its ghostly glare appeared to be dark and bright at the same time, and even though it served as the only source of illumination, it still cast enough of a glow to reveal that the entrance hall seemed to be comparatively normal.

(Obviously, there's the palpable creeping dread it instilled in every fibre of their being, the ominous, ethereal figures that seemed to be skulking in the shadows ready to attack them at a moment's notice, and the overriding sense of impending doom that threatened to tear down any semblance of bravado that may have existed within the group, thus causing them all to flee screaming into the night with their nerves in shreds and their minds in tatters, but that's just splitting heads.

Other than those tiny issues everything was tickety boo).

"It's downstairs," said Deirdre. "Whatever it is, it's under the ground. That's where we need to go."

"I didn't know the hospital had a downstairs," said Mrs. Ladle, who'd stayed there twice during her time in Skullenia.

The first time, she'd sustained some rather decent burns when she blew up her kitchen and half the front room trying to boil an egg, and then again a fortnight later when exactly the same thing happened whilst attempting to cook the very same dish.

Stubborn didn't even begin to cover it.

Well it did, but not very much.

Not as much as the egg, anyway.

Undeterred, Deirdre moved further into the building, and whilst not possessed in the traditional sense (i.e. flailing about like an electrocuted octopus, having bodily contortions akin to those of a rabies victim who's had too many blue Smarties, speaking in peculiar tongues that even a drunken Glaswegian couldn't reproduce, and generally making a massive arse of oneself. Or, to give it its medical name, Derekus Acorahitis), it was clear to the others that some external force was drawing her onward.

'At least she seems to be in control of herself, thank goodness', thought Ollie. And he was right to be grateful for that, because if she did succumb to something horrible, they'd be even more clueless than they already were.

Just as Ollie was about to enquire as to where they might find the way down, on account of neither him nor Stitches being overly familiar with the inner architectural workings of the hospital, a dread howl rang out through the hall, and though horrifying in its suddenness they detected traces of sadness and impotence in its tone, a call of anguish and despair wrought from the very depths of a blackened soul. It was as if the creature it came from were crying out for help to be rid of whatever abominable fate had befallen it.

Ollie, Stitches, and Mrs. Ladle looked at each other in sudden and silent agreement. The voice, as strangled and misanthropic as it was, sounded familiar.

"If I didn't know any better," said Stitches, who with that one sentence captured the essence of what each and every one of them was feeling, "I'd say that sounded a lot like Constable Gullett. But that would be silly wouldn't it. Wouldn't it? Please say yes."

Neither Ollie nor Mrs. Ladle voiced an opinion on the matter but they'd both thought exactly the same thing.

As the cries petered out, Deirdre moved onwards once more. She led them passed the empty chairs of the waiting area and into the corridor beyond.

Ollie flicked a light switch but wasn't surprised when it failed to come on, a fact he mentioned to Stitches.

"Did you honestly expect anything else?" said the zombie, trying to make out something, anything in the darkness stretching away in front of them.

"See if this helps," said Mrs. Ladle. She flicked her lighter on, having far more success than Ollie did with the light switch.

As its pale glow fought against the darkness, indistinct figures scattered from its periphery. More substantial than lurking shadows, but still like fleeting apparitions, they fled the moment their presence had been discovered.

"Eyes and ears open everyone," said Deirdre. "I have a feeling we're not going to get through this without encountering some kind of resistance."

"I don't suppose there's much chance of that resistance being a travelling group of underwear models offering free massages, rather than whatever the hell those scary things are, is it?" said Stitches.

No sooner had Stitches finished speaking than a door ahead and to their left burst open, releasing two hunched and cowering figures that approached them with barely disguised evil intent.

"Be gone from this place," said one, its voice dry and rasping. "There's nothing for you here."

"Only death and torment await," said the other.

"I take it the massage deal is a definite no go then?" said Stitches.

As the cursed interlopers moved about, the shuffling of their dragging heels on the frigid, marbled floor echoed throughout the confined space, and their breath came in ragged, bronchial wheezes.

Mrs. Ladle raised her lighter higher, thrusting it forward just a couple more inches in the hope that it would force the begotten creatures to return to the wretched obscurity from whence they had come.

Shocked gasps issued through the gloom as the quivering flames danced over the uninvited entities.

"Oh no!" said Ollie, shock evident in his outburst. "It's Grendle and Mandeep."

And indeed, it was, but they seemed to be pale and flaccid imitations of themselves and not the vibrant beings they once were.

They were caricature like in facet, blemished imposters perhaps striving for the appearance of normality but not quite accomplishing it. It *was* them, and then again it wasn't. Whatever personality that had been there was lost, or perhaps stolen, wrenched from them leaving nothing but barren, empty vessels.

"Grendle..." said Ollie, but he got no further.

Without warning, the two creatures rushed forward, barrelling towards them at high speed, focused, imbecilic freaks that closed the gap in the blink of an eye.

Before any of them knew what was going on, Grendle and Mandeep crashed into them full force, and due to the restrictions of the corridor, all six instantly went down in a tangled heap of confusion. And it was there, amidst the flailing morass of thrashing limbs that Mrs. Ladle dropped her lighter to the floor where it spluttered and went out plunging them all into a darkness that seemed to be infinitely more profound than before.

Shouts, yelps, and the odd curse word punctuated the sounds of the struggle, and then, just as quickly as it had started, it was over, leaving only the sound of heavy breathing.

"Is everyone alright?" said Ollie, slowly getting to his feet. He didn't relax, though, and kept his muscles tensed in case of a further attack. "Deirdre?"

"I'm fine, dear," said the medium, her voice a tad shaky. She was leaning against a wall and trying to get her breath back. She put a hand to her chest and fanned her face with the other. "Nothing a nice cup of tea and a lie down won't cure."

"Ordinarily, I'd say we're in just the right place for that treatment method but given what's just happened I'm not a hundred percent convinced their bedside manner is up to much at the moment. I'm going to write a stiff letter of complaint I can tell you," said Stitches, who'd just finished popping his left wrist back into place.

As far as injuries went, though, it could have been a lot worse, so he counted himself lucky and didn't complain about it. He'd learned from past experience, lots and lots of past experience(s), that intense, physical activity of any kind had the capability to cause him damage of some sort or another, so it was something best avoided.

For example. It was only a few weeks back that he'd attempted to retrieve a book from a shelf in Ollie's office and nearly ended up without his head. Now, obviously it wasn't *that* straightforward, and there were several other factors at play in the little vignette which I'm about to describe, so don't be fooled into thinking that his head has the habit of coming loose and falling off à la willy nilly.

Not that Mr. William Nilly was there at the time. He was off doing things that he hadn't planned in as random and chaotic a manner as was conceivable, because, if nothing else, Willy Nilly is a bit of a silly billy, especially when his willy gets all silly.

On second thoughts, I think it's best we disregard all that silly billy willy nonsense, as Willy Nilly can be a bit sensitive about his name, and the last thing I need is Willy Nilly being a silly billy about silly willy, especially as he and young Silly Willy had a falling out over something daft that Dr. Silly Billy said whilst he, Willy Nilly, and Silly Willy were having a Frilly Chilli at Mrs. Willie's Willy.

Damn, I mean Mrs. Strudel's, don't I? They were at Mrs Strudel's Willy. No, they weren't. It's cafe. I meant to say they were at Mrs. Cafe's Willy having a Willy Strudel. Hang on, that's not it, either. Give me a mo.

Okay.

I think I have it now.

As far as I can recall, it went something like this.

Willy Nilly got all silly sitting in his chair,
Cos Silly Billy told Silly Willy some things that were unfair

'Your chilli he pinched, but that's isn't all,
His middle name is Milly.
And if that isn't bad enough,
His socks are pink and frilly'.

So, Willy Nilly, ire now chilly,
Decided to retort,
So threw piccalilli at Silly old Billy,
And said, 'You listen up, sport'.

'I think you'll find my socks aren't frilly
Nor pink as you have told.
They're green at the top, and white underneath,
And the frills are not frills, that's just mould.

And as for the chilli, I took of it not,
Your story is ever so silly,
But I have to admit, as here I do sit,
That my middle name's certainly Milly'.

A lady then spoke, to our three dining chaps,
She was sitting somewhere just behind.
She was pretty and trim, had a hat with a brim,
And a face that looked ever so kind.

'Excuse me', she said, 'If it's alright with you,
There's a few things I'd quite like to say.
I only came in for a nice cup of tea
And you're flipping well ruining my day.

I heard what you said about pink socks and names,
And something regarding a chilli,
But nobody cares, so please keep it down,
And oh, by the way, my name's Lily.

Contrite were they then, those three grown up men
Known as Silly, and Willy, and Nilly
Fancy them causing such a big fuss,
And upsetting a beauty like Lily.

'Good woman', they cried to the keeper of shop,
Their voices arising so shrilly,
'More food if you please, for ours has gone cold,
And a fresh pot of tea for our Lily'.

Then laugh did all three, and made fun of the fact
That the owner must cook yet more scoff
And such was their glee, that they said, 'Is it free?'
And drew something quite rude on the cloth.

And so Mrs. Strudel, that genial host,
Did approach and was pleasant with charm.
She knew of these types, they came in now and then,
And so were no cause for alarm.

So, she took out her pad, and licked of her pen,
To make of a note, maybe two,
But then put them away, when that Willy did say,
'My goodness this place is just poo'.

Then angry she got, that dear, sweet old thing,
Who worked hard to make everyone bright.
So, a cleaver she fetched, and all three she did kill,
And said, 'There, that'll serve them all right'.

So now if you go for a meal at that place,
Be warned should you order the chilli.
There's three you could have,
And they all taste unique,
They're called Silly, and Willy, and Nilly

My goodness that got a bit sil...daft, didn't it?
Right, we'll say instead that, 'his head didn't have
the habit of falling off at the drop of a hat', which is a
lot easier, a very nice play on words, and hasn't got
anything to do with willy's and/or billy's, be they

silly, nilly, or anything else ending in 'illy that I've got to find a rhyme for.

Okay, back to the scenario, the thing I hinted at about three hundred years ago, and one that I really should be setting up. Let's see now. Ah, yes.

Stitches was on his own, the book was rather weighty, and it was on the top shelf.

Not being able to reach, he'd used his leather chair to stand on, which would have been okay for a more up to date item of furniture, but seeing as how this particular seat was extremely soft with age and squidgier than a baby otter made of marshmallow, it had started to dip the moment he'd stepped onto it. Once the weight of the book was added, the pressure had become too much not only for the chair, but also the zombie's ankles, knees, spinal column, rib cage, and just about every other part of his body to take. Consequently, everything liable to buckle under the pressure, buckled under the pressure, and he toppled backwards.

Now you might think that was bad enough, and indeed it would have been under relatively normal circumstances, should they ever have arisen. Sadly, though, fate decided that the situation clearly *wasn't* bad enough, and therefore in need a bit of a tweak.

Such was the abruptness of Stitches' reverse inertia, the book shot upwards at rather a rapid rate, paused, then plummeted back down like a literary missile where it connected with his forehead. Now, you might think that *that* was bad enough, bearing in mind we'd decided it was already bad enough in the first place as previously discussed, but no.

Fate was in a bit of a mood that day after tripping over a pair of shoes she'd left on the landing the night before (it was bound to happen, but try telling her that), so even more unfortunately, when the book struck, Stitches hadn't finished landing and it had knocked his head backwards thus elongating the fossilised and desiccated tendons in his neck to the point that they couldn't support its weight.

And so, he'd ended up sitting on the floor, unable to stand, and with the back of his head resting between his shoulder blades, an unusual position that gave him an equilibrium confusing, vertigo inducing upside down view of the world.

Thankfully, he'd managed to bum shuffle himself outside where Constable Gullett had seen the zombie's dire predicament and rendered immediate assistance.

After he'd finished laughing, anyway.

Okay. Back to the hospital.

Slowly feeling his way through the almost tactile gloom, Ollie walked unsteadily towards his companions. In spite of his enhanced vision the darkness was so intense that he was having trouble seeing clearly.

"We'll have that light again if you please, Mrs. Ladle," he said. There was no immediate reply. "Mrs. Ladle," he said again.

As he moved forwards his right foot knocked against something on the floor that clattered as it moved. It didn't feel big, and seeing as it hadn't ripped his leg off, he decided it wasn't an immediate threat, so he picked it up.

He weighed it in the palm of his hand, and even though he couldn't see it properly he could tell straight away that it was a cigarette lighter. He struck it, once again affording them the benefit of its meagre glow.

Stitches and Deirdre coalesced before him as if they were being reconstructed from faintly glowing pieces.

"She's gone," said the zombie, his voice trembling with fear and upset. "And so have Grendle and Mandeep."

* * *

Count Jocular was back in his study and staring out of the window, a doleful, gloomy, unadorned, and searingly curtainless square of transparent space that had occupied his every waking moment for goodness knew how long. At least since he'd woken up, certainly.

Try as he might he hadn't been able to resolve the accursed curtain, or lack thereof, issue to any sort of satisfactory conclusion, and as loathe as he was to admit it, without Egon's help it was as good as he was going to get.

After another failed attempt he'd taken a short break to relax a bit (he'd given the remains of Meat a damn good kicking) and then tried to remove the annoying crease one final time. Count Jocular was many things, but he wasn't a quitter.

Thusly emboldened he'd faced down the disobedient drapery once more, but when the cantankerous cotton crevice wouldn't shift, he'd lost his temper in a big way, to wit, he'd had a major hissy fit, hit the thing furiously, torn it down, ripped it to shreds, and chucked the resultant confetti like mess into a corner.

And so, no longer disturbed, diverted, or distracted by the disastrous decorative debacle, he was once again pondering why his vast and empty castle was so empty in its vastness.

In the last half hour or so he'd considered many and varied scenarios, premises, hypotheses, and theories that could explain the current situation, but the only conclusion that he'd arrived at that made any sort of sense (in that it made none whatsoever whichever way he looked at it) was that every single one of his servants had decided to take the night off.

Count Jocular shook his head. That couldn't be right, surely... but still.

Logically, it did seem to be the unlikeliest of unlikely occurrences because, to a creature, they all knew what the probable consequences of such naughtiness would be, and ordinarily that'd definitely be enough of a threat to curtail even the merest thought of such behaviour, but seeing as he really couldn't think of anything else vaguely sensible he went with it.

As he gazed outwards, his thoughts a wandering, he felt a push. It wasn't a physical one, of course; no one in their right mind would dare have the temerity to touch him without permission. Not if they wanted to continue opening their own bottles of ketchup, and rather liked having their internal organs on the inside, anyway. No, this was more like a mental shove, as if something had crawled into his head and given his subconscious a tap on the shoulder. It didn't feel overtly powerful as such, at least not as formidable as he, and no doubt wasn't any cause for concern, but it was certainly something that didn't happen very often, which is why it gave him a bit of a shock.

A bit of a shock! Count Jocular! But how?

As was natural with a vampire lord of his standing, you see, his innate psychic prowess was redoubtable and would brook no assault from any other being, so to say that this was an unusual occurrence was, well, unusual to say the least.

He focused his thoughts and tried to home in on the signals source. He reckoned it must be a creature of quite formidable ability to be able to penetrate his psyche like this, and that being the case, its threat, however significant or insignificant it may be, was one that needed to be identified as soon as possible.

He sat at his desk, put his elbows down, and placed his head into his hands.

"Zo," he whispered quietly, "who dares to breach my zsychic defences. Are you brafe enough to refeal yourself?"

There was another faint nudge then. The probing was subtle, indistinct, and barely registered at all, but it was definitely there. Or was it? He wondered if he could be imagining it. Was he going mad? Was his mind playing tricks on him? It had happened to his father who, at the age of seven hundred and thirty-eight, had succumbed to a form of brain sickness known as Gellar's Syndrome, an illness particular to vampires. It was akin to the human disease, Alzheimer's and displayed many of the symptoms associated with that wretched, and debilitating condition such as forgetfulness, getting lost in familiar places, not recognising people that you know, forgetfulness, getting lost in familiar places, not recognising people that you know, and repeating the same things over and over again.

But no, there it was again, only this time there was something else. A marker or signifier. A barely detectable hint of mental recognition burrowing its way into his grey matter like a determined parasite.

(Now, if all that sounds a bit odd in a mumbo jumbo way and you're wondering, 'what's this silly author on about?', think of it as a psychic fingerprint, a strange DNA quirk that we all have, but one which the majority of us have forgotten how to use.

Everyone's is different, and like all other physical and mental traits, it's dependent on certain inherited and naturally occurring factors such as latent psychic ability and cognisance of same, intelligence, family history, and having the wherewithal to be able to tap into it in the first place.

In most of us it just lies dormant, but those individuals who do have access to it can read it in others even if it's slumbering in the furthest reaches of their subconscious.

To those who have the natural ability to recognise the signs, high functioning persons present as a series of brightly coloured waves that undulate gently like a calm sea, whereas those less intellectually able appear as grey, formless blobs that have barely any motility at all. Even non sentient living things emit such a force, although it is very hard to trace. Except for Flug, that is, whose psychic output has been an unchanging flat line since the day he'd been created. Even an elderly button mushroom has a more robust psychic signature than poor old Flug, and not an overly intelligent one at that).

And then Jocular had it, finally recognising the person in his head. It was Deirdre, the lady who'd turned up at the castle.

There was only one reason that could enable a mere mortal to summon up the strength to get through to one such as himself. She was in terrible danger, and if that were the case there was every likelihood that his friends were in trouble as well.

And so, Count Jocular, lord of all he could see and quite a bit that he couldn't, master over all of the creatures within his domain, random slaughterer of the innocent on a ridiculously massive scale without thought or conscience, and interior decorator of questionable ability and taste, decided that he would seek her out and help the dear old thing.

No one was going to hassle a granny on his watch.

* * *

Deirdre led Ollie and Stitches ever further into the gloomy innards of the building where, thankfully, and much to their unending relief, they hadn't seen anything untoward for the last few minutes. The greeny/blue glow did seem to be becoming ever more intense, though, and every now and again the silence that'd descended was shattered by mournful cries and plaintive shrieks that didn't do an awful lot for their sense of wellbeing.

Eventually, they came to a junction and turned left, and not ten feet later Deirdre stopped. To her right was a door and on it was a faded sign that read 'SUPPLIES.'

"I think this is where we need to go," she said. "It's where I'm being drawn to. The pull seems to be getting stronger."

"I wonder what's inside?" said Ollie.

"A Chinese bloke waiting to make us jump?" said Stitches, ever the one for a witty line, an offhand remark, or a touch of light-hearted racism circa 1974.

Deirdre, still very much in the lead, turned the handle and opened the door.

As it happened, and much to their relief, they weren't greeted by an overly excited Oriental, and when Ollie put Mrs. Lightles lader on... (oops. I seem to have typed a bit of a Spoonerism there. Not that I'm going to hit the backspace button. When words get muddled up like that it's like unearthing a golden comedy nugget for free. 'Hypodeemic nerdle' is an obvious one, hypodermic needle, as is 'opporknockity tunes' instead of opportunity knocks, but my all-time favourite has to be, 'I laughed my head off at the Michael McIntyre concert last night,' instead of, 'I can't believe I paid forty quid to watch a fat bloke talk about herbs and wobble his head for an hour and a half. I've had funnier dental abscesses.'

Now, whilst I do admit that last example doesn't quite follow the rules of the aforementioned language related faux pas, you can't argue with the sentiment so there you go).

When Ollie shone Mrs. Ladle's lighter into the room they discovered that it was, indeed, very much full of, surprise surprise, supplies.

Not that it was much of a surprise it being full of supplies because, as was hinted at by the sign on the door, it was a supplies cupboard, after all.

So, what with it being a supplies cupboard and not a surprise cupboard, no great surprise there, there wouldn't have been any surprise supplies in the supplies cupboard that could've surprised them, anyway.

In fact, they couldn't have been less surprised to see supplies if they'd wandered into a supplies cupboard that wasn't a supplies cupboard and found it full of surprise, surprise, surprise supplies, which would have made it a supplies cupboard masquerading as a surprise cupboard.

Then again, they could have entered an actual surprise cupboard expecting to get a surprise, only to find that it was full of supplies, which would be a surprise in itself.

Right, I'm done with all this nonsense now because, surprise, surprise, I've got a stinking headache.

I think I better get some supplies.

In the cupboard they found the usual hospitally stuff. There were bandages, plasters, bottles of holy water, coffins and the like, as well as speciality items such as troll ointment, werewolf de-louser, phantom pregnancy kits, and ogre gloves (they did horrendous damage to their knuckles if they weren't paying attention, which they invariably didn't).

"Not really seeing much of a way down," said Stitches, as he followed the light into the room. "Are you sure that… WAAAHHHHHH!" THUMP. "I can't be a hundred percent sure, but I think I may have found it."

Ollie went over to where the noise had come from and looked down. "You should have used the ladder," he said, indicating the handy climbing down contraption to his left.

He was glad Stitches fell when he did because he'd only been a pace away from falling down the hole himself.

Stitches colourful reply was masked by the sound of shoe on rung.

They'd entered some kind of hollowed out recess, and it had a passage leading off it.

"This looks quite recent," said Deirdre, looking round when she got to the bottom. She ran her fingertips along one of the walls. "The earth is still fresh, and these roots are still moist. No wonder Mrs. Ladle had no idea this was here, because up until recently I don't think it was."

"Interesting. Well, I suppose you learn something new every day," said Stitches, who'd learned not to blunder into a strange and darkened room when it may or may not have a gaping hole in the floor that lead to a spooky pit, which in this case it most definitely did.

"Right, well there's only one way out which is a bonus of sorts," said Ollie, pointing to the way out that there was only one of. "Still, at least it means we haven't got to choose, I suppose."

"Well, let's have a massive thank goodness for that shall we," said Stitches. "Having to make a choice about which mysterious tunnel is the most dangerous can get awfully tiresome."

As they left the pit and entered the passageway leading off it, Deirdre stopped for a moment and leaned against the bare, earthen wall as a shudder passed through her entire system, rocking her to her very core. It seemed to touch every fibre of her be-ing and left her breathless and disorientated for a second or two.

"My goodness that was a strong one," she said, a tremble evident in her voice. "I think we must be very close now. Or at least I hope we are. I'd hate to think how strong this thing might be if we still had some distance to travel. It'd be staggering."

Ollie put a hand on Deirdre's elbow because she was still a little shaky. He was coming to have tremendous respect for this elderly lady who'd turned up out of the blue, not knowing who or what she'd find when she got here. And despite seeing things that would leave most people dribbling onto their shoes and only allowed to use crayons for the rest of their lives, she still continued to put her life on the line to assist them in dealing with whatever malevolent force it was that was causing all this.

"Are you alright to carry on?" he said.

"Oh yes, dear, don't you fret. It'll take more than the unwanted attentions of a colossal supernatural powerhouse to get the better of me."

"I take it you've encountered a few then?" said Stitches.

"Not as such, no, but I was married for forty-seven years; I know how to cope with unruly personalities."

Suddenly, a high-pitched scream, the likes of which none of them had ever heard before filled the tunnel and battered their eardrums. It was so piercing that it was actually painful, and no matter how tightly they clamped their hands over their ears, none of them could keep the terrible noise out.

It sliced into the brain like an acoustic blade and caused instant migraine like symptoms. It was literally blinding in its loudness. Then, equilibrium and any sense of awareness battered into submission, all three of them collapsed to the ground where they writhed and howled in abject agony, although their cries of pain were lost in the auditory cacophony engulfing them.

When it finally abated, it took them a few moments to realise that it had actually ceased, such were the reverberations clattering around their skulls.

Deirdre, being blessed with mere mortal hearing, recovered first, and she was quickly able to ascertain that apart from being a trifle muddy and having a bit of a headache, she seemed otherwise unharmed.

When she was finally able to get through to Ollie he sat up and shook his head to clear his senses, and it was only then that he saw the concerned look on her usually friendly face.

By the light of Mrs. Ladle's discarded lighter he realised that three had now become two.

Stitches had vanished.

* * *

As is the case for many a vampire lord, Count Jocular is, by necessity and design, the flesh born equivalent of an out of control combine harvester let loose in a large crowd. Capable of slaughter and carnage on a scale that would have made Genghis Khan need a session or three with a PTSD counsellor, he relished his lofty position and took his responsibilities very seriously, which is why he wouldn't allow any unwanted interlopers within his realm, and the very reason that he was now rapidly descending towards the Skullenian town square.

A graceful, fearless master of the sky, he'd swooped magnificently over hill and vale, deftly rode the eddying thermals that rose through the air like invisible columns, and unflinchingly reached speeds that would have scared many mortal creatures to the point of incapacity. It was through the artful use of these aeronautical acrobatics that he was able to protect the lands over which he held sway, an ever present, ethereal guardian who traversed the skies like a magnificent and deadly bird of prey, imperious in his sovereignty to govern all of those who dwelt below.

The sky was his second home, his refuge, and he welcomed its frigid, shimmering embrace.

As long as it wasn't at an altitude any higher than about six feet that is.

Jocular suffered from a touch of acrophobia, you see, and being any higher than your average human male made him feel a tad on the poo side.

(Actually, it was more than a tad, a touch, a poke, or any other inconsequential contact if we're being honest, and was rather more reminiscent of receiving a pile driving right hook from an outraged Godzilla.

Any activity that involved an altitude any higher than a couple of yards usually resulted in the fearsome vampire lord suffering from dizzy spells, increased respiration, and the ground below becoming festooned with a pungent, scarlet shower so potent that it destroyed anything living that had the misfortune to be in its acidic path.

No one knew about his affliction, of course. Not only would it be a bit embarrassing, the last thing he needed was an enemy realising he could be captured using a medium sized stepladder and a sturdy net).

He returned to human form and alighted deftly next to the fountain in the town square. Then, thusly settled, he placed a giant hand against its rough stone surface, closed his eyes, took a deep breath, and waited for a wave of nausea to pass.

Once he'd recovered, he took in the scene. He couldn't believe how quiet it was.

On any given evening Skullenia was a veritable hive of activity, plus, whenever he arrived anywhere there was always a certain amount of shrieking, fleeing in terror, hiding in churches, and general crucifix based nonsense that went on, and that was from those who knew he was on his way, although why they just didn't pop out to the shops for a few hours was anybody's guess.

(My two-penneth worth would be that they're all exceedingly dense, a bit retarded, inbred to the point that they have webbed ears and twenty seven toes, converse in their own language, have parents who also qualify as siblings, and an inability to tie a shoe lace because their claws are too sharp.

Not that I've ever been to the wilds of West Yorkshire to make a direct comparison, of course.

To be accurate it's probably got more to do with the fact that this sort of terrified reaction to his attendance is what you'd refer to as an expected response, one that's part of the great tradition of sucking up to those of a higher authority. You know the sort of thing. It's why Queen Elizabeth thinks everywhere smells of fresh paint and causes her to wonder precisely what a queue is for. It's sycophantic workers laughing at their boss's jokes when they're about as funny as an anal fistula, and adoring fans telling Sarah Jessica Parker that she's beautiful when everyone knows she looks like a horse that got its head stuck in a threshing machine.

So, if like me you despise fawning subservience in all its manifestations, I'm sure I can count on you to agree with me no matter what you think, because it pleases me for things to be that way).

Even The Bolt and Jugular, that regular haunt of many of the citizens, was deserted, and was just standing there like an empty public house, which it very much was.

"Fery strange indeed," Jocular muttered to himself. "Vot is going on I vonder?"

Twenty minutes later, thanks to his supercharged internal set up, Jocular had conducted a thorough, ground based search of the entire town, the result of which was that he now knew things were slightly more off kilter than a Jehovah's Witness at a blood donating session.

And so, with absolutely no idea what was happening in and around his demesne, he decided that, as much as he didn't want to because the very thought of it made him feel queasy, he needed to risk losing his lunch and take a look from up on high, although to be fair if he jumped in the air he'd gain more altitude than usual.

(This was why, even after the several hundred years that he'd been in residence, there were certain parts of his castle that he avoided in much the same way that Frankie the Funky Fantom shied away from soap. Anything above the ground floor had the potential to cause him a bit of a problem and, of course, he'd be mortified if anyone found out that he sometimes staggered about the corridors with his eyes screwed shut and clinging onto the walls for dear unlife. He wouldn't be mortified for long, obviously, because the finder outer would end up deader quicker than the tale teller who told the finder outer in the first place).

Summoning up all of the courage that he could muster, Jocular did his transforming thing and took flight. Wobbly flight. Very wobbly flight. In fact, it was so wobbly that he looked like a wobbly jelly that had been made with extra wobble, then sat on top of a particularly wobbly jelly that someone with the wobbles was wobbling, thereby making it, and him, wobble.

And he didn't even want to think about what would happen to his tummy and its contents once he got to the astronomical height of fifteen feet. If he dwelt on that subject for too long there was every chance he'd feel even more wobbly than he already did.

As the old saying goes, 'If Evil wobbles it just might fall down.'

Just as he was about to spew forth in rancid, chunky gouts from his pursed, batty mouth, something caught his attention, a something that momentarily caused him to forget his overwhelming fear of flying.

In the distance he could see a strange greeny/blue glow.

A strange greeny/blue glow he hadn't seen before.

A strange greeny/blue glow that really shouldn't be there.

A strange greeny/blue glow that could be the sign he was looking for.

A strange greeny/blue glow that's going to lose any and all meaning if it's mentioned one more time.

And being a vampire lord who always had his finger on the pulse (or his fangs buried in it at any rate) he knew that the hospital lay in that very direction.

And so, thinking that maybe, just maybe someone, or something, had very stupidly taken it upon themselves to enter his territory unannounced and uninvited with the possible intention of attempting to usurp him as leader, protector, and general being in charge, he decided to make his way to the hospital with all due dispatch and have a look.

On foot though.

It was no use arriving there all wobbly now was there?

* * *

With their numbers dwindling faster than a South African sprinters chance of getting his gun licence renewed, Ollie and Deirdre continued their journey into the murky, earthen underworld beneath the foundations of the hospital.

They didn't speak as they strode forth, not only because they needed to keep all their senses on full alert, it just felt like the right thing to do. They were under no illusion that their presence had gone undetected, but that didn't mean they needed to advertise the fact that they were here. They'd lost three members of their party already and couldn't afford to lose anymore. If anything happened to the pair of them who knew what would become of their happy, little town.

Neither of them could have said exactly where they were with any degree of accuracy, either, consequently they were relying on Deirdre's psychic nose to guide them to where they needed to be, and whilst Ollie wasn't entirely sure how it worked, whatever instinct it was that was driving her on, he trusted it implicitly.

That trust came with a side order of wonderment as well. Even though she'd never been beneath the hospital before, or even to Skullenia for that matter, and shouldn't have had a clue where she was going, she clearly *did* have a clue where she was going even if she didn't have a clue that she had a clue and knew where she was going, when quite clearly she couldn't possibly have a clue where she was going because she hadn't ever been here before, and therefore even if she did have a clue where she was going she wouldn't know that she had a clue where she was going, so the whole point was moot anyway. If in fact there was a point to all that verbal nonsense in the first place, of course.

Strange noises continued to reverberate around them, and it was still difficult to ascertain exactly where they were coming from. One minute they seemed to be in front, then hovering above, and the next, an unintelligible whispering in an ear. When all things were considered it was scary enough to have put the willies up even the hardiest of souls.

After a few more minutes of wandering through the semi-darkness, the eerily weird sounds that had been their constant companion ceased to surround them, and instead coalesced, coming together ahead of them in a towering, concentrated vortex of lamentation.

"We're very close now," said Deirdre. "I have a feeling that any moment now we're going to come face to face with whatever it is that's brought us here. Take care, Ollie dear. Ollie?"

With a sense of inevitability akin to sticking a knitting needle in your eye and knowing that it's going to hurt ever such a little bit, Deirdre turned round and confronted the empty space that was behind her, a space that had been occupied by her half vampire friend mere seconds ago.

There hadn't been any noise, no howls or caterwauls, and not even so much as the scuff of a shoe on the ground.

"Oh my," she whispered to herself. "What a to-do. Ah well. Onwards I go."

With a firmness of spirit that would put most people to shame, and only the tiniest hint of trepidation scratching away at her iron resolve, she determined to see what she now thought of as her quest, to the end.

About twenty feet further on the tunnel took a sharp turn to the left, and a few yards further on than that, came to a complete dead end.

"Well that's a little inconvenient I must say," said Deirdre. She took one more pace forward for a closer look.

By the increasingly feeble glow from the cigarette lighter she was able to discern that the end she was confronted with wasn't quite as dead as she'd first thought. It was on its last legs, could do with being hooked up to a drip, and in need of total bed rest, but it definitely wasn't deceased.

A small recess had been fashioned in the earth and it was through this she could hear the raised voices more clearly.

And so here she was. Alone, in the dark, and with only a short crawl between her and the unknown force that had compelled her to leave Shark's Bay and venture forth.

She got down onto all fours, wincing as her knee joints protested, clamped the lighter between her teeth, and slowly inched herself forward.

It wasn't long before she rounded a slight bend and was met by what, for all the world, looked like a fancy-dress ball where the only stipulation was to come as a shambling mess.

Dozens of figures were there, congregated in what could only be described as a hollowed-out cavern, but one so large that it seemed more exterior than interior.

And the figures weren't milling about but swaying in place like a cluster of metronomes set to larghissimo. God alone knew what was keeping them up. Such was the angle some of them were at she was amazed they were able to stay on their feet. It reminded her of that trick people do, the one where their feet stay in place but they're able to swing back and forth to extreme angles without falling over (I can't recall if it's magicians or drunks, but that doesn't really matter. They're both irritating and need locking up).

At first it appeared they were dotted about the place randomly, but a closer inspection revealed they were assembled in a rough circle, with all their attention seemingly focused on something, or someone, that Deirdre couldn't yet see.

As she watched, a spider that resembled a squash ball with legs scuttled across the back of her left hand. It frightened her so much that the intake of breath she took almost caused her to swallow the lighter.

As the giant arachnid moved away, she watched in disgust as it joined the gathered throng. It was almost as if it too were being drawn to whatever had brought the others here.

As she moved again, removing all thoughts of creepy crawlies from the back of her hand to the back of her mind, the words that Mrs. Ladle had spoken outside came back to her.

'So, what's the plan then?'

In light of that still unanswered question, she thought about beating a hasty retreat in order to formulate a decisive course of action along the lines of the twice hinted at P word, but was halted in her mental tracks by a distinct and clear voice that said, "Don't worry about it. Just keep going," (which was probably just as well. Thanks to her aged joints, the retreat she'd have been beating wouldn't have been in the least bit hasty, and extremely liable to grab a hold of a stick and hit back).

She glanced over her shoulder, for that was where the voice had come from. There, not two feet from her and in exactly the same crouching position was Mrs. Strudel. Or what was left of Mrs. Strudel, anyway.

Gone were the soft, grandmotherly features and gentle demeanour. Her gaze had become harsh and mean spirited, her friendly face transformed into a pallid disarray of grey flesh that now carried a sneering leer of pestiferous intent.

But it was her eyes. Once a pair of sparkling orbs that radiated an intelligent glow and seemed so full of joy, they now bespoke of her apparent retreat into nothingness, mere windows to the dead and empty void that had her floundering consciousness imprisoned within its icy clutches. They appeared as lifeless as a doll's eyes, a mournful brace of tarnished, marble like globes staring out from her once pleasant countenance.

"I said move on."

Realising that she had no choice, and even if she did it wouldn't be a good one, Deirdre crawled forwards.

Once out of the tunnel she stood up, grimacing as her knees popped and cracked. As she attempted to rub some life back into them, Mrs. Strudel appeared beside her in an instant. She took a firm hold of Deirdre's right arm at the elbow, squeezing much harder than she needed to.

"That hurts, dear," said Deirdre. "Come on, gently now. It's not as if I'm going anywhere is it?"

Mrs. Strudel responded by squeezing even tighter, thereby causing the medium even more pain.

Despite her age, the cafe proprietor had fingers like steel and a grip like a top class tugger of war. It had developed naturally during years of handling oversized kitchen equipment that wouldn't have looked out of place on a building site, portions of food that weighed more than she did, and plates the size of manhole covers (or, as in the case of January Pineapple, manhole covers served on a plate the size of a manhole cover.

A strange chap, he'd taken to gorging on the metal discs on account of him being afflicted by a rare medical condition called Pedicabo Ego Stulta

Inordinatio, or as it's more commonly known to most, Silly Bugger Disorder.

Now, ordinarily, his choice of fodder would've been alright and gone unnoticed in the grand scheme of things because let's face it, a bit of round metal wasn't ever going to be the most unusual of items that got consumed in town. Grimoire the Bleak likes Pop Tarts for goodness sake.

The reason it came to light was that beings of all descriptions were suddenly suffering injuries after falling down manhole shaped holes left in the street, so, ever the resourceful one, Mrs. Strudel had used her oven to forge January his meal of choice.

As it turned out, it wasn't all that difficult a baking concept, and she'd come up with a viable recipe in very short order, which was no great surprise.

She was well versed in the preparation of diverse cuisine, and some bloke choosing to dine on cast iron pancakes wasn't even close to the strangest dish that had ever left her kitchen.

In the past she'd extracted the life force from a living being and put it into a pie so that a psychic ghoul could have lunch, made a loaf of bread containing insect parts, fortified drinking chocolate, and distilled apathy for a depressed dwarf, and cooked a chocolate curry for Flug.

One time she'd even been asked to put a slice of gherkin into a burger, but she'd had to draw the line at that because it was flat out disgusting. Besides, it would have sullied the taste of the flame grilled colon nestling between the buns).

Trying to ignore the discomfort in her arm Deirdre had a look around. The space she'd been forced into seemed to be an expanded version of the roughly hewn tunnel that she'd recently traversed i.e. it was simply a vast dugout.

As she was led forward the crowd parted giving her a first glimpse of who was at the centre.

'Is this some sort of joke?' she thought to herself.

She looked behind wondering if someone was going to leap out to the sound of canned laughter and announce in a very loud voice, "GOTCHA!"

Sadly, they didn't.

If the situation hadn't been so dire, the big reveal would have been laughable to say the least, and not a little disappointing, because the being that had managed to capture some of the most powerful supernatural beings ever to have existed and bring the entire town of Skullenia to the point of collapse, was a little girl. She couldn't have been more than nine or ten years of age, to all outward appearances anyway, and pretty to the point that even now, it was obvious she'd be a stunningly beautiful heart-breaker when she reached adulthood.

'They'll write poems about you,' thought Deirdre.

She had long blonde hair tied in a ponytail, the most stunning blue/grey eyes, and was wearing a dusky pink dress. In her right hand she was clutching a well-worn, and obviously cherished teddy bear.

"Hello, Deirdre," she said, her voice all sweetness, light, and innocence. "I'm glad you could come to my party."

Deirdre decided to play along. Not only was she outnumbered lots and lots to one, it would be most unseemly for a lady of her age to engage in an all-out bout of fisticuffs. Better to follow the old maxim, 'Lie through your teeth so you don't get your head kicked in.'

She also had a nagging feeling at the back of her mind, but at the moment she couldn't quite put her psychic finger on it.

A frigid shiver ran the length of her aching back. As ridiculous as it sounded, something wasn't quite right here.

"Well, thank you for inviting me, dear," she said. "And what's your name?"

"Ava."

Her next response would determine whether she was dealing with an actual child, or some mass murdering hellion wearing the most inappropriate disguise of all time.

"That's a pretty name. And what a lovely dress you're wearing. You look just like a beautiful princess."

The girl gasped in excitement, clapped her hands together, and beamed with unalloyed pride.

"Thank you," she gushed. "My mummy bought it for me. It's my extra special party dress. I'm wearing it because it's my birthday."

"I thought as much," said Deirdre. "And what a wonderful party it's going to be. When are your mummy and daddy going to get here?"

Ava's face darkened, but it wasn't through anger or annoyance. She looked bleak and bereft, troubled to the point of distraction.

Powerful psychic waves washed over Deirdre like an emotional tsunami, and she reeled as she was pummelled by a veritable barrage of utter sadness and melancholy.

Ava's eyes moistened and tears dripped from her long lashes and rolled down her smooth, rosy cheeks.

The feeling that all was not as it seemed, intensified.

Despite the lugubrious surroundings and the funereal atmosphere, Deirdre just couldn't connect the invading presence in her mind with the child standing before her. She clearly had some sort of power, but…no, try as she might, she couldn't put it together.

Deirdre placed a hand up to her own face and realised to her astonishment that she was crying as well.

"They can't come," said Ava, her voice thick with unhappiness.

"Why's that, dear?" said Deirdre.

"They're dead."

Deirdre reached out into the ether, but there was no one trying to contact the child.

"You won't find them. He said they were gone. Gone forever."

"Who'd say such a thing?"

"The man. The one I've been hiding from."

Without seeming to move, Ava was suddenly standing right next to her. She waved Mrs. Strudel away and looked up at Deirdre.

"Can I show you something?" said Ava.

"Of course, you can, love. You can show me any-thing you want to."

Ava took a hold of Deirdre's hands in hers and closed her eyes, an action the medium felt com-pelled to emulate.

Images coalesced in the older lady's mind.

At first it was hard for her to discern exactly what it was she was seeing, but then the realisation dawned.

She was observing the scene through Ava's eyes, as if she were experiencing them for herself first-hand.

She was in the ordinary living room of what, no doubt, was an ordinary house. A table was covered in food of all types and at the centre was a cake. The mantelpiece to her left was bedecked with cards and the wall above it was garnished with a suitably gaudy banner that read, 'Happy Birthday Ava.'

She heard a voice from behind.

She turned and saw a man and a woman. Both were smiling. She felt safe and happy.

"Now, are you sure you don't want to come to the hospital with us to get grandma?" said the woman.

"No thank you, mummy. I want to enjoy my spe-cial party room as long as I can. It's the best one ever."

"Okay, sweetie. We won't be too long."

Both the man and the woman kissed her on top of the head and left.

Even though it was her birthday she didn't mind being left on her own for a bit because when they returned she would get to see grandma, even if she was, as daddy put it, 'a bit of a handful.' That's why they both had to go.

She helped herself to a few nibbles from the table, had a drink, then gave some sweets to teddy because he was hungry. They were sugar laden treats guaranteed to make her dentist tell her off if he ever found out, but she was sure he wouldn't mind, seeing as how it was her birthday.

She read her cards again, laughing at the funny jokes, and then chanced a glance at the wrapped boxes sitting in front of the fire. Her presents. She didn't mind what she got, of course, but she hoped one of them was a make-up kit. She felt she was definitely old enough for one and besides, she wanted to look as pretty as mummy when she put hers on.

After a while she grew a little restless. Mummy and daddy were taking a very long time to bring grandma home. The hospital wasn't that far away.

She sat on the settee and read for a bit.

She came to with a start and realised that she must have fallen asleep. And for quite a while it seemed because it was dark outside.

"Mummy, daddy!" she called out. "Grandma!"

She was answered by stony silence, then realised they couldn't be here. If they had arrived whilst she was asleep, they would have woken her up, especially today.

Not one for being easily scared she checked the rest of the house. No one else was here. She was definitely on her own.

'Maybe grandma's not quite well enough to come home yet,' she thought.

On balance, she decided that the sensible and grown up thing to do was to go to the hospital herself. After all, it didn't matter where she saw grandma on her birthday, as long as she saw her. And mummy and daddy wouldn't be angry with her because they let her walk to the shops on her own all the time, even when it was a bit dark.

She decided to leave her pink party dress on as she was sure grandma would want to see it, and to take teddy for company because she didn't want him being on his own. He was a bit of a scaredy cat.

After popping on her shoes, she wrote a note to let her parents know where she was and left it on the hallway table. She then turned off the hallway light and left the house, making sure to lock the front door. Even though Skullenia was a safe place she didn't like the idea of leaving her home insecure.

Skipping happily and confidently along, she politely said hello to everyone she passed, stopped to help Mrs. Flunk cross the road, and even exchanged pleasantries with Hugo Pepper, who could be a right old misery guts.

In spite of all this, though, and taking into account she had to stop twice to re-tie her shoes, she made good time, and it wasn't long before she reached the hospital gates.

(Twice was better than usual when it came to doing up her shoes. Quite often she had to fiddle with her laces five or six times, especially when she was playing. Mummy had shown her how to do it ages ago, but she still found it a bit tricky. She'd asked if the laces were faulty, which had made mummy laugh).

The idea of entering didn't faze her because she'd been here before when grandpa had been ill. Sadly, he'd died the next day, but the doctors and nurses had been really kind and friendly.

She went through the main doors and up to the reception desk. She knew that you needed to let the lady know you were here. Then she'd be able to tell you where you needed to go.

A little bell sat on the desktop. Next to it was a small sign that said, 'Ring for assistance,' which she did.

When no one came she rang it again, a little louder this time. Maybe the desk lady was busy and hadn't heard it the first time.

She turned as she heard footsteps from a hallway to her right.

"Hello there, young lady. How can I help you this fine evening?"

It was a man, and he was clearly a doctor because he was wearing a white coat, had a stethoscope around his neck, and a pen in his pocket, and she knew that all doctors had these three things with them all the time. He must also have been very busy indeed because his coat was spotted with red dots and he was holding something thin and shiny in his hand. It looked like a knife, which she knew was another important piece of doctory equipment.

"I've come to find my mummy and daddy," she said, confidently. "They came to collect grandma so she can come to my birthday party but that was quite a while ago."

The doctor walked right up to her and put a hand on her shoulder. She noticed it was slightly tinged with red, as were the underneath of his fingernails.

"I know exactly where they are, my dear," he said, smiling warmly. "And don't you go worrying your pretty little head about your grandma, either. She's absolutely fine."

He took her by the hand and led her through the brightly lit, yet empty corridors. It was a lot quieter than she remembered. The last time she'd been here there were nurses bustling about, visitors coming and going, and doctors flitting in and out of wards and side rooms.

"Where exactly is grandma?" she said, after they turned into yet another hallway.

"She's in a special ward for my extra special pa-tients," said the man. "And as you can imagine only very special people are allowed in there."

As they passed through a set of double doors and into the dimly lit room beyond, she noticed a strange smell. It was thick and tangy, disturbingly metallic, and cloying to the point that she could taste it in the back of her throat. It reminded her of the time she'd fallen over whilst skipping and cut her top lip open. The taste/smell was the same.

For the first time since entering the building, she was scared.

Before she could express her feelings, the ward was bathed in light, whereupon the full horror of what she had stumbled into became apparent, confirming the nagging fears that she'd had for the last few moments.

The walls, floors, beds, and even the ceiling were awash with blood. Thick gouts of it had sprayed across every surface making it look as if a sprinkler had been attached to a severed artery and switched on to full power.

Where it hadn't coagulated completely it dripped, heavy droplets thunking into semi liquid pools that had more or less ceased to spread.

Initially too shocked to speak, her attention was drawn to the beds themselves. She hadn't processed the images before but each one appeared to be occupied, but by whom, or by what, she didn't know.

Blood soaked sheets covered the formless, abstract shapes beneath them making it difficult to discern what they actually were, and she noticed that the sodden linen was drawn right up to the head board as if whatever was concealed there was hiding, the way a small child would when it hears an unfamiliar noise in the middle of the night.

Frigid tendrils of dread crept up her spine and she took an involuntary step back, but she was prevented from retreating any further by a strong hand placed in the middle of her back that firmly, but gently, urged her forwards.

As the guiding hand was only intended to let her know that she wasn't going anywhere but the intended direction, she should have stayed on her feet, but her left foot slipped in a turgid pool of congealed blood and she clattered to the floor, covering herself in the foetid, viscid mess.

"Aw, would you look at that," said the grinning man. "Your pretty dress is ruined. Ah well. Never mind." He reached down and dragged her to her feet. "Come on then, little lady. You don't want to keep grandma waiting. She's dying to see you."

She tried to get away but the hand gripping her squeezed ever tighter to the point that she could feel her delicate wrist bones grinding together.

She was led to one of the beds. It was just like the others, as one would have expected, but this one had two chairs next to it. Two occupied chairs. And like the bed, whoever was occupying them was covered in a grisly, scarlet shroud.

Without any warning or preamble, the man whipped the sheet off the bed revealing the shattered corpse of her beloved grandma. She'd been horrifically beaten leaving not one inch of her frail, elderly body without bruise, laceration, or contusion. She was barely recognisable, but Ava was able to identify her by the golden locket around her battered throat.

She screamed.

It was a short-lived exclamation, though. A rough hand clamped over her mouth stifling any further outbursts.

"Come now, dear," said the man. "That's no way to behave is it? That was loud enough to wake the dead."

With his free hand he lifted one of the deceased woman's arms, held it for a moment, and then let it go. It fell and slapped against the stained mattress sending out a shower of blood that slopped onto Ava's shoes. Jarred by the movement, the locket slipped round to her grandma's shoulder. "Well, not quite," said the man. He chuckled throatily, amused by his own joke. "And what would mummy and daddy think of your behaviour? Let's find out, shall we?"

With Ava in tow he made his way to the other side of the bed, and quickly and efficiently removed the sheets from the seated and shrouded figures.

If he hadn't have revealed what lay beneath, she still would've known what was there. Mummy and daddy. They were sitting bolt upright in their chairs, eyes wide open and staring vacantly at the ceiling, their faces frozen in anguish, their throats neatly slashed from ear to ear.

She was now beyond the capability for rational thought, but her involuntary fight or flight reflex kicked in and sent a bolt of adrenaline surging through her shocked system.

Managing to open her mouth she slid her face upwards across the man's slimy palm and bit down as hard as she could, burying her teeth into the soft, pliant flesh between the man's thumb and index finger.

Eyes closed with effort she clamped her jaws together until she felt the warmth of fresh, syrupy blood fill her mouth. Pungent and thick, it coated her tongue and ran down her throat, its coppery essence and cloying texture making her gag.

The man howled in pain and he snatched his hand from her face before she had the chance to bite him again.

Free from his grasp she ran. Away from the man, away from her parents, away from her grandma, and who knew how many other poor victims who'd fallen foul of this man's lunacy.

"COME BACK!" bellowed the man, his voice rich with anger. "IT'LL ONLY BE WORSE FOR YOU IF YOU RUN. MUCH WORSE!"

She heard the words and knew very well what they meant, but she paid them no heed. As fast as her legs and the slippery floor would allow, she sprinted towards the double doors, hoping that once she was through them, she would be able to remember the way out.

Then, about six feet from the exit, the lace on her right shoe came undone. Panicked at feeling the sudden loss of grip she scrunched up her toes and clamped them down onto the shoes inner lining, but it was no use. With an almost preordained inevitability the shoe slipped from her foot leaving her stockinged heel exposed. When she brought it down a second later, it slid on the blood strewn floor.

Unable to gain any traction her heel shot forwards forcing her legs into an awkward splits, and though she tried in vain to keep her balance she was moving much too quickly to prevent the outcome.

She landed in a heap and skidded in the glutinous ichor, coming to rest mere feet from escape.

She reached out a trembling hand but couldn't reach the freedom that beckoned.

As a shadow covered her, she glanced upwards, and as she saw the glint of steel in the man's hand only one thought occupied her mind.

'Who's going to look after teddy?'

Ava let go of Deirdre's hands.

The medium's eyes snapped open and her gaze focused on the little girl standing in front of her. Without uttering another word, she took the child in her arms and held her close and cried like she'd never cried before.

"He said when I was dead, I'd never be able to come back. He said my soul would be gone just like mummy's and daddy's, and grandma's. But I got away, and I've been hiding here ever since."

"Oh, you poor, sweet thing," said Deirdre, once she was able to speak.

Ava returned the affection and squeezed Deirdre for all she was worth, her head buried in the older lady's ample bosom. She felt safe now. Safe and loved.

"Is that what all these people are doing here?" said Deirdre. "Are they here for your party?"

Ava looked up. Her face was iridescent with moisture and her eyes puffy from crying, but a tentative smile broke through the veil of sadness.

"Yes," she muttered. "And I've been waiting for ages. I tried a few times before, but I wasn't strong enough to invite everyone. I just wish mummy, daddy, and grandma were here." Her smiled widened. "And a cake, of course."

"So why all the strange voices and theatrics to get everyone's attention? I'm sure this would've been more fun if everyone was awake," said the medium indicating the crowd.

"Who'd listen to a little girl?" said Ava.

It was the only explanation she was able to offer, but it was brutally truthful in its naive simplicity, and as such, totally and utterly valid.

How often are adults dismissive of the attentions of children? How many times are little ones ignored because parents are too busy, distracted by irrelevancies, or simply too indolent to be bothered?

"I thought if I pretended to be someone bad then people would come. Especially you."

"But why me?" asked Deirdre. "I live a very long way away. What am I doing here?"

Ava lost herself in Deirdre's chest once more.

"You remind me of my grandma," she said.

Deirdre's heart swelled with instantaneous love for the child and broke in two at the same time. Such loneliness would be hard enough to take for an adult, but for one as young as Ava to have go through it was almost beyond comprehension.

She stroked Ava's flaxen hair.

"I love you, Deirdre," the girl said.

"I love you, too," said Deirdre sincerely, because it was true.

Just then a roar came from the vicinity of the crowd, but it wasn't one of their number. A new figure had appeared. Gaunt, pale, and menacing it raised its hands into the air as if in triumph.

*"AT LAST I'VE FOUND YOU!"*

It strode towards Deirdre and Ava.

"OH NO. IT'S HIM!" screamed the girl. "THE MAN FROM THE HOSPITAL!"

*"I'M SO GLAD YOU RECOGNISE ME, ESPECIALLY AFTER SUCH A LONG TIME. I'VE BEEN TRYING TO FIND YOU FOR WHAT SEEMS LIKE FOREVER, BUT YOU HID FROM ME DIDN'T YOU, YOU NAUGHTY LITTLE THING. BUT WE DON'T NEED TO WORRY ABOUT THAT ANY MORE DO WE. NOW THAT I FINALLY HAVE YOU BACK, WE'LL HAVE THE WHOLE OF ETERNITY TO GET*

TO KNOW EACH OTHER. I SHAN'T LOSE YOU AGAIN. AND HOW I'M GOING TO EN-JOY YOU. FOR AGES I HAVE SUBSISTED ON LITTLE, SAVE FOR THE SCAVENGED, NOMADIC REMNANTS OF THOSE DISEM-BODIED ENTITIES UNFORTUNATE ENOUGH TO CROSS MY PATH, FEASTING SPARSELY ON THEIR WANING ETHEREAL FORCE AS I SLOWLY REGAINED MY STRENGTH FOR TODAY, THE DAY OF MY RETURN. FOR TOO LONG HAVE I EXISTED AS NEAR TO NOUGHT, BEREFT OF BODILY CONSTRUCT AND CONSTRAINED TO OBLIVION, NOTH-ING BUT INCONSEQUENTIAL FLOTSAM, A WANDERING MOTE CAST ADRIFT IN A SEA OF INFINITE VOID. OH, WHAT A VAPID HELL I'VE BEEN FORCED TO INHABIT. SOON THOUGH, THIS SEMPITERNAL TORTURE WILL BECOME NOTHING BUT DREADFUL MEMORIES, FLEETING IMAGES TO BE CON-SIGNED TO THE ANNALS OF HISTORY, A HISTORY THAT WILL BE SUPPRESSED AND EVENTUALLY FORGOTTEN NOW THAT I'VE MADE MY TRIUMPHANT AND BLOODY HOMECOMING. TOO LONG HAS IT BEEN SINCE I HAVE FELT THE FRAIL BRAWN OF

ANOTHER IN MY MONSTROUS GRIP AND FEASTED UPON THE LIFE GIVING FLUID SPILLED FROM WITHIN ITS SUCCULENT INNARDS."*

As the 'party guests' wandered, it felt its spirits soar as their very presence imbued it with an energy that would only build and build until finally, it could take on a more substantial form and walk upon solid ground once again.

All would then know of its existence, and those summoned would come to appreciate the divine calling and what it represented. If not, destruction and eternal damnation would be their only reward.

Then, a movement to his left caught his attention...

\* \* \*

"Vot on earth is going on down here?" said Count Jocular as he emerged from a second tunnel to Deirdre's right. "I vill not haff such naughtiness going on in my town. Who ze deffil are you, foul creature from somevhere else who seems to be suffering from a fery nasty case of ze verbal diarrhoeas? Speak, zo zat I may know ze name off zat vhich I am about to destroy."

Ignoring the interruption, the grim figure suddenly moved with a speed that belied its almost skeletal build and headed straight for the two cowering females.

'I am not beliefing it,' thought Jocular. 'Zis creature is defying me'.

It was clearly time for action.

Not the sort of shy and retiring chap to be outwitted, outthought, outmanipulated, outperformed, outclassed, outfought, outmastered, outstripped, outmuscled, outdone, outmanoeuvred, outflanked, outflummoxed, outdecorated, outthingamabobbed, or flipping well outanythinged else for that matter (especially so close to home where people might talk. He did have something of a reputation to uphold. It was outstanding), the vampire lord let forth with a roar so fearsome that dewy clods of earth, coiling tree roots, and a very surprised family of moles fell from the ceiling far above. Then, mustering all the supernatural powers at his disposal, Jocular set off to intercept the trespasser, the urge to rend the creature's spirit to wandering atoms rapidly consuming him.

In an instant, however, he realised that he might not make it...

Seeing what was going on, Deirdre held Ava as close to her as she could and placed a hand over the child's eyes to shield her from the sight of the venomous entity charging towards them.

'I wonder if this is my time?' she thought.

She'd never feared death, which bearing in mind her ability to converse with those already suffering from that most terminal of conditions, wasn't any great surprise.

'Bring it on, and let's enjoy the ride,' had always been her view, and if this was indeed to be her last hurrah then so be it. If nothing else, she'd finally get to meet everyone that she'd been in touch with over the years. And there was always the chance that she'd be lucky enough to find a friendly medium, someone who'd listen, pass on messages, and reassure her that all was well in the land of the quick. She'd only talk about important things though, and wouldn't go bothering them in the middle of the night with trivialities such as, 'Is the cat out?' 'Goodness, I fancy a cheese sandwich', or, 'What's that smell?'

As much as she was willing to accept her end, however, she was rather less inclined to let anything happen to Ava, so, turning her body slightly to protect the girl from the approaching menace, she steeled herself for what was to come…

* * *

Unbeknownst to the four people that still had their senses, Ava's childish, yet powerful hold upon the shambling, insensible members of the wretched group was beginning to lapse as she now focused her attentions on Deirdre.

Motility amongst the nomadic, wraith like forms was becoming slightly less spasmodic as if a certain semblance of control was being re-established. Eyes that had been devoid of any sign of intelligence had begun to take on that lustre once more as absent psyches returned from some unknown beyond, and they were all, to varying degrees, starting to come to their senses.

As the bumping and stumbling, jostling and shuffling grew less and less, and the cloak of nescient darkness that had shrouded them finally began to lift, some of the group started to take in their foreign surroundings. They tried to comprehend the unfamiliar sights and sounds assaulting their consciousnesses and questioned their presence in this strange environment because none of them knew exactly what had happened nor how they came to be here.

All were at a loss.

Except for one.

Ironically, it was the most pathetic creature of all who realised what was happening and reacted to it first.

With a burst of energy that no one would ever have given him credit for; Hector Lozenge detached himself from the group and charged at the threatening spectre bearing down on the ladies.

When he got close enough, he launched himself, diving forward with all the agile grace of a seasoned acrobat and the ferocious raw power of an attacking panther. Whilst still in mid-air he wrapped his arms around the interloper's midriff, and such was the force of the impact, Hector knocked him off course and took him to the ground.

"Unhand me, you boozy idiot," said the figure, glowing with unadulterated rage, "or I'll…"

He didn't get to finish the sentence because a powerful right hook connected with his jaw.

"Oh, shut up, you bloody arse-head," said Hector, putting together what was probably the most coherent sentence that he'd muttered for many a year. "And listen up. I've got something to tell you."

Hector began to mumble something, but such was its outlandish diction and unintelligible verbiage, anyone paying any attention would assume he was simply babbling away to his addled, rambling, inebriated self, as was normal. Or as normal as anyone is going to be with a blood alcohol level of just under one hundred percent.

By now the majority of the crowd had more or less regained their mental capabilities, but one of them in particular had snapped out of the imposed fugue state a lot quicker than the rest and realised straight away what was happening.

"HECTOR, NO!" screamed Mrs. Ladle when she realised what he was up to. "DON'T USE THAT ONE YOU STUPID, DRUNKEN OLD BUGGER!"

But it was too late. As he muttered a final few words, he turned his head to face the crowd and smiled, at which point a bolt of lightning crashed down from the ceiling of the cavern, splitting it in two.

Knowing it was coming, Hector rolled onto his back, thereby placing the struggling phantom atop his chest.

Unable to move because of Hector's bear hug, there was nothing the being could do but stare upwards in horror as the tip of the electrical serpent from beyond barrelled towards him.

"RELEASE ME! I COMMAND YOU TO RE..."

When the unstoppable atmospheric discharge punched into his chest, he howled in agony and despair as any and all vestiges of his tainted and blackened life-force were extinguished like a flame in a gale.

The lightning didn't stop there, however, its terrible power as yet undiminished. Once it had passed through the now still form of the phantom it continued its irrevocable journey towards the earth and plunged right through Hector's lean torso where it pierced his heart, stopping it in an instant.

Once the dust had settled and a certain nervous calm had descended upon those assembled, Ava approached and knelt beside the two corpses. Presently she was joined by Deirdre and Count Jocular.

"Who vas zis person?" said the vampire lord, nudging the corpse with his foot. It rolled off Hector and onto the floor "I haff neffer seen him before."

"No one seems to know," said Deirdre. "All we can be sure of is that he killed a lot of people at the hospital years ago. Murdered them in their beds. When Ava summoned all the towns' folk here, he used the power she'd generated to bring himself back."

"I see."

"What are you doing here anyway?" said Deirdre.

Jocular picked up the corpse of the murderer and slung it over his shoulder as if it were nothing but a big bag of nothing with nothing in it.

"I heard your call," he said. "You haff a powerful psychic gift, dear lady, vun of ze strongest zat I haff ever encountered. Vell, I can't stand around here gossiping all night. It looks like ze crowd is breaking up and I haff a sneaking suspicion zat ze lateness of ze hour means zat ze children of ze night are going to be razher peckish. It's vay past time for zeir dindins." He patted the carcass on the thigh. "It is a good job zey like ze takeavay, yes? Farevell, Deirdre Clownpuncher."

And with that he vanished (well, he wandered back up the tunnel that he'd come down, but he wasn't going to tell anyone. That reputation he was so adept at keeping could always do with a little shoring up).

Ava gently stroked Hector's cheek and tidied up the wispy strands of hair that had spilled untidily onto this forehead. A single tear fell from the end of her nose and landed on his ragged jumper.

"Thank you," she whispered.

"*You're welcome, sweetheart,*" said Hector's voice in her head. "*And look. I think you have visitors.*"

Ava stood up and turned around. Before her a shimmering mist hovered, an ethereal glow festooned with glistening, jewel like fragments of light.

"*Come closer,*" said another voice in her head. Or was it just one voice? "*Don't be afraid.*"

Ava felt compelled, but she wasn't fearful.

"Ava?" said Deirdre.

"It's okay," said Ava. "The danger's gone now."

When she reached the opaque mass, Ava stretched out a hand and touched it, whereupon it began to condense and coalesce into three separate forms.

As she watched, the trio of once indistinct blobs became recognisable, firstly as people, and then as people she knew.

"Mummy? Daddy? Grandma?"

"*Hello, sweetheart. We've missed you.*"

Ava allowed herself to be smothered by the three ghostly apparitions to the point that those watching lost sight of her.

"Is she going to be alright?" said Mrs. Ladle.

"Oh, yes," said Deirdre. "She's with those she loves."

After a few minutes the shapes started to break up. Wisps of smoke rose into the air where they ebbed and danced for a couple of seconds before winking out of existence, and before long Ava was visible once more with only a few vague tendrils left clinging to her clothes.

In time she returned to Deirdre, but of her encounter with the cloud she said nothing.

By now everyone had come to their senses, or to what senses they had in the first place at any rate and were engaged in speculation as to why they found themselves in a dank, earthen pit.

"Christ, I need to get the shop open," said Grendle, rushing off, muttering something about lost profits.

"I best check there's no looting been going on," said Constable Gullett, meandering away, although he would definitely need something to eat first. There was no crime that important that it would keep the policeman away from his food (or anyone else's if his ran out).

"Why all dese people in my bedroom?" said Flug as he lay down on the ground and fell asleep.

The next evening saw all of the townsfolk gathered at the cemetery to pay their respects to Hector Lozenge as he was laid to rest.

"What I don't understand," said Stitches, "is that of all the people that fell under Ava's spell, Hector was the one who came out of it first. I've not seen him coherent in all the time I've lived here."

"It's quite simple really," said Mrs. Ladle through a smoky, aromatic, and explosively carcinogenic veil. "He spent so many years functioning in a permanent state of drunkenness that a mere spell wasn't going to make him any more insensate than he already was. For him, I suspect it was akin to waking up with a mildly niggling hangover."

"Brave chap, though," commented Ollie, wiping away a tear and blowing his nose on a black, silk hanky.

"I'll miss him, actually," said Ronnie. "He'd always give me a prod with his broom if ever I fell asleep on the street in the early hours."

"At least he used it for something then," said Stitches with a chuckle.

As the coffin was lowered into the ground, Biddle the caretaker, groundskeeper, and all-round loon whose entire existence revolved around dealing with the dead and the planting thereof, said a few words about Hector.

He spoke about his life, his achievements, and the fact that despite having a brain that was more pickled than a jar of Professor Pickle's Ever So Pickly Pickled Pickles, he had managed to recall a decimation spell from his days as a young warlock and save the day.

Once the coffin reached its final resting place, but before the first shovel full of earth was placed onto it, Ava, holding Deirdre's hand, stepped forward.

"Are you sure you want to do this, sweetheart?" said the medium.

"Yes," said the little girl.

She leaned over the grave as far as she could and dropped teddy onto the wooden box, where it landed right above where Hector's chest was.

"I don't want Hector to be lonely. Teddy will look after him."

"Won't you miss teddy?" said Deirdre.

"I will. But I have you now."

* * *

A few hours later, Deirdre and Ava were crossing the town square.

"I just need to have a very quick word with Ollie before we go," said Deirdre as she opened the door to the building.

When she saw that the door to the office was shut Ava said, "Maybe he's sleeping."

"Oh, I doubt that very much," said Deirdre, pushing the office door open.

"SURPRISE!" came the shout from the dozens of people who'd been hiding in the office. "HAPPY BIRTHDAY, AVA!"

And what a treat it was. There were balloons hanging from every available surface, streamers over just about everything, and a big, pink banner over the fireplace that read 'HAPPY BIRTHDAY PRINCESS'.

(And before all you grammar Nazis out there start moaning, yes, I'm fully aware that the sentiment on the aforementioned decoration is grammatically incorrect to the tune of one comma. So, get stuffed, Fascists. She's a little girl for goodness sake).

And as you can imagine, Ava was lavished with gifts aplenty. They ranged from the thoughtful (a new pair of light pink party shoes from Ollie that caused Stitches to question his friends taste, eyesight, and sexuality), the inappropriate (a cigarette lighter from Ronnie because there's nothing worse than a little girl being stuck for a light ((apart from a little girl being stuck for a light, that is)), the stupid (a mug from Stitches bearing the logo, 'I love Skullenia' that contained a preserved, and very real eyeball at the bottom that winked when you drank), to the downright bizarre (Flug presented Ava with a model that he'd made all by himself. He said it was a cat, but if that were the case it was one that had either spent its formative years baking in a nuclear reactor, or as a main character in some morose and pathologically depressing, Lovecraftian nightmare. Or possibly both. Ollie was sure there were pincers in there somewhere. At least it was better than his original idea, though. Flug had wanted to give her Derek Strudel).

Ava had a wonderful time and finally, thanks to Mrs. Strudel, got her long-awaited birthday cake (Mrs. Ladle would have done it, but she didn't fancy having to redecorate. Again).

Being the kind girl that she was, Ava only took a small slice for herself so that everybody could have some, but she made sure that Deirdre got an especially big piece to go with her cup of tea.

Much later, with the party over and everyone having made their way home, Deirdre decided it was time to take her leave. As a special favour, Count Jocular sent Bill the Coachman to escort her home.

"I see she's decided to go with you then," said Ollie.

"Oh yes," replied Deirdre, the look on her face testament to how happy this made her. "But I've known she would since the very moment I laid eyes on her. I think it was meant to be from the start."

"The message on your window you mean," said Stitches.

"Yes. For whatever reason, when she first reached out, she managed to find me. And to achieve a feat like that over such a long distance has to mean something. Not that I'm complaining, of course. I never had children of my own, so I've got a lot of spoiling to catch up on."

"What I don't understand is how she's so…well…so solid, I suppose," said Ollie. "She is a ghost after all. Or was, anyway."

"Her family did that when she entered the cloud," said Deirdre. "Whatever vital essence they had left over they passed onto her. Don't worry about them, though. They're resting peacefully now, safe in the knowledge their little one can go on and have a happy and fulfilling life. I also have a sneaking suspicion that she's taken on some of the spirit of the town, or the people who live here at any rate. There's a lot of love in this strange place."

"SLOW DOWN!" screeched an excited Ava from her lofty position atop Flug's shoulders. The lumbering behemoth had taken quite a shine to the little girl and had resolutely decided that walking was no longer an option for her. Since the party she hadn't spent more than a couple of minutes on terra firma.

"It's not often that Flug has someone to look up to is it?" said Ethan. "And I've always said that two heads are better than one."

"I think you might be right about that. Still, he could have a potato up there and it'd double his IQ. Mind you, he does look happy, doesn't he?" said Stitches.

When Deirdre and Ava were finally settled on the coach, the medium leaned out of the window and took Ollie's hand.

"It's been special," she said. "Different certainly, but definitely right up there as one of life's highlights. Now you promise you'll come and visit."

"Of course, we will. Flug's already asked." He gave her a peck on the cheek. "You take care, Deirdre. Bye bye, Ava."

"Bye," shouted the little girl. "See you soon. Love you all."

"And don't forget what we talked about," said Deirdre.

As the coach moved off, Stitches inquired as to what she'd meant.

That all became clear a couple of days later when the Hector Lozenge Memorial Bench was unveiled. It was situated about forty yards from The Bolt and Jugular because that was the spot where the old boy had most often been found after one of his prolonged drinking sessions (on two occasions found standing up supported by nothing but his broom and the encrusted dirt on his trousers).

It was constructed of the finest ebony, had soft cushions, and glass holders at regular intervals.

As you'd expect it proved very popular with the towns drinkers, but to a creature not one of them would sit in the seat on the right hand side because, as a few of them pointed out, it felt as if you'd be sitting on something that was already there even though it was clearly empty.

"Maybe it's old Hector keeping an eye on things," people would say. "You know how much he loved this spot."

Now that may well be true, or it might just be a case of wishful thinking, but one thing was for sure. Despite never replacing Hector with a new town cleaner, no one saw any litter on the streets of Skullenia ever again.

THE END

# Ouch!

This is essentially a gambling game in which bets are placed on the amount of pain that a contestant can take.

Once the participant has placed their wager, it is up to them to attempt to make the other person say OUCH! by inflicting whatever torment he thinks may cause the most discomfort.

The rules themselves are very simple in that the contestants cannot be relieved of whatever life they may have, and at least half of their number of limbs must still be intact at the conclusion of the game. If the 'attackee' can withstand five assaults, then he wins and collects the money. Obviously, if he succumbs and says 'OUCH!' he loses. Please note that passing out and not saying OUCH! counts as a loss.

Although on the surface the game itself may seem brainless and rather violent, there is some thought required as there are no restrictions on how the pain can be administered. In one famous example, Completely Mad Malcolm, a psychopath who had a collection of weapons to rival a Roman legion, told Dolly Bookshelf that she had a backside the size of a small asteroid. Okay, so he had cut off three of her ears after that, but it just goes to show that subtle nuance and lateral thinking can be just as effective as wielding an axe that could chop a tower block in half.

The current champion is a troll called Patio who's so dense that a reasonably sized thermonuclear detonation wouldn't cause him any undue worry.

On a side note, the shortest game ever played was when a dwarf called Ouch Sturdyback asked to have a go, which only goes to prove that when entering into a game of any sort it pays to read the rules. And not have the intelligence of a house brick.

# How Many Fingers?

Although this pub game may not sound as overtly violent as OUCH! How Many Fingers is probably responsible for more disabling injuries and premature deaths than the casualties of two World Wars, the Spanish Flu Pandemic, The European colonization of The Americas, and Mrs. Ladle's plum duff combined.

Two protagonists sit opposite each other at a sturdy table onto which is placed, what can only be described as a surgical carousel. It's basically a circular contraption about the size of a car tyre attached to which are a variety of very shiny and very sharp cutting instruments, ranging from flick knives and cutthroat razors to scalpels and carving knives. At the centre of this forest of steel lies a golden cube about the size of a sugar lump, which is a remarkable coincidence in that it actually is a sugar lump that's been coloured gold. It's either that or one of the urinal cakes.

The machine, powered by a small generator, once switched on becomes a spinning, glinting round-about of amputation, and the idea of the game is to reach into this mobile mincer and grab the golden cube whilst remaining unscathed, although during the games long and messy history, unscathed is a term that has never been attributed to the winner. Neither has the word winner as it goes. Survivor is a more apt description, as is brutally disfigured corpse, fatally injured participant, remaining contestant despite catastrophic blood loss, and complete head case who's going to have to get used to drinking through straws, using ramps, and getting by with the mental agility of a turnip.

The resulting carnage is usually such that most landlords insist that the game not be played in the main bar but in the function room at the rear of the pub as this area is usually equipped to deal with spilled fluids on a massive scale. You know the sort of things. Easily wiped down walls, non-staining floors, a wide gutter, and a plug hole that can handle the odd foot, upper arm, or heavily lacerated torso.

The games name is interesting as well. Although very apt it's often misunderstood in that it doesn't refer to how many digits you have left at the end, but on how many you start with. If a contestant has the traditional ten and ends up with six then their score would be four, but if his opponent begins with seven and finishes with six then his score is one, so in effect the greater the potential loss, the greater the risk and therefore the greater chance of winning.

Sadly, it hasn't been played for a while. During a contest in Tonboot an ogre lost an arm and in the ensuing meaty tangle a fingernail had shot out of the machine and decapitated the landlord, and even though the spectacle of the contest was great for drawing a crowd, the brewery decided to ban it in all of their establishments for a bit because it was hard enough to get someone to take on the proprietorship in the first place without having to add into an employment contract that there may be a risk of death from airborne body parts. You might as well go to Iraq for that. At least you can get some duty frees on the way back.

The last game known to have been played is still talked about to this day because it resulted in several teeth, half an eyeball, most of a liver, and three nostrils stuck to the ceiling of a pub in Puke. Unfortunately, no one knows the final result because Dr Frankenstein heard about the deranged carnage and was last seen leaving the establishment with several rather squelchy shopping bags. He wasn't making anything in particular; he just likes to have spares to hand, and indeed, hands to spare.

Dear reader,

We hope you enjoyed reading *Intensive Scare*. Please take a moment to leave a review, even if it's a short one. Your opinion is important to us.

Discover more books by Tony Lewis at https://www.nextchapter.pub/authors/tony-lewis

Want to know when one of our books is free or discounted? Join the newsletter at

http://eepurl.com/bqqB3H

Best regards,
Tony Lewis and the Next Chapter Team

# About the Author

Ah, the author bio. What can I say about myself that'll be interesting? I could make it up I suppose, but who'd believe the fact that I've won the Nobel Prize for Literature and written two Oscar-winning screenplays. NO ONE! So here it is.

Born in Cardiff in 1967.

Moved to Kent in 1983.

Employment. Warehouse stuff with a bunch of loonies (hi, guys. You know who you are), some varied and not entirely wholesome activities assigned by an employment agency (long hours but at least I got night rate for the grave robbing), policeman (unbelievable but true), trainee barista (though why Costa needed a lawyer serving skinny lattes is beyond me), debt collector for the PTA (nasty lot), and now a hospital porter, a job I love.

I'm married to Sharon, have a son James, and two stepchildren, Joe and Eve.

That's it. You can read the book now.

# Books by the Author

The Skullenia Series
Wherewolf
Cup and Sorcery
Wuthering Frights
The Quest for the Bone Idol
A Witch In Time
Intensive Scare

Lightning Source UK Ltd.
Milton Keynes UK
UKHW011004231120
373921UK00001B/281